# The Daily Telegraph

## GUIDE TO

# PAYING
# LESS TAX

# The Daily Telegraph

## GUIDE TO

# PAYING
# LESS TAX

Everything you need to know
about cutting your tax bill

## NIKI CHESWORTH

MACMILLAN

First published 2002 by Macmillan
an imprint of Pan Macmillan Ltd
Pan Macmillan, 20 New Wharf Road, London N1 9RR
Basingstoke and Oxford
Associated companies throughout the world
www.panmacmillan.com

ISBN 0 333 90845 7

1 3 5 7 9 8 6 4 2

A CIP catalogue record for this book is available from
the British Library.

Typeset by SetSystems Ltd, Saffron Walden, Essex
Printed and bound in Great Britain by
Mackays of Chatham plc, Chatham, Kent

To Katie, who is never taxing.

# Contents

# Contents

# Introduction

So you want to pay less tax? One would assume everyone would agree to this – and certainly anyone reading this book. However, there is a vast difference between what most people want, and what they actually do in practice. Just as many of us want to lose weight/take up that sport/read *War and Peace*/give up smoking etc. . . . when it comes to applying ourselves with a bit of hard work, then we often give up or put off our plans to another day. The same applies with saving tax – or even getting round to filling in the dreaded tax return. It is all too easy to put off until tomorrow (which often turns out to be next month or even next year), what should be done today. But any delay could cost money.

Part of the problem is that many people have a mental block when it comes to dealing with taxation. Yes, the tax return could be made simpler. However, it is only a form. Most taxpayers need to fill in only a couple of dozen boxes on their return, but even that causes headaches (which is probably why almost one in nine people who have to fill in a return, fail to send it back on time and, as a result, are fined at least £100 each). And yes, so many different tax bands, tax rates, tax allowances and tax credits do make tax seem very complicated. However, once taxpayers know the basics, it is relatively simple for them to make the most of easy tax-saving opportunities.

This book aims to help readers overcome these problems – a combination of apathy, fear and a lack of knowledge – with jargon-free guides to the main taxes: income tax and capital gains tax as well as inheritance tax and National Insurance. Each chapter and section is packed full of tips on ways to pay less tax . . . legitimately. In a few cases, readers are advised to consult an accountant or a solicitor, but in most the tax-saving tips are so easy to implement they can be done without professional advice. All readers have to do is act on them.

Remember, those who delay, pay.

# WHY YOU NEED THIS BOOK

The chances are that one of the biggest bills readers have to pay each year is their tax bill. They may not realize this – particularly if tax is deducted at source from their salary, savings and investments. Yet unlike other bills such as mortgage, gas and electricity bills or even the weekly grocery or petrol spend, taxpayers tend to pay up without question. They may shop around for a better home-loan rate, scour the shops for the best price on a new electrical item or drive an extra mile to buy cheaper petrol, but when it comes to putting in time and effort to cut their tax bill they do nothing – even though the potential savings are often far greater and, according to IFA Promotion the organization that promotes independent finan-cial advice, as a result, Britons are wasting almost £6 billion a year in unnecessary tax.

It found that:

- Nine out of ten adults in the UK pay more tax that they have to.

- Forty-one million people could be better off if they made the most of easy tax-saving tips.

- On average, every person would be £140 better off per year if we all paid the right amount of tax.

- Two minutes filling in a form would save 4 million non-taxpayers an average of £75 in tax that they are paying unnecessarily on their savings interest.

- Every year almost one million taxpayers pay a £100 fine that is easily avoided by simply sending their tax return in on time.

- Over £550 million in tax could easily be avoided if everyone sheltered their investments and savings in an Individual Savings Account (ISA).

- Some £485 million in personal tax allowances is unused each year.

- An extra £1,240 million could go to chosen heirs instead of the tax man in the form of inheritance tax if more people planned ahead.

- Almost £1,000 million of tax relief could be claimed by optimizing contributions to personal or company pension schemes or by making additional voluntary contributions.

- Nearly £400 million could be saved simply by transferring assets between spouses to maximize capital gains tax (CGT) allowances.

The waste goes on . . . and on. All this money is needlessly given to the Inland Revenue, when – in many cases – these taxes could easily be avoided.

Every effort has been made to ensure the accuracy of this book, however, readers are still advised to check with their accountant or tax office before taking any major decisions. This is because tax law is constantly being challenged and revised, extra statutory concessions are made giving tax breaks that were not available before, and even when the rules seem clear different tax offices often implement them differently.

# 1 Paying Less Income Tax

This chapter looks at some of the easiest ways to pay less tax by ensuring all the tax allowances due are received, claiming the relevant tax credits and checking that the correct amount of tax is deducted from a salary or pension.

There are special sections for employees (including the most tax-efficient means of receiving employee benefits), for the over 65s and for families.

## INCOME TAX: THE FACTS

Income tax is an annual tax (the tax is based on the individual's income for the tax year, which starts on 6 April and ends on 5 April) with the tax charged at different rates on different bands of taxable income (income above the individual's personal tax allowance, which is the amount that can be earned before paying tax).

Individual taxpayers pay each rate of income tax only on income that falls within a particular tax band. This means they can pay tax at the lower rate, basic rate and higher rate if they have income that falls into each tax band.

## Tax Rates

| Tax Year | 2001/02 | 2002/03 |
|---|---|---|
| Starting rate | 10% | 10% |
| Basic rate | 22% | 22% |
| Higher rate | 40% | 40% |

These rates apply to non-savings and non-dividend income. So they are the rates that apply to earnings for employment and self-employment, for example, but not to savings interest.

Tax rates for savings income are charged at:

| Tax Year | 2001/02 | 2002/03 |
|---|---|---|
| Starting rate | 10% | 10% |
| Basic rate | 20% | 20% |
| Higher rate | 40% | 40% |

Savings income is added to other income to determine the rate paid. So an individual who pays tax at the basic rate may find that savings income is taxed at the higher rate as it pushes his taxable income into the higher tax band.

Tax on savings income is usually deducted at source at the rate of 20 per cent. This lower rate is the rate paid by basic-rate taxpayers – even though they pay 22 per cent on their other income.

Tax rates for dividend income are charged at:

| Tax Year | 2001/02 | 2002/03 |
|---|---|---|
| Non-taxpayers and basic-rate taxpayers | 10% | 10% |
| Higher-rate taxpayers | 32.5% | 32.5% |

## Tax Bands

The tax rates listed above apply to income that falls into each tax band. The tax bands apply to income above the individual's tax allowances (these allowances are the amount that can be earned each year before paying tax).

| Tax Year | 2001/02 | 2002/03 |
|---|---|---|
| Starting rate (10%) | up to £1,800 | £1,920 |
| Basic rate (22%) | £1,881–£29,400 | £1,921–£29,900 |
| Higher rate (40%) | over £29,400 | over £29,900 |

---

✎ **Tax tip**

It is important that each taxpayer knows the maximum rate of tax he must pay. Some savings and investment schemes are suitable only for higher-rate taxpayers while basic-rate taxpayers cannot claim higher-rate tax relief.

## Example

*Tom Taxpayer earned £30,000 a year as a store manager last year (the 2001/02 tax year). In addition, he earned £1,000 in savings interest gross (£800 after tax). He therefore believes that he is a higher-rate taxpayer as the higher rate starts at £29,400 and that he must pay higher-rate tax on his savings interest. However, he is wrong.*

*His net income chargeable to tax is the figure he needs to use. This is his taxable income after his allowances (the amount he can earn before paying tax) have been deducted. As a single man with no children he qualifies only for the basic personal allowance of £4,535 with no additional allowances or tax credits. This means that the first £4,535 of his earnings are tax free.*

*His taxable income therefore is:*

*(£30,000 salary + £1,000 savings interest) – £4,535 (the personal tax allowance) = £26,465*

*This is below £29,400 (earnings over this amount are taxed at 40%) so all of his income falls within the lower and basic-rate tax bands and he will pay tax as follows:*

*Salary:*
*0% on the first £4,535 (his personal allowance)*
*10% on the first £1,880*                  *= £   188.00*
*22% on the next £23,585*                 *= £5,188.70*

*Savings:*
*20% on his savings income of £1,000*         *= £   200.00*

*TOTAL income tax for the year*             *= £5,388.70*

*As all of this income tax is deducted at source (through Pay As You Earn (PAYE) for his salary and by his building society on his savings' interest) he has no further tax to pay. Note that his savings income is added to his other income when determining the top rate of tax he pays.*

---

### ✎ Tax tips

Basic-rate taxpayers can get caught out by the way tax is calculated on savings. The fact that savings interest and investment income is added to other income to calculate the top rate of tax can mean that an employee pays basic-rate tax on his salary but higher-rate tax on his savings. It is important to know what level of tax is due in order to plan ahead and avoid this tax.

While employees receive higher-rate tax relief automatically on contributions made to an employer's occupational scheme, higher-rate tax relief on personal pension or stakeholder pension contributions needs to be claimed. However, if the individual does not know that he or she is a higher-rate taxpayer this tax relief could go unclaimed. That is why it is important for all taxpayers to understand the tax rates and tax bands.

---

# TAX-FREE INCOME

Although most types of income – and even payments in kind – are subject to income tax, some escape.

- Income from tax-free savings schemes including ISAs, Personal Equity Plans (PEPs), Tax Exempt Special Savings Accounts (TESSAs), National Savings Certificates and the first £70 of interest from the National Savings Ordinary Account (see CHAPTER 2: SAVINGS AND INVESTMENTS for more details).

- Grants – education grants, scholarships, home improvement grants etc.

- Redundancy payments (up to £30,000) and certain other payments on loss of job.

- Some employee benefits such as a subsidized canteen (these are detailed in full later in this chapter under the section on BENEFITS IN KIND).

- Some social security benefits including:

  - *Child benefit and allowances.*

  - *Housing benefits.*

  - *Council tax benefit.*

  - *Maternity allowance.*

  - *Christmas bonus for pensioners.*

  - *Widow's payment.*

  - *Incapacity benefit paid for the first 28 weeks of sickness.*

  - *Incapacity benefit paid to someone who was receiving invalidity benefit paid before 13 April 1995, provided there has not been a break of more than eight weeks in the claim.*

  - *Attendance allowance and disability living allowance.*

  - *War disablement pension.*

  - *War widow's pension.*

  - *Working families' tax credit.*

- Maintenance payments from a former spouse.

- Premium Bond, National Lottery and other gambling prizes.

---

### ✎ Tax tip

While State benefits paid to those unable to work due to illness or unemployment (statutory sick pay and jobseeker's allowance) are both taxable, those who take out insurance policies to cover them against unemployment, accident, sickness, disability or infirmity will find that these benefits are tax free if the policy is:

- A mortgage payment protection policy – which pays the mortgage interest.

- Permanent health insurance – mainly taken out by the self-employed.

- Creditor insurance – which meets loan or bill payments.

- Long-term care insurance – but only if the policy is taken out before the need for care becomes apparent.

# TAXABLE INCOME

All other income including:

- Income from employment – including salary, bonus, overtime, tips or gratuities, holiday pay, maternity leave pay and sick pay.

- Many benefits in kind/employee perks (individuals are generally taxed on the value of these).

- Income/profits from self-employment or partnership.

- Savings interest and investment income/dividends.

- Pension income (pensions from employers, personal pensions and state pensions).

- Income from property.

- Certain state benefits including:

  - *jobseeker's allowance*

  - *statutory sick pay*

  - *statutory maternity pay*

  - *invalid care allowance*

are subject to income tax.

**Note:** The jobseeker's allowance, which replaced unemployment benefit in 1996, is a taxable benefit. However, it is not paid with tax deducted at source. If the individual had earnings from employment earlier in the tax year and is now due a rebate, no tax rebate can be claimed. Instead, this amount is used to cover the potential tax liability. At the end of the tax year – or when the individual resumes work – the Jobcentre will normally work out the individual's tax position and send any refund.

# TAX ALLOWANCES

Taxpayers do not have to pay income tax on all of their income. Everyone is entitled to what is called a tax allowance – the amount that can be earned before paying tax.

In most cases, individuals receive these allowances automatically. They are either included in their PAYE tax code and are used to reduce the amount of tax deducted from salaries (and pensions paid by occupational schemes which are paid to pensioners through the PAYE system), or, if the taxpayer is self-employed or not an employee, he will be able to claim allowances when filling in the tax return and deduct them from income when calculating the amount of tax that needs to be paid.

Allowances are covered on page 6 of the tax return under question 16.

## The Basic Personal Allowance

Everyone is entitled to the basic personal allowance. Worth £4,615 for the 2002/03 tax year, it is the amount that everyone – including children and pensioners – can earn before paying tax. The allowance usually rises at the start of each tax year in line with inflation (however, income tax allowances for the under 65s will be frozen in 2003/04). The allowance for 2001/02, the tax year covered by tax returns sent out in April 2002, was £4,535.

The allowance can only be used once. Those who have more than one job or who are employees and self-employed can only set the personal allowance against one lot of income – usually their main source.

## Age Allowances

The personal allowance is increased for those aged 65 and over to:

| Tax Year | 2003/04 | 2002/03 | 2001/02 |
|---|---|---|---|
| Age 65–74 | £6,610 | £6,100 | £5,990 |
| Age 75 and over | £6,740 | £6,370 | £6,260 |

Pensioners, therefore, can earn much more than those under 65 before having to pay tax.

**Note:** Each spouse qualifies for his or her own personal allowance. So if one spouse is over 65 and the other under 65 only the older partner will qualify for the increased age allowance. Likewise if one partner is aged 75 or over that partner will qualify for an even higher age allowance.

However, there is an allowance restriction which means that those with higher incomes benefit less than those on lower incomes. Those whose taxable income exceeds £17,900 (£17,600 for the 2001/02 tax year) will see their allowances reduced by £1 for every £2 earned over this limit.

The allowance only stops being reduced when it is cut to the basic personal allowance of £4,615 (£4,535 for the 2001/02 tax year). So the more a pensioner earns, the less tax savings he makes.

---

### ✏ Tax tip

To qualify for an age allowance, individuals must have reached the required age by the end of the tax year – not the start. Even those born on 5 April (the last day of the tax year) can still claim age-related allowances for the entire tax year once they reach 65.

---

**Note:** The personal allowance for those aged 65 or over will be increased by £240 over indexation in 2003/04. In future the increase in the allowance will be linked to the rise in earnings not inflation for the remainder of this parliament. This is an important concession as earnings tend to rise at a faster rate than inflation.

> ✐ **Tax tip**

Pensioners who earn more than the allowance restriction limit of £17,900 for the 2002/03 tax year should plan their investments carefully. If they can defer income to later years or switch to investments that produce capital gains rather than income, they can reduce their taxable income to below the threshold and make full use of their age allowances. They should also consider tax-free investments as even if these produce an income it does not affect the age allowance (see CHAPTER 2: SAVINGS AND INVESTMENTS).

This is how earnings reduce age allowances:

## Example

*Arthur Pensioner is 69 and had a total income from pensions and investments of £22,000 for the 2001/02 tax year. This exceeded the £17,600 threshold.*

*His age-increased personal allowance is £5,990 which will be reduced by £1 for every £2 of income in excess of £17,600.*

*£22,000 − £17,600 = £4,400*

*He therefore earns £4,400 more than the restriction.*

*The allowance will be reduced by £1 for every £2 of income over the restriction*

*£4,400 ÷ 2 = £2,200*

*His allowance will be reduced by £2,200.*

*£5,990 (Arthur's age allowance) − £2,200 = £3,790*

*However, this is below the basic personal allowance of £4,535.*

*However, the earnings restriction cannot reduce the allowance below the level of the basic personal allowance, so Arthur's tax-free allowance will be £4,535.*

*Arthur's problems do not end there. As he was born before 6 April 1935 he also qualifies for the married couple's allowance of £5,365 for the 2001/02 tax year.*

*Any earnings restriction that is not used up in reducing the age allowance, is then used to reduce the married couple's allowance.*

*The unused reduction is: £4,535 (the basic personal allowance) – £3,790 (what his allowance would have been cut to) = £745.*

*So his married couple's allowance will be reduced by £745.*

*£5,365 (the married couple's allowance) – £745 = £4,620*

**Note:** Just as the earnings restriction cannot reduce the age allowance to below the level of the basic personal allowance, it cannot reduce the married couple's allowance to below a set minimum – £2,070 for the 2001/02 tax year. This is explained in greater detail in the section on the married couple's allowance on page 12)

---

### ✎ Tax tips

If one spouse earns more than the income threshold and the other does not, consider splitting the ownership of income-generating assets differently so that neither exceeds the limit. See the tips in CHAPTER 2: SAVINGS AND INVESTMENTS.

To ensure that earnings do not exceed the threshold – and therefore cause the pensioner to lose age-related allowances – investors should try to keep within the total income limit by switching to tax-free investments such as ISAs or National Savings Certificates. See the tips in CHAPTER 2: SAVINGS AND INVESTMENTS.

When calculating total income (to see if an individual exceeds the earnings threshold which is £17,900 for 2002/03) note that not all income needs to be included. Only income that is assessable for tax need be added up. Income not assessable for tax is excluded. This includes:

- Interest credited to an ISA (or an existing TESSA).

- Dividends paid by a PEP or a venture capital trust.

- The growth in value of National Savings Certificates.

- Amounts withdrawn from insurance bonds (up to the 5 per cent limit).

- Income received under the rent-a-room scheme.

Pensioners with earnings reaching or exceeding the threshold should therefore consider the alternative sources of income listed above. That way their age allowances will no longer be reduced because of their earnings, or will be reduced by a lower amount.

Another way to reduce assessable income so that earnings do not exceed the threshold is to increase the amount of outgoings that qualify for tax relief. This could include making a gift to charity under the Gift Aid scheme. Donations through the scheme are treated as tax-allowable deductions and reduce the total income figure when calculating age allowances. To donate £100 to charity, taxpayers only need actually donate £78 – the remaining £22 is claimed from the Inland Revenue by the charity. Even so, when calculating their income pensioners can reduce it by the full £100.

It will pay to put income-generating investments and assets in the name of the older spouse as he or she will qualify for a higher age allowance and therefore be able to earn more before paying tax.

Just as individual partners each qualify for their own age allowance, when calculating whether or not their allowances should be reduced because their income exceeds the earning threshold, individual partners need to do separate calculations. So if one partner has an income above the threshold he or she will suffer a reduction in the age allowance even if the other partner has earnings below the threshold. This is why it pays to split the ownership of assets – and therefore the income they generate – so that neither exceeds the threshold.

# Married Couple's Allowance

This is no longer given to married couples unless they were born before 6 April 1935.

---

**✐ Tax tip**

Even though this allowance was scrapped for younger couples at the end of the 1999/2000 tax year, they may still be able to benefit from it. If they failed to claim the allowance (i.e. did not notify their tax office that they had married), they have five years and ten months after the end of the tax year to which the claim relates in which to claim the allowance. In most cases, those who have been overlooked will not have received a tax return and not realized that they were entitled to the allowance. Note, however, that it is too late to change the way the allowance is given. It will automatically go to the husband – as any election for half or the whole amount to be given to the wife had to be made before the start of the tax year.

---

Pensioners who qualify for the married couple's allowance receive the following allowances depending on age:

| Tax Year | 2002/03 | 2001/02 |
| --- | --- | --- |
| Born before 6 April 1935 | £5,465 | £5,365 |
| Aged 75 or more | £5,535 | £5,435 |

This allowance may be reduced if earnings exceed £17,900 (£17,600 for the 2001/02 tax year). The personal allowance will be reduced first and only after that has been reduced to the level of the basic personal allowance, will the married couple's allowance be affected. Even then, there is a minimum amount that must be given of £2,110 (£2,070 for the 2001/02 tax year).

The rate of tax relief on the married couple's allowance for people born before 6 April 1935 is 10 per cent. So even though the allowance for the 2001/02 tax year was £5,365 the maximum benefit was only 10 per cent of that amount – tax bills were therefore reduced by only £536.50 (£543.50 for those aged 75 and over).

The replacement for the married couple's allowance is the children's tax credit, given to those with children under 16. See the section on TAX CREDITS later in this chapter for details.

---

### ✎ Tax tips

The married couple's allowance is given if either spouse has reached the required age at the end of the tax year. It is still given even if one partner is much younger.

Couples can choose for the minimum allowance of £2,110 (£2,070 for the 2001/02 tax year) to go to either spouse (if they both agree) – or to be split between them (a wife can elect to receive half the allowance without her husband's consent). However, if no choice is made, the allowance will always be given to the husband.

An election must be made before the start of the tax year for which it is to have effect using Inland Revenue Form 18. There is no need to make a new election at the start of subsequent tax years unless the couple wish to change the way the allowance is given.

Even if an election is made, if the wife then has insufficient income to use her part of the married couple's allowance she can transfer the excess back to her husband.

While couples can elect to split only the minimum allowance (£2,110), the whole lot (£5,465 or £5,535) can be transferred if the husband has insufficient income to use it himself. This election must be lodged with the Inland Revenue within five years and ten months from the end of the tax year. Couples where the husband is the lower earner should ensure that any unused allowances are transferred to the wife. If they are not, these allowances will be wasted.

---

As has been discussed in the previous section, AGE ALLOWANCES, if those in receipt of an age allowance earn more than a certain threshold – £17,900 for the 2002/03 tax year – their allowances are reduced by £1 for every £2 of income in excess of this threshold. In the first instance, the higher age-related personal allowance is reduced but it cannot be reduced to below the personal allowance. If there is any unused reduction this will be used to reduce the married couple's allowance. Once again this cannot be reduced to below the minimum of £2,110 (£2,070 for the 2001/02 tax year).

The level of allowance given is always based on the husband's total income even if:

- He is under 65/75 and only qualifies for the married couple's allowance because of his wife's age.

- All or part of the minimum married couple's allowance has been transferred to the wife and her total income exceeds the earnings threshold of £17,900 (£17,600 for the 2001/02 tax year).

If the husband dies, the married couple's allowance is set against his income in the year of his death – even if the couple had elected to share the allowance. If the wife dies, the husband will continue to receive the married couple's allowance for the whole of the tax year in which she dies. However, if a couple marry they are entitled only to a proportion of the married couple's allowance reflecting the number of months out of the year they have been married.

---

**✎ Tax tip**

Even though the married couple's allowance is set against the husband's income in the year of his death, any unused part can be claimed by the wife.

---

## Parents of Dependent Children

The additional personal allowance given to those with dependent children living with them was abolished with effect from 6 April 2000. These taxpayers should now claim the children's tax credit along with married couples of non-pension age with dependent children who now no longer benefit from the married couple's allowance.

---

### ✎ Tax tip

Even though the additional personal allowance has been abolished, some parents could still benefit from it. Married couples with children used to receive an additional tax allowance. But single, separated, divorced or widowed parents with dependent children may not have realized they were also entitled to the same allowance. If they had failed to claim the allowance they have five years and ten months from the end of the tax year to which the claim relates in which to claim the allowance.

## Blind Person's Allowance

This is given to those who are registered as blind. In England and Wales this means the person's name appears on the local authority's register of blind persons. In Scotland and Northern Ireland taxpayers simply need to be so blind that they cannot perform any work for which eyesight is essential.

The allowance for the 2002/03 tax year is £1,480.

---

### ✎ Tax tips

If both the husband and wife are blind they can each claim a separate blind person's allowance.

If the husband has insufficient income to use all his blind person's allowance he may be able to transfer the allowance or part of it to his wife (or vice versa if she is blind) – whether or not she is also blind. The claim must be made using Revenue Form 575 within five years and ten months of the 31 January following the end of the relevant tax year.

## Widow's Bereavement Allowance

This allowance has now been abolished. However, it can still be claimed by widows whose husbands died in the 2000/2001 tax year or before. The allowance was given in the year of death, provided the couple were living together at the time of death. The rate for the 2000/01 tax year was £2,000 with relief given at 10 per cent, giving a tax saving of £200.

> **✎ Tax tip**
>
> Widows who were unaware that they could claim the allowance have five years and ten months from the end of the tax year for which they are claiming in which to claim the allowance.

## How Allowances Reduce Tax Bills

A tax allowance is the level of income that can be earned before paying tax, not the amount of tax saved.

The reduction in the amount of tax for each taxpayer depends on their top rate of tax (unless the allowance is given at a restricted rate). This is because allowances reduce each taxpayer's total taxable income. If, as a result, they reduce the amount of income that falls into the higher-rate tax band, then the taxpayer saves more than if the allowances only reduced the amount of income that falls into the basic-rate tax band.

This is how the basic personal allowances for 2001/02 benefited higher earners more than lower earners:

40% (the higher rate of tax) × £4,535 (the amount of income that is no longer taxed at the higher rate because of the personal allowance) = £1,814

If, however, the taxpayer paid tax at only the starting and basic rate this means that he no longer had to pay the basic rate of tax on £4,535 of income:

22% (the basic rate of tax) × £4,535 (the amount of income that is no
longer taxed at the basic rate because of the personal allowance) = £997.70

So the higher-rate taxpayer saved far more than the basic-rate
taxpayer.

It is only possible to save the higher 40 per cent rate on income
that falls into the higher-rate tax band. If, before the personal
allowance, only £1,000 of that taxpayer's earnings would have fallen
into the higher-rate bracket, then he will only save 40 per cent tax
on £1,000 of the personal allowance. The remainder of the allowance
(£3,535) would lead to savings at the basic rate.

## Using Allowances Effectively

Each year millions of pounds are wasted by those taxpayers who
fail to use up their allowances – or use them effectively.

Anyone who earns less than their allowances cannot carry these
unused allowances forward to another tax year – so they are lost for
ever. Couples should therefore ensure that both partners use up
their allowances by transferring income-generating assets to the
spouse with no or a low income.

The same applies to couples where one spouse is a higher-rate
taxpayer and the other falls well within the basic-rate tax band. By
transferring income to the lower-earner's name, more income will
fall into the basic rate rather than the higher rate, leading to overall
tax savings for the couple.

---

### ✎ Tax tip

It is not possible to transfer unused basic personal allowances to a
spouse. However, the whole of the higher age-related married couple's allowance may be transferred to the wife if the husband has
insufficient income to use it himself. In addition, the blind person's
allowance can be transferred.

**Example**

*Eric Earner had an income of just £2,400 a year in the 2001/02 tax year because he lost his job and had been unable to find any employment other than occasional days of casual work. In addition, he earned £1,000 gross interest from the joint savings account he held with his wife Emily. She earned a good salary of £18,000 a year. She also received £800 in interest from their joint savings account after tax – which is the equivalent of £1,000 in gross interest.*

*Even though Eric earned less than the basic personal allowance (£4,535 for the 2000/01 tax year), he cannot transfer this unused allowance to his wife, so the tax savings are lost. His unused allowance was £4,535 – £2,400 (earnings) – £1,000 (savings interest = £1,135. For a basic-rate taxpayer this would mean a tax saving of 22% × £1,135 = £250. So £250 of potential tax savings were wasted by Eric.*

*However, if Emily had transferred all their savings into Eric's name he would then have been able to earn the interest on the savings free of tax – because even when the savings interest was added to his other income he would still not have exceeded the basic personal allowance.*

*The couple would therefore have saved:*

*20% tax (the rate applying to savings interest) × £1,000 (savings interest) = £200*

*Eric as a non-taxpayer, should be receiving his share of the interest, tax free, by registering to receive it gross.*

# TAX CREDITS

These are a relatively new introduction and taxpayers may find that even though they are entitled to a tax credit, they do not receive it because they have failed to claim it.

Tax credits reduce the amount of tax payable on income or are added to pay or given as a cash payment. Unlike tax allowances, tax credits do not reduce the amount of income that an individual can receive without paying tax, instead they reduce the amount of tax paid/due by a set amount. The exceptions include the tax credits that replace state benefits including the working families' tax credit which can either be given as a tax credit, be added to pay if the individual is a non-taxpayer or claimed as a cash payment.

## Children's Tax Credit

Introduced on 6 April 2001, this tax credit is worth up to £529 a year (£520 for the 2001/02 tax year). The credit was first announced in the Budget of 1999 as a replacement for the married couple's allowance. However, unlike the allowance it replaces, it is not given to all married couples. It can only be claimed by single people and couples (whether married or not) of any age if they have a child under 16 (at the start of the tax year) living with them during the tax year (for at least part of the tax year).

It can only be claimed by a parent or someone maintaining a child. The child can be their own child, a stepchild, an adopted child or a child they look after at their own expense. If someone else can claim for the same child, the parents or guardians may have to share the tax credit. However, if a couple has more than one child and they live together they can only have one credit between them.

Note: only one tax credit is given to parents even if they have more than one child.

The rate of tax relief is restricted to 10 per cent. So although the tax credit for the 2002/03 tax year is £5,290, the rate of tax relief is restricted to 10 per cent giving a maximum benefit of only £529.

In addition, if the main earner in the family is a higher-rate taxpayer the allowance is further reduced, with some couples qualifying for no tax credit at all because the credit is reduced by £1 for every £15 of the claimant's income taxed at the higher rate.

From April 2002 the tax credit is almost doubled in the year parents have a baby and the higher amount paid for the child's first year. This will give a tax credit of £10,490 in the first year. However, remember that the tax relief on this is also restricted to 10 per cent, so the maximum benefit will be only £1,049.

| ✎ Tax tip |
|---|

Even if a couple are unmarried and the mother bears the bulk of the cost of bringing up the child, if the couple live together then it may be the father who receives the tax credit not the mother. This is because the tax credit is generally given to the parent who pays tax at the higher rate, so that the credit can be reduced if earnings exceed the higher-rate tax threshold. If one parent pays tax at the higher rate, it is not possible to escape the reduction in the tax credit by getting the lower earner to claim the credit.

Note that when the children's tax credit is replaced by the child tax credit in April 2003, the credit will be based on joint incomes with those earning up to £58,000 a year qualifying for help.

| ✎ Tax tips |
|---|

If both parents pay tax at the lower rate then either one can claim the children's tax credit or they can even have it split between them. However, both partners have to agree if the partner with the lower income is to have all of the credit.

If the partner that claims the credit does not pay enough tax to use all of it, he or she can transfer any unused credit to the other partner after the end of the tax year.

If one parent is self-employed (and neither is a higher-rate taxpayer), then the employee should claim the credit rather than the self-employed parent. This is because the credit is paid through PAYE and the employee will get the benefit of paying less tax immediately. While employees receive the tax credit through their PAYE tax code, the self-employed need to claim the tax credit when they fill in their tax return – so there will be a delay before the credit is paid.

Even if the child reaches the age of 16 during the tax year, the parent can still claim the tax credit for the whole year as long as the child lives with them during the period before their 16th birthday.

Note that the tax credit has to be claimed – it may not be given automatically. To claim the tax credit complete form CTC1 which is available from tax offices or from the special Inland Revenue helpline on 0845 300 1036.

## How the Tax Credit Reduces the More the Parent Earns

Those earning in excess of £41,000 are unlikely to receive any credit because the amount of the credit is reduced by £1 for every £15 of income that falls into the higher-rate tax band.

Note that it is the higher-rate taxpayer that must claim the credit.

### Example

*Paul and Pippa Parent have a three-year-old daughter and they can therefore claim the children's tax credit. Paul, as the higher earner, needs to make the claim. However, as he pays higher-rate tax on some of his income, the amount of tax credit will be reduced. He earns £35,000 a year.*

*First he needs to calculate how much of his income falls into the higher-rate tax band. This is his calculation for the 2001/02 tax year:*

*£35,000 – £4,535 (the personal allowance) = £30,465*
*Higher-rate tax is payable on his earnings above £29,400*
*£30,465 – £29,400 = £1,065 of earnings in the higher-rate tax band*
*The credit is reduced by £1 for every £15 of his earnings in the higher-rate band, he will therefore see his credit reduce by £1,065 ÷ 15 = £71*
*The value of the credit is therefore cut to £520 – £71 = £449*

*On PAYE Tax Coding Notices the reduction may be expressed as £2 of the allowance withdrawn for every £3 of income in the higher rate band.*
*To calculate every £3 of income in the higher-rate tax band:*

*£1,065 ÷ 3 = £355*
*Then this is withdrawn at the rate of £2*
*£355 × 2 = £710*
*£5,200 (the tax credit) − £710 = £4,490*
*Divided by 10 (relief is restricted to 10%) = £449*

*So he has lost out by £71 a year (£520 − £449) because he has some earnings in the higher-rate tax band.*

If Paul earned less and Pippa earned more, and he was no longer a higher-rate taxpayer then they would suffer no reduction in tax credit even if their overall income was the same.

In this sense the tax credit is unfair. There could be two families both with the same family income, but because in one family there was a higher-rate taxpayer that family would receive a lower − or even no − children's tax credit.

This is why the credit is being replaced by the child tax credit.

## The Child Tax Credit

This will be paid to the main carer, usually the mother, with all families earning less than £50,000 a year entitled to the full credit and those earning up to £58,000 a year entitled to a reduced credit along with those earning up to £66,000 a year for the first year of a child's life.

It will be based on family income (not the income of the higher earner as is the case with the children's tax credit) and will combine elements of state benefits such as income support and the job-seeker's allowance as well as the children's tax credit and the working families' tax credit.

The child element of the tax credit will be worth £1,445 a year in the 2003/04 tax year for families with a total income of less than £50,000. For families earning £50,000–£58,000 the credit will be worth £800 to £1,400 with it being withdrawn at the rate of £1 for every £15 above the £50,000 threshold.

This tax credit will be paid directly to the main carer rather than through wage packets under PAYE.

---

### ✎ Tax tips

As with other tax credits, the new child tax credit must be claimed. However, only those claiming the existing children's tax credit (those households where the higher earner was earning up to £34,000 a year) will be notified. And, as there has only been a 65 per cent take up in this credit because of the form filling it involves and the fact it needs to be claimed, many who will be entitled to the new credit will not get it. As the new credit is given to higher earners – those in the £34,000 to £58,000 band (£66,000 in the first year of a child's life) with a non-earning spouse – even those not entitled to the existing tax credit may now qualify. The Inland Revenue will be allowing families to check their eligibility online.

The tax credits will be based on annual income for a tax year calculated on circumstances at the start of the tax year.

---

## Pension Tax Credit

This will be introduced from October 2003 benefitting five million pensioners by £400 a year. It will guarantee a minimum income and reward those who have modest savings or second pensions.

Under the current system, pensioners on the minimum income guarantee (MIG) lose a pound of benefit for every extra pound of their second pension or earnings income. Or, if they have a small amount of capital their benefits are dramatically reduced. To address these problems the pension credit will revise the current capital rules, abolish the weekly means test and reward those who have saved for retirement.

Around half of all pensioner households will be entitled to the credit. To illustrate this, under the current arrangements a pensioner in 2003 with a basic state pension of £77 a week and an occupational pension of £14 a week would have their income topped up by £9 to the level of the minimum income guarantee, £100 a week. They would therefore see no gain at all from their occupational pension. Under the new arrangements they would receive £17.40 a week of pension credit taking their income to £108.40 a week.

Based on current figures, those with second pensions or earnings which give them incomes of up to £135 a week for single pensioners and £200 for couples will benefit from the credit.

The credit will be given to those who have reached pensionable age. The guaranteed minimum income is expected to be around £100 for single pensioners and around £154 for couples in 2003.

In addition, those with additional income (from a second pension or savings) will qualify for a savings credit which is expected to be around £77 per week for single pensioners and around £123 for couples in 2003, but below a set threshold (expected to be around £135 per week for single pensioners and around £200 per week for couples in 2003). The amount payable through the savings credit will be 60p per week for each £1 of retirement income above the level of the basic state pension (expected to be around £77 per week for single pensioners and around £123 for couples in 2003). Once income exceeds the guaranteed minimum (£100 for single pensioners, £154 for couples) the credit will be reduced by 40p for each pound of income.

The couple's joint savings and income will be taken into account regardless of whether they are held in separate accounts. Income from the first £6,000 of capital will be ignored. The pensioner will be assumed to have an income from the balance which will be set at £1 per week for every £500 over £6,000 (£10,000 for those in residential care and nursing homes).

The credit will replace income support for those aged over 60 and will need to be claimed. It can be claimed regardless of whether or not the individual pays tax (so it is not like the children's tax credit, for example, which is only paid to taxpayers).

## Working Families' Tax Credit

The WFTC is a tax credit available to families on low incomes with at least one adult in remunerative work for at least 16 hours a week and who are responsible for at least one child under 16 (under 19 if in full-time education up to A level or equivalent standard). It is payable to one-parent as well as two-parent families. However, it will be extended to all of those on low incomes – not just those with dependent children – from 2003.

From October 2001 the minimum income guarantee for a family on WFTC has been £225 a week (assuming that one earner is in full-time work – working 35 hours a week – and receiving the national minimum wage).

The credit is complex and can be made up of:

• A basic tax credit of £60 a week (which will rise by £2.50 from June 2002).

• An additional credit if one partner works at least 30 hours a week of £11.65.

• A tax credit of £26.45 for each child from birth and £27.20 from the September after their 16th birthday until the day before they are 19.

• A childcare tax credit of up to 70 per cent of eligible childcare costs to a maximum of £135 a week for one child, or £200 a week for two or more children.

• An extra £35.50 per week for a child with a disability.

• An enhanced disability payment.

As with other tax credits, the WFTC is reduced when earnings exceed a set amount. Currently it is reduced by 55p for each £1 of net income above £94.50 per week (from 2003 this rises to £97). For this calculation, net income (including some state benefits) is earnings less tax, National Insurance and half of any pension contributions.

Savings also reduce the tax credit.

---

### ✎ Tax tips

Couples can choose which partner receives the WFTC – but they cannot split it between them. However, as the credit is calculated using family income – rather than one spouse's income – there is no benefit in terms of tax savings.

Even if the parent does not pay much tax (their earnings are low), they still benefit from the full tax credit. While an allowance reduces the amount of income which is taxable, the WFTC is worth a set amount (other than for those who earn more than £94.50 a week). If a parent is entitled to a credit of £50 then that amount will be added to weekly net income (after tax and National Insurance).

Even non-earners can benefit from this tax credit as payments can be made directly – the credit does not have to be paid through the PAYE system.

---

### ✎ Tax tip

Claiming the WFTC requires a lot of paperwork – payslips, proof of childcare costs etc. – however, once the claim is made it applies for 26 weeks. Even if, during that time, the claimants' income increases this will not affect their entitlement. Under the new working tax credit, claims will be for 12 months and will only be adjusted if income rises by more than £2,500.

---

Application forms for the WFTC are available from benefit agency offices, Job Centres, post offices, tax enquiry centres and the tax credit office. Alternatively call the Tax Credit Helpline on 0845 609 5000.

## Working Tax Credit

The WFTC is being replaced by the working tax credit and extended to cover low-earning couples with no children provided they work at least 30 hours a week and are aged 25 or over. The new working tax credit will also replace the disabled person's tax credit and New Deal 50 plus employment credit.

Couples with income of less than £14,000 and single people with an income of less than £10,500 will be eligible. On top of the national minimum wage, the tax credit will provide a minimum weekly income guarantee of £183 a week for couples and £154 for single workers.

It will be paid to employees through the wage packet, topping up wages.

As with the WFTC, it is made up of several elements including:

| | 2003/04 weekly rates |
|---|---|
| • Basic element | £29.20 |
| • Additional couple's and lone parent element | £28.80 |
| • 30 hour working week element | £11.90 |
| • 50 plus return to work payments (19–20 hours) | £20.00 |
| • 50 plus return to work payments (30+ hours) | £30.00 |
| • Childcare element | |
| Maximum eligible cost | £200 |
| Maximum eligible cost for 1 child | £135 |
| Percentage of eligible costs covered | 70% |

## Childcare Tax Credit

This is a component of the WFTC and the disabled person's tax credit and will be a component of the new working tax credit. The maximum payable is £135 a week for families with childcare costs for one child and £200 for families with two or more children. Up to 70 per cent of the eligible childcare costs will be paid.

---

### 🖉 Tax tip

It is not possible to try and boost the amount of tax credit by claiming that a friend or relative is providing childcare. Eligible childcare costs are currently restricted to registered childminders, after-school clubs, nurseries and crèches and other formal childcare arrangements and evidence of the costs is required.

However, in the 2002 Budget the Chancellor announced that it would be extended to cover childcare in the home.

---

## Disabled Person's Tax Credit

This is similar to the WFTC but the disabled do not have to be looking after children to receive it. In this instance the disabled qualify if they are at a disadvantage in getting a job and work at least 16 hours a week. They must also receive a disability benefit (or have received it up to 182 days prior to the date of application).

As with the WFTC it is made up of a number of components:

- A basic weekly credit – £62.10 for single people and £92.80 for couples (rising by £2.50 from June 2002).

- An extra £11.65 for those working at least 30 hours a week.

- A tax credit for each child: £26.45 from birth and £27.20 from the September after their 16th birthday until the day before they are 19 (the DPTC can be claimed for children up to 19 provided they are in full-time education).

- An extra £35.50 for each child who receives disability living allowance or is registered blind.

- A childcare credit (see the section above – it is the same as for the WFTC).

- An enhanced disability payment of £16.25 for parents and £41.75 for a child.

The DPTC will be replaced by the new working tax credit in April 2003, see the earlier section in this chapter for details. The disabled worker element of the new working tax credit will be £39.15 from 2003. Both the new and the old credits are reduced for those earning more than certain amounts and with savings.

The minimum income guarantee for a couple on DPTC with one child is £257 a week from October 2001. This assumes that one earner is in full-time work working 35 hours a week and being paid the national minimum wage.

---

### ✎ Tax tip

The DPTC cannot be transferred to a spouse, it can only be claimed by the disabled person.

---

# TAX CODES

This section applies to employees and those in receipt of occupational pensions (these are usually taxed under the PAYE system for collecting taxes).

It is essential that taxpayers understand their tax code as the incorrect amount of tax could be deducted if it is wrong.

Tax codes only apply to those paid through the PAYE scheme. These codes tell employers how much tax to deduct. The Inland Revenue issues a code for each employee or pensioner.

Employees (and pensioners) are usually sent a coding notice from the Inland Revenue telling them their tax code and how it is made up. Those who have not received one should find their coding notice on their payslip or pension notification.

Some taxpayers receive several coding notices a year and others, who have straightforward tax affairs, may not receive one at all.

Most notices are sent out in January or February giving details of what will apply from the next tax year.

---

✎ **Tax tip**

Anyone who receives a PAYE Tax Coding Notice should check it thoroughly. It is not unknown for mistakes to be made – particularly if the individual's circumstances have changed. A leaflet should be enclosed telling taxpayers how to correct any errors.

Tax codes are made up of a letter and a number. So the code could, for example, be 453L.

The letter tells the employer the type of taxpayer (see below). It enables employers to alter code numbers in line with Budget changes.

The number tells the employer how much tax-free pay each employee is allowed in each tax year. The last digit is then deleted. So those with a personal allowance of £4,535, should find the number 453 on their tax code – the last digit having been deleted. This means they can earn £4,535 a year before paying tax.

---

**Note:** This allowance is spread evenly throughout the year. It does not mean that the first £4,535 earned in any one year is tax free, which would mean a tax-free April and May and a heavily taxed February and March. Those who are paid monthly will be able to earn one twelfth of their allowances each month before paying tax.

Those who cannot earn any tax-free pay before tax is deducted – for example, if they owe the Inland Revenue money – still receive a tax code. For details of how these are calculated, see the K code, below.

## PAYE Tax-code Letters

These are easier to check than the tax-code numbers.

L     This is given to taxpayers who get the basic personal allowance.

H     This is given to taxpayers who get the basic personal allowance plus the full children's tax credit (those taxpayers are usually basic-rate taxpayers).

P    This is given to those taxpayers aged between 65 and 74 who get the full higher age-related personal allowance..

V    This is given to taxpayers aged 65 to 74 who get the full higher age-related personal allowance and, for those born before 6 April 1935, the full married couple's allowance (these taxpayers are usually basic-rate taxpayers).

Y    This is given to taxpayers aged 75 and over who get the full age-related personal allowance.

K    This is given to taxpayers if their total taxable deductions exceed their taxable allowances (i.e. they receive no untaxed pay). Instead of being given an allowance each month (or pay period) the excess tax they owe is deducted (this is done by adding the excess to their income each pay period before the tax owed is calculated so they are effectively taxed on more than they earn). For example, those with allowances of £4,535 and deductions of £5,535 will have a negative amount of allowance for the year of £4,535 – £5,535 = £1,000, so they will have a code of 100K. This means that £1,000 will be added to their annual income before calculating the tax they must pay. (They do not actually receive an extra £1,000 – it is just added when the amount of tax owed is calculated.) If they are higher-rate taxpayers this will result in an extra £400 of tax being deducted. Every month all of their salary will be taxed and an additional £400 ÷ 12 = £33.33 of tax will also be deducted.

T    Tax will not be adjusted by the employer but by the tax office. These codes are issued if the tax office needs to review the tax code.

DO  This is given to taxpayers who have earnings elsewhere and tells the employer to tax all earnings from this source at the higher rate, and that allowances have been allocated elsewhere.

BR  This is given to taxpayers who have earnings from elsewhere and tells the employer to tax all earnings from this source at the basic rate and that all the allowances have been given elsewhere.

NT  No tax is paid on this income.

> ✎ **Tax tip**
>
> Those who do not want their employers to know personal details such as their age or marital status can ask for a T code.

# PAYE Tax-code Numbers

The figures in the tax code show the amount that can be earned in a tax year before paying tax. The figure is made up of allowances less deductions.

## *Allowances*

The Inland Revenue adds up all the tax allowances to which the individual is entitled including the basic personal allowance and may add on a sum to give higher-rate tax relief due for personal pension plan contributions.

There may also be a sum for job expenses – this is to ensure tax-payers are not taxed on expenses that are allowable and not taxable.

In some cases the allowances will appear on both sides of the Tax Coding Notice – on the left-hand side which is for allowable expenses and the right-hand side which lists deductions. This is not an error. Some allowances do not qualify for full tax relief. In the case of the children's tax credit which is £5,290 for the 2002/03 tax year, the rate of tax relief is limited to 10 per cent giving a maximum benefit of £529. If the allowance were simply listed as £5,290 then the Inland Revenue would be giving away too much. An 'Allowance Restriction' is then listed under the 'Amounts taken away from your total allowances' section of the coding notice.

The same applies to other allowances which are restricted including the married couple's allowance and maintenance relief for those born before 6 April 1935. To check that the amount given is correct involves a quick calculation.

**Note:** The married couple's allowance was abolished in April 2000 for all married couples. It is now given only to older couples.

## Example

*David Dad is a basic-rate taxpayer qualifying for the children's tax credit (CTC) because he has a child under 16.*

*His PAYE Tax Coding Notice covering the 2001/02 tax year lists under his allowances:*

| | |
|---|---|
| *Personal Allowance* | *£4,535* |
| *Children's Tax Credit* | *£5,200* |

*If there were no adjustment this would mean he could earn £9,735 a year before paying tax. However, the CTC was restricted to a maximum relief of £520 for the last tax year. So on the right-hand side of his PAYE Tax Coding Notice under 'Amounts taken away from your total allowances' is an adjustment:*

*Children's Tax Credit Restriction    £2,836*

*This gives him a total children's tax credit allowance of £5,200 − £2,836 = £2,364*
*However, this does not mean that the value of the allowance is now £2,364*
*This sum must be multiplied by David Dad's highest rate of tax. As he is a basic-rate taxpayer this is 22 per cent.*

*£2,364 × 22% = £520 (the maximum relief allowed)*

*This gives David Dad a tax allowance of:*

*£9,735 − £2,836 = £6,899*

*This is explained on the bottom of the form where the tax coding notice lists: Your tax free amount for the year. In this case it is £6,899 giving a tax code of 689H.*

*The 'H' applies because John Dad is entitled to the basic personal allowance and the children's tax credit and is a basic-rate taxpayer.*

Payments that qualify for tax relief may also be shown on the left-hand side under 'Your Tax Allowances'. These figures are often what the Inland Revenue expects the taxpayer to pay in the coming year. The only information that the Inland Revenue has to go on is what was paid last year. So if a higher-rate taxpayer increases contributions to a personal pension plan – and therefore is due even more tax relief – this will not be taken into account.

In addition to tax allowances, the following payments that qualify for tax relief can be listed on the left-hand side of the Tax Coding Notice:

- Payments for allowable expenses incurred in your job.

- Professional subscriptions that are essential for your work.

- Payments to personal pension or stakeholder plans (also to pre-1988 personal pensions known as retirement annuity contracts).

- Payments to free-standing additional voluntary contribution schemes.

- Tax allowable payments to charity.

Those who make contributions to personal pension plans or other items listed above may not see these listed on their PAYE Tax Coding Notice. This is because basic-rate tax relief is given automatically on stakeholder and personal pension contributions and charitable gifts. With a personal pension, for example, a £78 contribution by the individual means a £100 contribution in total to the pension plan because the Inland Revenue automatically pays the basic-rate tax relief of £22 to the pension scheme. Higher-rate tax relief, however, needs to be claimed.

## Deductions

The right-hand side of the PAYE Tax Coding Notice lists 'Amounts taken away from your total allowances'. These deductions are added up and the total subtracted from the total allowances to give an individual's tax-free amount for the year – the number that makes up the tax code.

Deductions are usually employee perks and benefits in kind such as use of a company car or private medical insurance. In addition, there are deductions if any allowances are restricted. Any tax owed for previous years may also be included. These deductions reduce the allowances. As a result, the amount of tax-free pay will be less and the amount of tax paid will be more.

Deductions can include:

- Employee perks and fringe benefits (known as benefits in kind). Not all of these are taxable but ones that are will be listed here and include company cars and private medical insurance. For a full list of which benefits in kind are taxable and which are not, see the section BENEFITS IN KIND later in this chapter.

- Any other income from employment that is not taxed under PAYE such as commission.

- Taxable state pensions and benefits (see sections TAX-FREE INCOME and TAXABLE INCOME earlier in this chapter for a list of which state benefits are taxable and which are not).

- Investment income received before tax has been deducted (higher-rate taxpayers who need to pay additional tax on investment income will have this collected under the heading higher-rate adjustment).

- Taxable rental income.

- Tax owed from previous years.

> ### ✎ Tax tips
>
> Those who owe small amount – less than £1,000 – of tax can have this collected through a change in their tax code. This gives them an entire year to pay off the tax owed in instalments (interest free) rather than them having to pay the bill in one lump sum. See page 7, question 19 of the tax return.

Taxpayers due a rebate should ask for this to be paid to them rather than given to them as an adjustment to their tax code. That way they get the money quickly, rather than having the tax repaid over the year.

When circumstances change, taxpayers should tell their tax office and not assume that their tax code will alter automatically. Failure to notify the tax office can result in too much tax being paid or a later demand for tax underpaid. These changes in circumstances can include:

- Birth of a first child (to qualify for the children's tax credit).

- Increases/decreases in contributions to a personal pension plan or stakeholder pension if they are higher-rate taxpayers (taxpayers do not have to notify of any changes to an occupational pension scheme run by their employer).

- Taking up a second job (the personal allowance will only be given against your main employment and earnings from the second employment will be taxed in full).

Ensure the tax code includes the correct allowances. These reduce the amount of tax paid by increasing the amount of tax-free pay. See the section on TAX ALLOWANCES earlier in this chapter to check entitlement.

Those aged 65 or over may see an estimate of their total annual income on their tax code. This is listed as Estimated Income. The reason for this is that age-related allowances depend on income. Check that the Inland Revenue is not overestimating the amount. See the section TAX SAVING FOR THE OVER 65s later in this chapter for more details.

## Additional Information on the Tax Coding Notice

PAYE Tax Coding Notices should be kept safe. They contain much valuable information including:

- the address of the taxpayer's tax office

- tax office telephone number

- tax reference number

- National Insurance number

- tax code

---

### 🖉 Tax tips

Tax codes give employees the opportunity to calculate just how much a perk is costing. If the costs outweigh the benefits to the individual employee they should consider forgoing the benefit to save tax. See the section BENEFITS IN KIND later in this chapter for help in calculating the cost of perks.

It is the taxpayer's – not the employer's or the Inland Revenue's – responsibility to check that their tax code is right. Do not assume it is correct!

## TAX SAVING FOR EMPLOYEES

Employees have tax deducted from their taxable income from employment which includes:

- salary

- overtime

- bonuses

- commissions

- tips or gratuities

- holiday pay

- sick pay including statutory sick pay

- statutory maternity pay and any maternity pay from the employer (the state maternity allowance is not taxable)

- taxable benefits in kind (these are perks of the job such as company cars)

> ### ✎ Tax tip
>
> Although sick pay is normally taxable, if the amount is less than the tax-free pay to which the employee is entitled (less than their personal allowances) then the employee should receive a refund of tax already paid in addition to the sick pay.

## Employees and PAYE

Employers deduct tax and National Insurance from each employee's salary and pay this over to the Inland Revenue under PAYE and, as explained earlier in the chapter, each employee has a tax code which tells the employer how much to deduct.

> ### ✎ Tax tip
>
> Employees who suddenly earn more than usual in one month – for example, as a result of a bonus or some overtime – can find that the amount of tax that has been deducted seems to be far higher than expected. This could be because the increased earnings in that month have pushed them into the higher-rate tax bracket.
>
> However, if they are basic-rate taxpayers and their income over the entire year does not push them into the higher rate, they will not lose out. The tax tables used by employers automatically adjust the amount of tax deducted so the correct amount should be deducted by the end of the tax year.

## Moving Jobs

When employees move jobs they need to hand over a form P45 to their new employer so that the correct tax code is used when calculating the amount of tax to be deducted through PAYE.

**✎ Tax tips**

Those who do not have a P45 may be told they will be given an 'emergency' tax code. Many taxpayers wrongly interpret this to mean that they will be taxed at a far higher rate than they should be. This is generally incorrect. The 'emergency' tax code – 453L for the 2001/02 tax year – is the same as the tax code for those who are only entitled to the basic personal allowance. Those who are single and do not have children under the age of 16 will generally have the correct amount of tax deducted.

Those who have not been working for part of the tax year could find that they pay too much tax if they do not have a P45. This is because those who are paid monthly are allocated a twelfth of the personal allowance for each month of the tax year before paying tax. Those who have, for example, not worked for the first two months of the year will miss out on two months of their allowance.

It is essential when starting new employment after a gap, that employees ensure they provide their employer with the correct information.

Those who have not got a form P45 should be given form P46 by their new employer. This form is then passed on to the Inland Revenue to work out a tax code. Until one is issued, employees will be taxed using the emergency tax code with the calculations assuming that this pay period is the first of the year (regardless of when the employee starts work during the tax year), so no account is taken of any period of no earnings. Once the correct code is issued, the employer will refund any tax overpaid.

# Losing a Job

Employees whose income suddenly drops – for example, because they have been sick or have lost their job – will have paid too much tax. This is because tax allowances are allocated evenly throughout the year. Someone paid monthly will receive a twelfth of their allowance each month. Remember the allowance is the amount that can be earned before paying tax.

**Example**

*Jenny Student stopped working in August – five months into the tax year – and did not have another job to go to as she was starting university.*

*During the five months she had earned £6,000 and paid tax on this amount. Her personal allowance of £4,535 for the 2001/02 tax year was divided by 12 when calculating how much tax she owed, so each month the first £378 (the personal allowance of £4,533 divided by 12) was not taxed.*

*Of the £1,200 she earned each month therefore, only £822 was subject to income tax.*

*During the 2001/02 tax year the first £1,880 of taxable income would be taxed at 10 per cent. On a monthly basis this works out at £157 per month taxed at the 10 per cent rate. The remainder of her taxable salary was taxed at the basic rate of 22 per cent, and on a monthly basis this worked out at £665 a month at the 22 per cent rate.*

*Her monthly tax bill was:*

£157 @ 10% = £ 15.70
£665 @ 22% = £146.30

TOTAL          £162

*Over five months she paid £810 in tax.*

*However, as she earned only £6,000 in the entire tax year her tax bill should have been:*

£6,000 – £4,535 (the personal allowance) = £1,465 taxable income

*As this was below the £1,880 threshold for the starting rate of tax all of her income should be taxed at the 10 per cent rate, i.e. £1,465 × 10% = £146.50*

*As she had already paid £810 in tax she was therefore due a rebate of £663.50.*

If she had earned less than her personal allowance, any unused entitlement could have been used to set against the taxable amount of any jobseeker's allowance, if she had become unemployed.

## Benefits in Kind

It is not just an employee's salary that is subject to income tax. Any perks or benefits in kind are also taxable. Even though the employee receives no hard cash, he is taxed on the taxable value of these perks – such as the use of a company car, free private health insurance or a membership of a gym.

The way perks are taxed means they are valuable tax breaks. This is because employees do not pay the full cost of the perk, only a maximum of 40 per cent (the higher rate of tax). How? This is how the tax on benefits works:

### Example

*Wayne Worker has the benefit of free private health insurance as a perk of his job. This costs his employer £400 a year. If he wanted to buy the same level of cover for himself it would probably cost him even more as his employer has negotiated a group discount.*

*The £400 cost of the perk is deducted from his personal allowances (and reduces the amount of earnings that escape tax) as part of his PAYE tax code so that he is taxed at source on the benefit. As he is a basic-rate taxpayer he pays tax – at the basic rate of 22 per cent – on £400 of income that would otherwise have been tax free. So the perk costs him: 22% × £400 = £88*

*If he was a higher-rate taxpayer the cost would be: 40% × £400 = £160*

*This is still far less than the £400 cost of the perk.*

So benefits in kind cost less than the actual benefit – even for higher-rate taxpayers. Benefits are always charged at the highest rate of income tax an employee has to pay. So for every £1,000 cash equivalent of perk (usually the cost to the employer) a higher-rate tax-payer is charged £400 in tax.

---

> ### 🖊 Tax tip
>
> If an employee pays towards the cost of the benefit, the amount paid
> is usually deducted from the taxable value or cash equivalent. How-
> ever, this is not always the case. In some cases – as for example with
> company car drivers who benefit from free fuel for private use – the
> entire cost of the perk must be reimbursed to escape tax.

---

## Rules for Those Earning Under £8,500

It may seem ludicrous today but when the tax rules for benefits were devised, higher earners were classed as those earning over £8,500. Those earning under this threshold were classed as lower earners and pay less tax on their benefits. In fact, they pay no tax on most fringe benefits, including company cars and fuel, and only the second-hand value of benefits that can be sold, or otherwise turned into money.

However, these rules do not apply to company directors and those who control more than 5 per cent of the share capital of the company. The exemptions to this rule are that the director:

- Is a full-time working director or works for a charity or a non-profit making company.

- Is not also a director of an associated company.

- Does not own (either on his own or together with close family members and certain other associates) or control a total of 5 per cent or less of the shares in the company.

- Earns below the £8,500 limit.

All of the above have to apply for the director to escape tax on fringe benefits.

Even if an employee earns under £8,500 a year, he can still be taxed at the full rate on perks. This is because the earnings include not just basic salary but also any bonuses, commissions and financial payments as well as the taxable value of any benefit (known as the cash equivalent).

## Example

*Louise Lowearner earns just £7,000 a year and gets a company car in order to do her job because it involves visiting clients. As she can also use the car for private use it is taxed as a perk of the job.*

*The car has a taxable value of £1,550. Although she receives no bonuses or commissions, the fact that her taxable perk, once added to her salary, totals more than £8,500 (by just £50) means she is treated as a higher earner. Therefore the tax concessions given to those earning less than this amount do not apply. She must therefore pay tax on her company car.*

Earnings are worked out on an annual basis. Those who are employed for part of the year must work out the figures pro rata as though they worked for the whole year. So if an employee earns £5,000 for six months' work – the equivalent of £10,000 a year – this means he will exceed the £8,500 threshold.

---

### ✐ Tax tip

Those earning near the £8,500 limit should consider the value of benefits carefully. One model of company car could push them over the threshold and mean that they are taxed on their benefits in kind while another type of car, one that is more environmentally friendly, may have a lower taxable value and mean they escape tax on their perks.

# Tax-free Perks

Generally if an employee wants to escape tax on employee benefits and expenses, these benefits must be 'wholly, exclusively and necessarily incurred' in the performance of duties of office or employment. This definition is important. Employees cannot claim travelling home from work as a tax-free expense because their duties of employment do not start until the place of work is reached and end when they leave to start their journey home. (There are special rules for those who work from home or from more than one office or building.)

However, there are exceptions and the following benefits are exempt from tax:

- Canteens: tea and coffee and also free or cheap meals provided these are available to all employees.

- Meal/luncheon vouchers – but only a very low amount of just 15p a day.

- Childcare in a workplace nursery but not nursery place vouchers or free or subsidized places at nurseries unconnected to the workplace.

- Medical check-ups provided these are routine.

- Pension scheme contributions made by the employer into approved pension schemes.

- Any perks that do not cost the employer money or do not incur an additional cost. For instance, if an employee works for an airline, theatre, bus or train company which gives cheap seats to its employees this will not usually be taxable.

- Sports facilities provided they are available to employees generally.

- Incidental expenses while working away from home for things like telephone calls and laundry. Employees can receive £5 for every night spent away from home on business in the UK and £10 if abroad. If they receive more than this allowance, the payment cannot be tax free and the total amount (including the £5 or £10 concession) becomes taxable.

- Free parking at or near work.

- Directors' and employees' liability insurance.

- Training expenses for those who need to acquire new skills for their job. The expenses can include books, travel to and from the course and the reasonable cost of meals.

- Clothes specially needed for work (but not everyday work clothes such as suits) and the cost of cleaning or repairing protective or functional clothing.

- Discounts on goods and services provided there is no cost to the employer – for example, shop staff who are allowed to buy goods at the wholesale price.

- Employee parties and outings including staff Christmas parties – normally the maximum allowed is £75 per head.

- Provision of travel, accommodation and subsistence due to disruption caused by industrial action.

- The value of outplacement counselling services provided in the UK to full-time employees (with a minimum two years' service) who are made redundant.

- Fees and subscriptions to professional bodies – provided the organization is Inland Revenue approved and the employee needs to be a member for his job.

- Personal gifts on marriage or retirement (but not money on retirement).

- Relocation expenses within certain limits – generally up to £8,000 if the employee has to move home (i.e. it is no longer within reasonable daily travelling distance from their employment). Costs that can be paid for include: removal expenses, legal fees, estate agency costs and even the costs of buying new domestic goods if the old ones are not suitable for the employee's new home.

- Season ticket loans and other interest-free or cheap loans up to a total of £5,000.

- Life insurance provided it is part of the company pension scheme.

- Some low-rent or rent-free job-related living accommodation – if it is necessary for the job (for example, for a caretaker) or if it enables the employee to do their job better (for example, a publican) or if the employee has to live in it for security reasons.

- Long-service awards if given for service of 20 years or more with the same employer (no more than £20 per year of service – so that is a very ungenerous £400 for the minimum 20 years).

- Scholarship and apprenticeship schemes provided the employee is enrolled for at least one academic year and attends full time for an average of at least 20 weeks a year and the amount of payment including lodging, travelling and subsistence but excluding tuition fees is not above £7,000. If more is received, the full amount is taxable.

- Shares bought cheaply or given for free in an employer's company through an approved company shares scheme – see the section on EMPLOYEE SHARE SCHEMES later in this chapter for further details.

- Staff suggestion scheme awards – up to an overall maximum of £5,000 for the scheme.

- Certain travel costs (see the sections later in this chapter).

- Some of the heating and lighting costs of the employee's home and some of the telephone bills and other costs if the employee has to use his home for work.

- Gifts and goods from business contacts costing up to £150 provided that the gift is not in recognition of particular services and hasn't been procured by the employer

- The value of any entertainment, such as a meal, provided by someone other than the employer or an associate company.

---

📝 **Tax tips**

Check which benefits can be received tax free. Employees should make sure they know which benefits will cost money and which will not – and then claim every tax-free benefit they can and ask for additional tax-free benefits when negotiating remuneration with their employer.

Some manual workers who have to pay for the cost of the upkeep of tools and special clothing out of their own pockets, rather than receiving these as a benefit, can claim a flat-rate allowance from the Inland Revenue ranging from £40–£135 per year.

---

## Taxable Perks

Any benefit that is not 'wholly, exclusively and necessarily' needed to do a job and is not a tax-free perk listed above will be taxable.

### *Company Cars*

One of the most popular employee perks, the company car, is valuable in many ways: the tax on the perk is usually far less than the costs employees would face if they ran their own car and they do not have the additional hassle of servicing, taxing, MOTing and insuring the vehicle.

From this year (starting 6 April 2002), the charge on the benefit of a company car is now graduated according to carbon dioxide ($CO_2$) emissions.

In the past, mileage was reduced for drivers who exceeded 2,500 and 18,000 miles a year on company business and for those driving cars more than four years old at the end of the tax year. These were valuable ways to save tax that no longer apply.

The charge will now start at 15 per cent of the car's list price when new. This basic charge will apply for cars emitting $CO_2$ at or below the qualifying level. It will then build up in 1 per cent steps for every 5 grams per kilometre (g/km) over that level. The maximum charge will be 35 per cent of the car's price. The qualifying level will gradually be reduced as cars get more fuel efficient.

### Car benefit charges depending on $CO_2$ emissions

| 2002/03 | 2003/04 | 2004/05 | % of car's price taxed |
|---|---|---|---|
| | ($CO_2$ emissions in grams per kilometre) | | |
| The exact $CO_2$ emission should be rounded down to the nearest 5g/km. | | | |
| 165 | 155 | 145 | 15 |
| 170 | 160 | 150 | 16 |
| 175 | 165 | 155 | 17 |
| 180 | 170 | 160 | 18 |
| 185 | 175 | 165 | 19 |
| 190 | 180 | 170 | 20 |
| 195 | 185 | 175 | 21 |
| 200 | 190 | 180 | 22 |
| 205 | 195 | 185 | 23 |
| 210 | 200 | 190 | 24 |
| 215 | 205 | 195 | 25 |
| 220 | 210 | 200 | 26 |
| 225 | 215 | 205 | 27 |
| 230 | 220 | 210 | 28 |
| 235 | 225 | 215 | 29 |
| 240 | 230 | 220 | 30 |
| 245 | 235 | 225 | 31 |
| 250 | 240 | 230 | 32 |
| 255 | 245 | 235 | 33 |
| 260 | 250 | 240 | 34 |
| 265 | 255 | 245 | 35 |

Add 3 per cent if the car runs solely on diesel up to the 33 per cent tax level when this drops to 2 per cent and then to 1 per cent at the 34 per cent level. The maximum charge is 35 per cent so there is no diesel supplement for cars taxed at this level.

Cars without an approved figure of $CO_2$ emissions will be taxed according to engine size as follows:

| Engine size | % of car's price on which tax will be charged |
|---|---|
| 0–1,400cc | 15% |
| 1,401–2,000cc | 25% |
| 2,001cc+ | 35% |

Diesel cars are subject to a 3 per cent supplement, but this will not take the maximum charge above 35 per cent.

Cars registered before 1 January 1998 will be taxed according to engine size as follows:

| Engine size | % of car's price on which tax will be charged |
|---|---|
| 0–1,400cc | 15% |
| 1,401–2,000cc | 22% |
| 2,001cc+ | 32% |

If a car has no approved figure of $CO_2$ emissions and no cylinder capacity it will be taxed on 35 per cent of the car's price (or 32 per cent if the car was registered before 1 January 1998) unless it runs solely on electricity, in which case the charge will be 15 per cent of the car's price.

## Example

*Penny Petrol drives a company car, which has a list price of £15,000. The new car, which runs on petrol, was bought in March 2000 and had an approved $CO_2$ emission factor of 197g/km*

*Her tax charge is calculated as follows:*

*197 g/km rounded down to 195 g/km (the nearest level – see table)*
*The rate at this level of emissions for 2002/03 is 21%*
*21% × the list price of £15,000 = £3,150*

*However, this is not the amount of tax she will pay. She pays tax on this charge at her highest rate. As a basic-rate taxpayer this will be:*

*22% (the basic rate of tax)* $\times$ *£3,150 = £693*

*Her colleague David Diesel drives a car with the same list price but the approved $CO_2$ emission factor of his vehicle is 240g/km.*
   *His car benefit charge for 2002/03 is:*

*The rate at this level of emissions, 240 g/km, is 30%*
*Plus the diesel supplement of 3% = 33%*
*33% $\times$ the list price of £15,000 = £4,950*

*As David is a higher-rate taxpayer he will suffer a tax liability of:*

*40% (the higher rate of tax) $\times$ £4,950 = £1,980*

---

### ✎ Tax tips

In the past, company car drivers could reduce the amount of tax they paid on their vehicle by increasing their business mileage or by not renewing their car and driving an older model. This is no longer the case. The only way to reduce the tax liability is to change the type of vehicle driven opting for one with a lower $CO_2$ emissions rate. Employees about to receive a new company car should check how environmentally friendly it is.

Drivers with cars registered before 1 January 1998 will find that they could be charged more tax than those drivers with similar cars registered after this date. This is because older cars are taxed on engine size, not the emissions rate.

It may not make a style statement, but driving a company van may be a better bet than a company car – particularly if the employee can make private use of the van (ferrying the cricket team's equipment to matches, loading up with DIY equipment if doing up a house; driving to France to stock up on wine). This is because for the private use of a van, taxpayers pay tax on a flat amount of £500 (which works out as tax of just £110 for basic-rate taxpayers).

## Free Fuel for Private Use

Employees with company cars are taxed on any fuel paid for by the employer which is for private use. So a company car driver who is allowed to submit petrol receipts regardless of whether this petrol was used on company business miles or to go to the shops, will pay tax on this benefit.

Rather than pay tax on the value of the actual amount of fuel used on private mileage, employees are usually taxed using the fuel scale charge. This sets a value on the worth of private fuel depending on the engine size of the car.

In the 2002 Budget, the Chancellor announced that charges will in future be based on $CO_2$ emissions not engine size, ranging from 15 to 35 per cent of a set figure for the year.

Below are the fuel scale charges for 2002/03. Rates for 2001/02 are in brackets:

| Engine size | Petrol | Diesel |
| --- | --- | --- |
| 1400cc or less | £2,240 (£1,930) | £2,850 (£2,460) |
| 1401cc to 2000cc | £2,850 (£2,460) | £2,850 (£2,460) |
| Over 2000cc | £4,200 (£3,620) | £4,200 (£3,620) |

### ✎ Tax tip

Employees with company cars who use these cars very rarely for private use (they may have a second car they prefer to use, or live centrally in a city and have little need for a car other than for business journeys) should consider paying their employer for any private mileage. The scale charges apply automatically unless the employee is required to make good all the costs of fuel provided for private use, including journeys between home and the permanent workplace, and in fact does so. Paying for some – instead of all – of the fuel used on private journeys does not mean the driver escapes the tax.

**Example**

*Dan Driver is a young, single sales representative from Manchester who lives in a warehouse conversion in the heart of the city. Although he drives thousands of miles a year on business, he rarely uses his car for private use as he shops locally and when he goes out in the evening does not want to risk a conviction for drinking and driving.*

*His employer gives staff the option of opting out of the free fuel for private use system. Although it means Dan has to keep detailed mileage records he does this anyway so his boss knows how much he spends on each visit to his clients. At the end of the tax year he calculates he has spent just £125 on fuel for private use.*

*He therefore saves:*

*40% (he is a higher-rate taxpayer) × £2,460 (the fuel scale charge for a 1,600cc car) = £984 (the tax paid on the perk)*
*£984 (the amount of tax he would have paid) – £125 (the cost of fuel for private use) = £859.*

**Note:** Business mileage does not include journeys between home and the permanent workplace. These are classed as private use of the car.

## *Employees' Own Vehicles*

Employees who use their own vehicles for company business can find that this works in their favour. This is because they are given an authorized mileage allowance which is often higher than the actual cost to the driver – so they make a profit, tax free.

As from this year, 6 April 2002, the previous system of authorized mileage rates geared to a car's engine size is being replaced by a single rate. This will apply to all cars and vans regardless of engine size. The employer will be able to pay up to this amount per mile without generating a tax or National Insurance Contribution (NIC) charge.

Note that these are the maximum allowable rates. Employers may not be so generous in practice.

*Rates for 2002/03*

The tax and NIC free mileage rates are:

Cars and vans:

| | |
|---|---|
| On the first 10,000 miles in the tax year | 40p per mile |
| On each additional mile over 10,000 miles | 25p per mile |
| Motor cycles | 24p per mile |
| Bicycles | 20p per mile |

These are the rates per mile that can be paid without the employee incurring a tax liability (without the payments becoming a benefit in kind).

---

### ✏ Tax tips

Employees who work for employers who are less generous and pay less than the statutory rate, can claim tax relief up to the level of the mileage allowance. So even if their boss is a little mean, they do not lose out.

Employees can no longer claim for part of the cost of purchasing the car (capital allowances or interest on loans to purchase the car) when making a mileage claim. Under the previous system they could make claims for expenses based on actual motoring expenditure and could claim for some of the cost of buying the car. This would have been beneficial if the costs were higher than the mileage allowance.

Employers who are more generous and pay above the statutory rate will generate a tax and NIC liability, which is paid on the amount in excess of the statutory rate. So if the employer pays 5p above the allowance, this 5p will be subject to income tax at the individual employee's highest rate. The National Insurance is paid by the employer.

Employers are also allowed to pay up to 5p per mile free of tax and NICs for each passenger carried. However, the passenger must be a fellow employee making the same business trip. And this only applies where employers pay extra for carrying passengers. If no

payments are made for carrying business passengers, employees will
not be able to claim any tax relief.

## Business Travel

Employees are not taxed on any expenses claim – or money paid –
for business travel either from the employee's home or place of
work (travel from home to work is not allowed). There are special
rules for site-based workers who can be paid for travelling costs
when posted to a different site of work. However, those who have
more than one workplace cannot claim for the travelling costs from
home to either place of work.

## Employers Who Pay for Journeys Home

If an employer pays for an employee's journey between the workplace and home, this is usually treated as a benefit to the employee.
The cost to the employer forms part of the taxable income from
employment for the employee.

---

### ✎ Tax tip

There is an exemption to this rule. If the employee is occasionally
required to work late but those occasions are not regular, then the
cost of getting home (usually a taxi fare) can be claimed from the
employer without being treated as a taxable benefit in kind.

However, either public transport between the workplace and home
must have ceased, or it would not be reasonable in the circumstances
for the employer to expect the employee to use it (the service is
irregular, runs rarely or would take too long). Working late means until
9 p.m. or later.

---

## Employer Gifts

Employers cannot get round the rules by giving staff goods or
services instead of hard cash. Assets that can either be converted

into cash or sold are taxable. However, employees may only pay tax on the second-hand value.

If the employer gives an employee his company car when he leaves employment, then the employee will be taxed on its second-hand value – minus anything paid towards the cost by the employer. As cars depreciate rapidly, this could work in the employee's favour.

Employers can, however, lend some items of equipment to their employees tax free.

---

### ✎ Tax tip

To encourage wider computer use and computer skills among employees there is no benefits tax charged on computers and computer equipment worth up to £2,000 lent by employers to employees for up to £2,000 worth of computer equipment.

---

## Employer Loans

Loans are a fairly common perk. Although cheap or interest-free loans such as season ticket loans of £5,000 or less are tax free, if a loan is for more than this amount the entire amount is taxable. In most cases, these larger loans will be subsidized mortgages.

The taxable value is based on the difference between the interest paid by the employee and the official rate of interest (this was 6.25 per cent for 2000/01 and dropped to 5 per cent from 6 January 2002). This rate is set for the entire year and is announced just before a new tax year begins.

---

### ✎ Tax tip

Even if a subsidized loan from an employer is taxable, it will still usually be cheaper than if the employee had to pay the full cost of the loan. For example, if the subsidized rate led to a £1,000 interest saving each year (compared to the official rate of interest), even a higher-rate taxpayer would only suffer tax of £400 (40% × £1,000). So the employee would be £600 better off with the subsidized mortgage, even after tax. Basic-rate taxpayers would make even larger savings.

### Example

*Harry Homebuyer works for a bank which has a subsidized mortgage scheme. He has borrowed £50,000 at 4% interest. The official rate of interest was 6.25%. His taxable amount is therefore:*

| | |
|---|---|
| *£50,000 at the official rate of 6.25%* | *£3,125* |
| *Less interest at 4%* | *£2,000* |
| *Taxable amount* | *£1,125* |

*This will be shown on Harry's PAYE Tax Coding Notice as a deduction:*

| | |
|---|---|
| *Employers loan benefit* | *£1,125* |

*However, the cost to Harry is only 22% (he is a basic-rate taxpayer) of that amount.*

*22% × £1,125 = £247.50*

Employees can get tax relief for loan interest if the loan is for certain qualifying purposes:

- to purchase a share in a partnership

- to acquire an interest in a close company

- to buy plant and machinery including a car for use in trade or employment

- to pay inheritance tax

## Example

*Caroline Car is an estate agent and needs a car in order to do her job. Her employer lends her £7,500 at 2% to help her buy a car. She pays £150 of interest. During the tax year, she drives a total of 12,000 miles – 4,000 of these are in the course of her job. The taxable benefit is:*

| | |
|---|---|
| *Interest on the loan at the official rate of 6.25% × £7,500* | *£468.75* |
| *Less interest actually paid* | *£150* |
| *Taxable benefit* | *£318.75* |

*She then needs to claim tax relief on the business proportion of this benefit.*

*Of the total amount of interest ⅓ (4,000/12,000 of the miles are for business) is attributable to her employment duties. She can therefore claim tax relief on this amount in the qualifying loans box on the tax return, box 15.2, calculated as:*

*£468.75 (total interest) ÷ 3 = £156.25 of tax relief.*

*This leaves her with a total tax liability for low-cost car loan of £162.50.*

For more information see Inland Revenue leaflet IR145: Low Interest Loans Provided by Employers.

## Employee Share Ownership

Employee share ownership is not only lucrative (many employees make sizeable profits when they sell their shares), it is also tax efficient.

There are several types of share scheme. Save As You Earn (SAYE) Sharesave and the Company Share Option Plan (CSOP) are the two main types of existing scheme. In addition there is the new All Employee Share Ownership Plan (AESOP) now known as the Share Incentive Plan (SIP).

**Note:** The Approved Profit Sharing Scheme is no longer running. After 2002, schemes have to be moved into new plans for the tax breaks to continue.

## The All-employee Share Ownership Plan (AESOP)

The AESOP or SIP was designed to be a way of ensuring all employees can have an interest in their company's success. Companies have been able to offer AESOPs since July 2000.

- Under the new Employee Share Ownership Plan employers can give employees up to £3,000 of shares each year free of tax and National Insurance. Some or all of these shares can be awarded to employees for reaching performance targets.

- In addition to being given shares by their employer, employees can buy what are known as partnership shares out of their pre-tax salary (gross income before tax and National Insurance is deducted), up to a maximum of £1,500 a year.

- Employers can match partnership shares by giving employees up to two free shares for each new partnership share they buy. So if an employee buys 100 shares, the employer can give them a further 200 for free.

- Employees who keep their shares in the plan for five years will pay no income tax or National Insurance in respect of those shares.

- Employees who keep their shares in the plan for three years will only pay income tax and National Insurance on the initial value of the shares – any increase in their value will be tax free.

- Shares must be held within the scheme (they are held by trustees) for three to five years. Any growth in their value during this period is free of CGT. If the employee sells the shares after five years there is no tax liability. If, however, the employee holds onto the shares once they have come out of the scheme, there is a potential CGT liability but only on any increase in the value of the shares since they came out of the scheme.

- Shares have to come out of the plan when employees leave their job. Companies can decide whether employees lose their free shares or not if they leave within three years.

- Up to £1,500 of dividends may be reinvested in shares tax free each year.

- Shares are exempt from stamp duty when employees buy shares from an AESOP trust.

---

### ✎ Tax tip

Stamp duty is no longer payable on shares bought through this scheme.

## Save As You Earn (SAYE) Sharesave

The SAYE scheme gives employees the option of buying shares in their employer's company at a discounted price of up to 20 per cent. Employees do not initially pay for these shares and instead save a regular amount until the maturity date – usually five years later. They then have the choice of (or option of) buying the shares at the agreed discounted price or taking their cash out of the scheme. If, as is usually the case, the company's shares have risen in value, it makes financial sense to purchase the shares as they will cost far less than the stock market price and can then be sold for an instant profit. There is no tax or National Insurance charged on the discount or on the gain made when the option is exercised (the shares are bought).

Employees can save a fixed monthly amount of between £5 and £250 for three, five or seven years. At the end of the savings contract a tax-free bonus is payable.

To qualify for these tax breaks these schemes must be eligible to all employees. They are not affected by the new all-employee share ownership plan.

✎ **Tax tips**

These schemes require employees to save a fixed amount each month usually for five years before the options can be exercised. As the schemes run on a cyclical basis with new schemes often launched every year, employees can ensure that they escape any CGT on profits made when they sell the shares by limiting the number of shares they sell in each tax year (only selling as each plan matures), so that they do not make a gain that exceeds their CGT threshold. This ensures that the shares are not only free of income tax but also of CGT.

Once shares have been realized (i.e. the employee has bought the shares), there is a 90-day window in which they can be transferred directly into an ISA. The maximum that can be transferred is £7,000. The advantage? Once in an ISA they can be sold free of CGT and any future dividends are free of income tax. The disadvantage? The investor's ISA limit is then used up. However, if, by transferring some of the shares into an ISA the investor escapes a hefty CGT bill it will be worthwhile.

Investors do not have to realize their shares (i.e. purchase them) for up to six months after the maturity date comes up. They then have a further 90 days within which to transfer any shares into an ISA. This extra time can mean that a capital gain is deferred into a new tax year. Alternatively, if an employee has used up this year's ISA allowance and faces a CGT bill, it may be possible to delay realizing the shares until they can be transferred into an ISA once the new allowance is given on 6 April.

If the employee's company has performed badly and the shares are 20 per cent or more below the price at which the option was granted, then the shares do not have to be purchased. The proceeds of the SAYE savings will be repaid in cash, tax free.

## Enterprise Management Incentives (EMI)

This scheme is designed to help small but growing companies (often in the high-tech sectors) to attract staff who may need an incentive to accept what could potentially be a risky or less rewarding job. Companies can grant up to £3 million of shares under the Enterprise Management Incentives (EMI) scheme.

EMI share options can be granted by trading companies, quoted or unquoted, with gross assets of no more than £30 million. These companies can reward up to 15 key employees with tax-advantaged share options, with each receiving options worth up to £100,000 at the time of the grant.

Options are normally free of income tax and National Insurance charges on grant and on exercise. When the shares are sold, CGT taper relief normally starts from the date the options were granted. For a full explanation of taper relief see the section on Taper Relief in the Chapter on Capital Gains Tax.

---

### ✐ Tax tip

Employees who own shares in non-trading companies, which are mainly companies that deal in land, securities or other financial instruments, are in banking or insurance, provide legal or accountancy services or are property-backed businesses such as hotels (the EMI applies to trading companies) where they work, can benefit from an additional CGT break provided they do not have a 'material interest' of more than 10 per cent in the company. They can claim the business assets rate of taper relief when they sell their shares which means that the effective rate of CGT reduces from 40 per cent to 10 per cent after just four years for a higher-rate taxpayer compared to reducing to 24 per cent after a much longer period of ten years for non-business assets.

---

## Company Share Option Plan (CSOP)

Under this scheme employees are granted options to acquire shares at the market price at the time of grant. So, unlike SAYE Sharesave there is no discount. However, this does not mean there is no profit. Between the time share options are granted (i.e. the option is taken up by the employee) and exercised (i.e. the shares are actually bought by the employee), they should, in theory, rise in value. When they are purchased, the market value should be much higher than the price the employee actually pays – giving an instant profit.

Employees may be granted options over shares worth up to £30,000 at any one time.

There is no tax or National Insurance charged on the gain made when the option is exercised, provided that the options are held for at least three years and there is a gap of at least three years between each tax-relieved exercise. Options need to be exercised (bought) within ten years after they are received.

For options granted after 16 July 1995, there is an additional requirement. The price paid for the shares must not be below the market value when the option was granted.

These schemes are not affected by the AESOP.

---

✎ **Tax tip**

By timing the granting and exercising of options carefully (ensuring there is a three-year gap), employees can ensure that they escape tax on their share options.

---

## Unapproved Share Options

The schemes already covered in this chapter are what are known as approved schemes, which simply means they are approved for tax purposes and therefore tax breaks.

Unapproved schemes – although they may sound slightly dubious – are simply unapproved when it comes to tax breaks.

However, this does not mean these share options are not worth having. Unapproved share options tend to be offered by fast-growing, young companies and the shares have potential for substantial growth in value. However, while no income tax breaks are given, these profits could be subject to CGT.

## Example

*Roger Rich was given the option to buy 1,000 shares in his employer's company Wealth Ltd at a price of £3 per share. After five years he exercised the option, paying £3,000 to buy the 1,000 shares. However, they had risen in value to £7 a share during those years so he will pay income tax (not CGT) on the profit made, even if he does not sell the shares. Tax is payable when the option is exercised.*

| | |
|---|---|
| *Market value* | £7,000 |
| *Less amount paid* | £3,000 |
| | = £4,000 *taxable profit.* |

In addition, NICs are charged on gains arising when share options are exercised outside an Inland Revenue approved scheme and the shares are readily convertible into cash. The NICs are payable by both employer and employee.

It is, however, hard for employers to plan for NICs on share options, particularly where the share price is volatile. As a result, legislation was introduced in July 2000 to allow the employee to bear the employer's NIC on share option gains. Employees were then given tax relief for any of the employer's NICs that they paid against the taxable gain on the share option. In the example above, if the employee agrees to pay his employer's NICs, they will be deducted in arriving at the taxable amount.

In the 2001 Budget the amount of NIC payable on options granted between 6 April 1999 and 19 May 2000 was capped – limited to the gain attributable to the growth in the company share price up to 7 November 2000.

# TAX SAVING FOR THE OVER 65s

Retirement may be a time when most people want to put their feet up and take life easy, but the Inland Revenue does not see it that way. Tax gets more complicated for the over 65s. They are entitled to tax allowances not available to younger taxpayers but then lose some or all of these allowances if they earn more than a certain threshold.

The age allowances are covered in detail earlier in this chapter under TAX ALLOWANCES and TAX CREDITS. The over 65s should read these sections carefully as they contain valuable tax-saving tips.

# Pension Income

Most pension income is taxable including:

• The basic state pension – which, although paid gross (without tax deducted), is taxable, if, once it is added to all other income, the individual's total taxable income exceeds his allowances.

• The State Earnings Related Pension Scheme (SERPS) – or any other additional state pension.

• Occupational or employers' pensions – these are paid net of tax through PAYE.

• Income from a compulsary purchase annuity.

However, the war disablement and widow's pensions are not taxable and neither are cold weather payments.

---

### 🖉 Tax tips

Those about to retire should contact their tax office to tell them that they plan to draw a pension. They should give their tax office an estimate of income after retirement – including income from the state pension and from savings. This is so the Inland Revenue can issue a PAYE code.

The tax deducted from an employer's pension using this PAYE code may seem higher than when the individual was an employee. This is to reflect the fact that the retiree now receives untaxed income (such as the state pension). Tax due on this income is collected through the PAYE code.

On retirement the PAYE code should be adjusted automatically to reflect the fact that the individual has reached 65 and now qualifies for higher age-related tax allowances. Even so, individuals should check that their PAYE code is correct.

- A code ending with a V means the pension is receiving the married couple's allowance for those born before 6 April 1935 and pays tax at the basic rate.

- A code ending with a P means the individual receives the higher age-related personal allowance for those aged 65–74.

- A code ending in a letter Y means the individual receives the higher age-related personal allowance for those aged 75 or over.

- A code ending in a T means the individual does not receive the full age allowances because his income exceeds the threshold (£17,900 for the 2002/03 tax year).

The higher age-related allowances are given to all taxpayers who reach 65 during the tax year – even if they have their 65th birthday on 5 April, the last day of the tax year. They are entitled to the allowances for the entire tax year, not just from the date they reach 65.

Those who work past state pension age will have their state pension added to other taxable income when determining the amount of tax they need to pay. However, they will not have to pay any more National Insurance once they reach state pension age. (Those who are self-employed will continue to pay Class 4 contributions until the end of the tax year in which they reach state pension age.)

Those who want to work past state pension age can defer taking the state pension for up to five years. As a result, they will receive a higher pension when they do retire. It will be increased by 7.5 per cent for each year retirement is put off.

## Non-taxpaying Pensioners

Pensioners who are non-taxpayers can register to receive any savings interest paid gross (without tax deducted) by filling in form R85 available from banks and building societies. Any tax already deducted can be reclaimed.

Those who only need pay tax at the starting rate of 10 per cent, can also claim a tax refund. See CHAPTER 2: SAVINGS AND INVESTMENTS for more tips.

Pensions paid by employer pension schemes will be paid without tax deducted if the pensioner's income is less than the personal and age allowances (the amount that can be earned each year before paying tax). So no tax should be paid, and no tax should need to be reclaimed.

Pensions paid by annuities purchased by the proceeds of a pension are usually paid after basic-rate tax has been taken off. Pensioners whose total taxable income is less than their tax allowances, can ask for this income to be paid without tax deducted. Ask for form R89 from the retirement annuity provider.

Those who need to pay some tax, but who can also receive some annuity income free of tax, will need to claim a tax refund from the Inland Revenue.

## Tax Relief for the Over 65s

Just as the over 65s (well, those who were born before 6 April 1935) are entitled to now-abolished tax allowances such as the married couples' allowance, they are also entitled to tax relief not available to taxpayers in general.

### Home Reversion Schemes

The elderly are often equity rich but income poor with the bulk of their wealth tied up in their home while they struggle to live on a low income. The solution to this is a home income scheme – a loan is taken out with, or part of the property is sold to a home income company in return for an income. One method of providing this income is to use the capital to purchase an annuity – a life insurance product that provides an income for life.

Interest on such loans taken out before 9 March 1999 to purchase an annuity from an insurance company still attract tax relief at 23 per cent (the basic rate of tax at that time) provided:

- The borrower was 65 or over at the time the annuity was purchased.

- 90 per cent of the loan taken out on the property on which interest is payable went towards buying the annuity.

- The property in question is the borrower's main residence.

As with the old mortgage interest tax relief (MIRAS) the maximum amount of the loan on which tax relief is allowed is £30,000. Tax relief does not have to be claimed as it is taken into account in the payments made to the lender.

## *Maintenance Relief*

Provided one spouse (either the payer of maintenance or the recipient – a divorced or separated spouse) was born before 6 April 1935, then tax relief on qualifying maintenance payments can be claimed. Individuals can claim 10 per cent tax relief on payments up to £2,110 for the 2002/03 tax year (giving maximum tax relief of £211).

Tax relief is not given on maintenance paid to, or for, children. The spouse receiving maintenance does not have to pay tax on this amount.

# TAX AND DEATH

The married couple's allowance is not reduced in the year of death of either spouse. In addition, both are entitled to the full personal allowance and any age-related allowance for the entire tax year in which they die.

The bereavement payment is also tax free. This £2,000 payment is paid as soon as an individual is widowed but is only paid if the late husband or wife was not entitled to the state retirement pension when he or she died, or the surviving spouse was under state pension age at the time of death.

Benefits paid on death – the widowed parent's allowance and bereavement allowances – are both taxable.

---

### ✎ Tax tips

If the husband's income does not exceed his allowances, then any unused married couple's allowance can be transferred to the widow. However, unused personal allowances cannot be transferred. The married couple's allowance will first be used against the husband's income – even if the couple shared the allowance. If the couple shared the allowance, any unused part can be transferred to the wife upon her death.

The widow's bereavement allowance was abolished in the 1999 budget. However, widows who failed to claim the allowance can still do so. The allowance was given to widows in the year of their husband's death and for the next year, provided they did not remarry. Widows have six years to claim an allowance – so that means they have until 6 April 2003 to claim any allowances for the 1996–1997 tax year.

The widow's bereavement allowance was worth £197 in 1999/2000. Those who claimed the allowance in the 1999/2000 tax year could claim an allowance worth £200 in 2000/01.

---

# TAX SAVING FOR FAMILIES

Husbands and wives are taxed separately on both their income and gains rather than as a family unit and are both entitled to individual personal tax allowances. However, couples often fail to use their allowances to their maximum benefit or to capitalize on the fact that one partner may pay tax at a lower rate. See the sections on TAX ALLOWANCES and TAX CREDITS earlier in this chapter for valuable tax-saving tips.

---

### ✎ Tax tip

When filling in their tax returns, spouses need only include half the income from any savings accounts, shares or property (unless they have elected to receive this income in different proportions). It is not unknown for couples to make the mistake of entering the total income – rather than just their share.

Children, too, are taxed as individuals and are entitled to their own personal allowance (so they should not have to pay tax on income from holiday jobs or interest from savings). However, parents cannot reduce their income tax liability by putting savings into their children's names because if this capital generates more than £100 in interest (gross) in a tax year, the whole amount (not just the excess over £100) is then taxable as the parent's income. For tax tips on ways to invest for children see CHAPTER 2: SAVINGS AND INVESTMENTS.

It may seem that there are no longer many tax advantages to being married particularly since the married couple's allowance was scrapped in April 2000 (other than for the over 65s).

However, couples do not normally pay CGT on gifts or transfers made between them – something that unmarried partners do not benefit from – and similarly upon death, anything inherited by a spouse escapes inheritance tax. See CHAPTER 4: CAPITAL GAINS TAX and CHAPTER 5: INHERITANCE TAX for more tax tips.

This is important as giving away assets that generate income (such as savings or investments) is an easy way to reduce income tax.

## Example

*Ian Investor had built up a substantial share and unit trust portfolio over the past few years and not only faced a large CGT liability when he sold the investments but was now earning a significant amount of income from his portfolio which was taxed at his top rate of tax, 40 per cent.*

*He decided to give his wife Iona £20,000 worth of investments which were transferred into her name. They generate an income of £800 a year, which is paid net. Although the tax credit (this is the name given to the 10 per cent tax automatically deducted from dividends before they are paid to investors) is not reclaimable by Iona, Ian no longer suffers the higher-rate of tax on this dividend income.*

*In addition, when Iona comes to sell the shares she can sell them in batches using up her CGT allowance each year to escape CGT. This still leaves Ian with his own CGT allowance.*


## Tax and Divorce

Couples do not normally pay CGT on gifts they receive from each other. This continues to apply in the year of separation. However, after that date, any gifts received from a separated spouse or former spouse are liable to CGT.

So, if a divorce settlement takes time, the partner required to transfer assets to the former spouse could find that he or she is liable to CGT. This is because CGT is payable when an asset is disposed of – which includes giving it away as well as selling it.

---

### ✐ Tax tips

The CGT exemption applies to transfers made during the tax year in which the couple have been living together – provided they were living together at some time.

Those separating at the start of the year have longer in which to make transfers. Those separating at the end of the tax year – February or March, for example – only have a few weeks within which to make transfers free of CGT.

The exemption is also lost on divorce. However, there is no inheritance tax to pay on:

- Money paid as a divorce settlement.

- Maintenance payments to a former partner or children including adopted and step-children who are under 18 or in full-time education.

Tax relief on maintenance payments is no longer given for younger families. Only if one of the partners in the marriage was 65 or over on 5 April 2000 will tax relief be given.

## Tax for Unmarried Couples

Now that the married couple's allowance has been abolished, those cohabiting are in much the same tax position as those who have tied the knot when it comes to income tax. However, the valuable CGT and inheritance tax concessions for married couples do not apply, and bereavement benefits paid to widows or widowers are not paid to those who are cohabiting, only those who were married.

---

     ✎ **Tax tip**

Unmarried parents who have a child living with them could claim the additional personal allowance (which was the same as the married couple's allowance) until this allowance was abolished from 6 April 2000. Those who were eligible for the allowance from 6 April 1997 until it was abolished, who did not claim it, can still do so.

---

# OTHER WAYS TO PAY LESS TAX

## Charitable Donations

Give to a good cause, not to the Inland Revenue – and at the same time save tax. However, charitable gifts have to be planned. It is not possible to put a few pounds in a collection box. Instead, all donations must be made through one of the Inland Revenue approved schemes.

## Gift Aid

Donations to charity through the Gift Aid scheme qualify for basic-rate tax relief. The scheme has no minimum donation (the £250 minimum was abolished at the end of the 1999/2000 tax year).

Higher-rate taxpayers can claim higher-rate tax relief on any donations. Although the charity receives the basic-rate tax relief, it is the donor who gets an 18 per cent tax relief (the difference between the basic- and higher-rate tax rates). This must be claimed through the taxpayer's tax office. From 2003, higher-rate taxpayers can carry back their 18 per cent tax relief to the previous tax year.

---

### 🖉 Tax tips

Non-taxpayers or starting-rate taxpayers should think twice about using Gift Aid as it could cost them money. They will have to repay tax reclaimed by the charity (in part or whole depending on their rate of tax).

Pensioners whose income is close to or slightly above the maximum allowed before age-related allowances are reduced (see the AGE ALLOWANCES section earlier in this chapter) can keep their income within the limit by deducting the gross amount of gifts made during the tax year.

In order to calculate tax relief due, donors must work out the gross and net amount of gifts.

---

### Example

*Gary Generous decides to make donations to his favourite charity through Gift Aid, as he knows they can benefit from tax relief.*

*He wants the charity to receive £1,000. However, he realizes that if he gives that amount, once tax relief is added he will in fact be giving far more. So he needs to calculate the net amount to donate.*

*£1,000 − £220 tax relief (22% of £1,000) = £780*

*So he donates £780, and the charity claims £220 in tax relief bringing the total amount up to £1,000.*

For those who pay tax at the higher-rate the calculation is slightly more complex.

*Harry Highearner decides to give £500 to charity and wants to calculate how much tax relief he can claim as a higher-rate taxpayer.*
*He makes a £500 donation through Gift Aid on which the charity can claim 22 per cent tax relief.*
*To gross up his donation he divides £500 by 78 and multiplies the answer by 100.*

*£500 ÷ 78 × 100 = £641*

*So once the 22% tax relief of £141 has been claimed by the charity the total donation is £641.*
    *If Harry was a basic-rate taxpayer then he need take no further action.*
*However, as a higher-rate taxpayer he can claim higher-rate tax relief.*
    *This is calculated as follows:*

| | |
|---|---|
| *Tax relief at 40% (40% of the gross donation of £641)* | *£257* |
| *Less 22% tax relief claimed by charity* | *(£141)* |
| *Higher rate relief (reduction in Harry's own tax liability)* | *£116* |

**Warning:** If Harry was a non-taxpayer, he would have to repay the £141 tax relief claimed by the charity. However, if he was a lower-rate taxpayer he would probably escape paying all of this money and provided he paid £141 in tax at the lower rates he would not have to make good the tax relief paid to the charity.

It is also possible to give listed shares (shares in stock market quoted companies) and units in a UK authorized unit trust or shares in an open-ended investment company to a charity and obtain tax relief. Tax relief is based on their market value (inclusive of any costs of disposal). Tax relief is now also given on donations of land or property.

For more information ask for Inland Revenue Leaflet IR178: Giving Shares and Securities to Charity.

---

### 🖉 Tax tip

Those facing a hefty CGT bill – or wanting to reduce their gains to below the threshold of £7,700 (£7,500 for the 2001/02 tax year) – can consider giving some shares to charity. No CGT arises on these gifts. So in addition to receiving income tax relief at 40 per cent, higher-rate taxpayers can make CGT savings too.

---

### Example

*Sarah Shareholder knows she is going to face a hefty tax bill this year as she has cashed in a large part of her share portfolio. To reduce her tax bill she decides to give shares with a market value of £10,000 to charity. Had she sold the shares they would have realized a capital gain of £5,000.*

*As the shares are a gift under Gift Aid, no CGT is payable. As Sarah had already used up her annual CGT allowance, if she had kept the proceeds, she would have faced a CGT bill of:*

$$40\% \times £5,000 = £2,000$$

*In addition she receives higher-rate relief on her gift:*

$$18\% \times £10,000 = £1,800$$

*Total income tax and CGT saving = £3,800*

### Deeds of Covenant

This is a term that no longer applies. Deed of covenant payments are now treated as Gift Aid donations.

*Payroll Giving*

These schemes, run by employers, enable staff to make regular donations from their salary. As donations come straight from gross pay before tax, employees effectively increase the value of their contributions. So, unlike with the Gift Aid scheme, higher-rate tax-payers cannot claim any additional tax relief.

However, the scheme does mean more money for charity at less cost for them. In addition, the government is adding 10 per cent to all donations until April 2003.

Employees have little choice about these schemes as they must be run by the employer. So they cannot, for example, ask their employer to set up a scheme just for them for one particular cause. However, they can enlist the support of colleagues and ask their employer to set up a scheme.

For more information ask for Inland Revenue Help Sheets IR342: Charitable Giving and IR65: Giving to Charity by Individuals.

# Tax Relief on Life Insurance

Tax relief on life insurance premiums (paid into qualifying life assurance policies) was scrapped in the mid-1980s. However, those who took policies out before 14 March 1984 still qualify for the tax relief, which is given at a fixed rate of 12.5 per cent. Premiums are paid after the deduction of the tax relief so there is no need to claim it and, as it is at a fixed rate, higher-rate taxpayers cannot claim any additional relief.

If the premium is £100, the Inland Revenue pays £12.50 reducing the amount that the policyholder pays to £87.50.

The maximum premiums that can be paid are £1,500 or one sixth of total income before allowances, whichever is the greater.

> ### ✎ Tax tip
>
> Those who have these older life policies should think twice before cashing them in or discontinuing the premiums as they will lose their tax relief. Also, if the benefits are varied or extended, tax relief is lost, so they cannot extend the term of the policy or convert it into an endowment.

## *Life Insurance as Part of a Pension*

Although tax relief on life assurance premiums has been scrapped, it is still possible to receive tax relief on life insurance bought with a personal or stakeholder pension plan.

Employees pay their contributions net of tax relief at the basic rate. Only higher-rate taxpayers need claim higher-rate relief of 18 per cent (the difference between the higher and basic rates). The self-employed need to claim tax relief when filling in their tax return.

> ### ✎ Tax tip
>
> Buying life insurance through a pension plan is one of the cheapest ways to buy cover – as premiums qualify for tax relief. So if the annual premium would usually be £400, this would only cost a higher-rate taxpayer £240 through a pension plan with the remaining £160 being tax relief.

## Tax Relief

There are very few ways to get tax back from the Inland Revenue now that most forms of tax relief including Mortgage Interest Tax Relief (MIRAS) and relief for vocational training costs have been scrapped.

Investing in a pension is the easiest way. Tax relief is given at the individual's highest rate – see CHAPTER 9: INVESTING FOR RETIREMENT. In addition, tax relief is given on certain investments – the Enterprise Investment Scheme and Venture Capital Trusts. See CHAPTER 2: SAVINGS AND INVESTMENTS.

Tax relief is also given on certain charitable donations (as has been discussed earlier in this chapter) and on some maintenance payments (see the section on TAX SAVINGS FOR THE OVER 65s earlier in this chapter).

Although MIRAS was abolished from 6 April 2000, it is still possible to get tax relief on the interest paid on certain loans including:

- Loans to purchase an annuity – home income plans – provided the scheme was taken out before 9 March 1999. This tax relief is usually given automatically.

- Loans to purchase investment properties – the interest can be offset against any rental income when calculating profits. See CHAPTER 7: LAND AND PROPERTY.

- Loans to invest in a partnership or to fund a close company (generally owned by fewer than five investors) – claimed in box 15.2 of the tax return.

- Loans to buy plant or machinery for your work – see the section earlier in this chapter on LOANS BY EMPLOYERS.

For more information ask for Inland Revenue Help Sheet IR340L: Interest Eligible for Relief on Qualifying Loans.

---

### ✎ Tax tips

Now that tax relief is no longer given on mortgage interest, it will make sense for those with spare savings to repay their mortgages as quickly as possible. This is because the interest earned on savings is generally lower than the interest charged on the mortgage – and the individual is taxed on this savings income.

It is also possible to claim tax relief on payments to a trade union or friendly society for death benefits. So that part of any trade union subscription that covers superannuation (pension), life assurance or funeral benefits can be claimed as tax relief. Only one half of that part of the subscription can be claimed. This is done in box 15.10 of the tax return. However, note that many trade unions have an agreement with the Inland Revenue for a block payment of tax relief to be made and this therefore leads to reduced premiums.

# Moving Offshore

Thousands of UK residents leave these shores each year to live abroad – often retiring to a sunnier climate. However, this does not always mean that they escape UK tax.

Even if an individual is not resident in the UK he is still liable for tax on any income 'arising' in the UK. If the individual is classed as a UK resident for tax purposes he will be liable to UK tax on all of his worldwide income.

> ### ✎ Tax tip
>
> Those planning to live overseas should ensure that they are no longer classed as UK residents for tax purposes. That way they escape UK tax on their worldwide income. However, they may have to pay tax in their new country of residence – so they should check that the tax regime there is more favourable than in the UK.

## Non-resident Rules

Generally, an individual will be taxed on any money earned overseas as well as any UK income, unless he is absent from the UK for an entire tax year.

However, trips home are allowed provided the non-resident:

- Spends less than 183 days in the UK in any tax year.

- Spends less than 91 days a year over a four year average in the UK.

Note that days of arrival and departure are not normally included in this test.

> ### ✎ Tax tips
>
> Those who fail to meet these requirements may find that they are taxed in the UK on their worldwide income and taxed in the country where they now live. As a result they will be taxed twice. There are treaties in place to ensure that this does not happen and that any double payment of tax can be reclaimed.
>
> Non-residents may be able to continue to claim the UK personal tax allowance of £4,615 (£4,535 for the 2001/02 tax year) against any income subject to UK tax.
>
> The rules covering residency relate to entire tax years. However, this does not affect personal allowances. Those arriving or leaving the UK part way through the tax year can still claim the full personal allowances (they are not apportioned depending on the number of months spent in the UK).
>
> Non-residents should transfer investments overseas so that income can be earned free of UK tax in the years they are non-resident for UK tax. A bank in an offshore tax haven will pay interest gross (without tax deducted).
>
> Those non-resident in the UK should make the most of their tax status selling assets to generate tax-free capital gains in the years they are overseas.
>
> Those planning to rent out their UK property when they move overseas should note that rental income is subject to UK tax even if the individual is not a UK resident for tax purposes. Tax should be withheld at the basic rate by the tenant or managing agent. However, if the landlord is registered for self-assessment and has up-to-date tax affairs he can apply to receive rent gross. See leaflet IR140, Non-resident landlords, their agents and tenants.

> ✎ **Tax tip**

Non-residents can also apply to receive interest from savings gross (without tax deducted).

**Note:** The government is reviewing the residence and domicile rates, so those planning to move abroad should ensure they are prepared financially for any changes.

# 2 Savings and Investments

Savers and investors squander almost £1 billion in each tax year by not making the most of the tax breaks on offer according to research from IFA Promotion.

Most of this tax could easily be saved if investors and savers made the most of ISA allowances and CGT allowances. Other easy ways of paying less tax include investing in a pension, splitting assets between husband and wife to make the most of tax allowances and investing in schemes that either grow tax free or pay a tax-free lump sum on maturity.

In most cases, investors do not need to use the services of a sophisticated investment adviser specializing in tax planning, and they do not necessarily need to invest large sums. While the super rich may need to take advantage of offshore tax havens to escape paying tax, for most investors there are adequate tax shelters at home.

In fact, it is possible to save and invest over £27,000 in tax-free schemes sold in local high streets – more if the investor already holds TESSAs and PEPs and existing National Savings products.

In addition, tax relief at up to 40 per cent can be given on pension contributions of up to £38,000 (depending on age and earnings) and 20 per cent tax relief is given on up to £250,000 of investments in venture capital trusts and enterprise allowance schemes.

Making the most of the CGT allowance of £7,700 for the 2002/03 tax year gives further tax-free profits and employees who can join company share schemes can cash in on the growth in shares in their company, free of tax.

With so many tax-efficient ways to invest that are so accessible, it is surprising how many taxpayers – and in some cases, non-taxpayers – are still paying tax on their investments.

## SAVINGS

# How Savings are Taxed

Income from savings can be paid in three different ways:

- Taxed and paid net – interest is paid net of tax with the tax deducted at source. This is the usual case for bank and building society savings accounts.

- Taxable but paid gross – no tax is deducted at source but the saver is still liable for tax on this income and needs to declare the interest and pay tax unless he is a non-taxpayer. Some National Savings products pay interest gross.

- Tax free and paid gross – no further tax needs to be paid. This is the case for cash ISAs.

Tax on savings income is usually deducted at source (by the bank or building society, which pays this tax over to the Inland Revenue). It is deducted at the rate of 20 per cent.

Although tax has already been deducted, individual savers may not be liable for tax at all – if they are non-taxpayers – or may need to pay tax at a different rate. While tax is deducted at the rate of 20 per cent, the amount an individual taxpayer owes will depend on his own taxable income. The three rates applying to savings interest are:

- 10% starting rate

- 20% basic rate

- 40% higher rate

Non-taxpayers escape paying tax.

While the basic rate of tax is 22 per cent, basic-rate taxpayers are taxed at only 20 per cent on their savings income. Those people who fall into the lower-rate tax band now pay the starting rate – 10 per cent – on all their income regardless of whether it is savings interest or other earnings (although some people may still believe they are taxed at the basic rate, as the starting rate of tax did not apply to interest on savings until April 1999).

Savers who fall into the higher-rate tax band pay 40 per cent on savings and other income above the higher-rate threshold and must pay additional tax on savings interest even if it is already taxed at source, because only 20 per cent tax is deducted at source by banks and building societies. They therefore need to pay an additional 20 per cent tax to bring the total tax paid up to 40 per cent. Savings interest should be declared on the tax return. In some cases, additional tax can be collected via an employee's PAYE tax code.

However, things can become more complex if savings income pushes the total taxable income of an individual into a higher tax band, because savings income is added to other income when determining the rate that needs to be paid. If an employee's salary is just below the higher rate threshold, but he has an extra £1,000 a year in savings interest, most of this interest will be subject to 40 per cent tax even though he believes he is a basic-rate taxpayer, because this additional income falls into the higher-rate tax band.

Likewise, a taxpayer who pays the starting rate of tax (10 per cent) on his pension may find that his savings interest is taxed at 20 per cent because this additional income falls into the basic-rate tax band.

---

### ✎ Tax tip

It is important that savers know what rate of tax they will pay on their savings income as some tax-efficient schemes may be worthwhile only for higher-rate taxpayers. They also need to check that savings income does not push them into a higher tax band.

---

### Example

*Arnold Account was tempted by the high interest rate on a two-year savings bond on offer by his bank. As a pensioner on a low income he needed to maximize the return on his savings. But he wanted to make sure that even with the interest he would earn he would still have an income that was less than his allowances (the personal allowance and additional age-related allowance). That way he would escape paying tax on this savings interest.*

*He calculated that he would still just earn less than allowed and as such he registered to receive interest gross (without tax deducted).*

*However, he failed to realize that the bank only declared all the interest earned on the bond once it matured after two years. Once two years' interest was added to his other annual income, he found that he had earned more than his allowances and was liable to tax on some of the savings interest.*

*Savers should check if interest is declared yearly or at the end of the bond term to ensure that they do not earn more than expected in one year. Had Arnold known he faced a tax liability, he would have opted for a cash ISA. As it was, he did not think a cash ISA was worthwhile because he thought he did not need a tax-free savings scheme as a non-taxpayer.*

---

### ✏ Tax tip

Couples need to know what rate of tax they each will pay on savings income. This is to enable them to minimize their tax liability. If one spouse is a basic-rate taxpayer and the other a non-taxpayer, then savings can be put in the name of the non-taxpayer so that interest is not taxed. However, if one partner is a basic-rate taxpayer and the other pays tax at the starting rate, there may be no savings at all as the additional savings income could push the starting-rate taxpayer into the basic-rate tax band.

## Example

*Alan and Anne Saver have £10,000 of savings on which they earn 5 per cent interest. This gives them gross (without tax deducted) interest of £500 a year and net interest of £400. Because Alan had a savings account before he met Anne, and the building society where he held the account is near his work, he has always put their savings into this account even though it is in his name only.*

*Anne does not work because the couple have two young children. Alan has recently had a large pay rise and for the first time, is now a higher-rate taxpayer.*

*When he comes to fill in his tax return he will be in for a shock – he will now have to pay higher-rate tax on his savings.*

*The total amount of tax due is:*

*40% (the higher rate of tax) × £500 (the amount of gross interest) = £200*

*As £100 has already been deducted at source (at the 20 per cent rate), he owes another £100 to bring the tax rate up to 40 per cent.*

*This may not seem a large amount but if the savings had been in Anne's name, no tax would have had to be paid at all – she is a non-taxpayer and the £500 in gross interest is below her personal allowance. This would save the couple £200 a year in tax. However, she would have to register to receive income gross (see below) and the couple would not be able to save tax retrospectively.*

*Alternatively, they could open a joint account and split the interest 50/50. This would cut their tax bill by £100 as only Alan would be liable for tax, or, Alan could open an ISA. Each year he could put £3,000 into a cash ISA and would, depending on the rate of interest, save £60 a year in tax on this amount.*

---

### ✎ Tax tips

When filling in the savings section of the tax return, remember that couples need only enter half of any joint sources of income – not the full amount. Failure to apportion interest could result in twice as much tax being paid as is necessary.

It is possible for couples to elect for another split in interest paid on joint accounts than the assumed 50/50. However, this cannot be done retrospectively. So savers cannot assume a different split when filling in their tax return (although they can use the additional information box on page 8 to ask to make an election). They need to inform their tax office before the start of the tax year that their savings are split differently for it to apply for the following tax year. The tax office will also want to know that the assets are actually owned in different proportions rather than interest merely being split differently to save tax. It is therefore usually easier for couples to open separate accounts if they want to split interest differently. The added advantage is that the new split will apply from the date the account is opened – with an election to split interest differently there will be a delay until the start of the new tax year.

Savers who are non-taxpayers or pay tax at the starting rate (10 per cent) will find that they are paying 20 per cent tax on their savings income unless they do something about it.

# CLAIMING TAX BACK

**Non-taxpayers**: A single non-taxpayer under 65 entitled to the basic personal allowance can earn up to £4,615 a year (the rate for the 2002/03 tax year) including savings income and still receive interest gross. Those over 65 can earn up to £6,100 (for the 2002/03 tax year) and those aged 75 and over, £6,370. Some people may have higher allowances – for example, if they have a child living with them or are married – so they should read the section on TAX ALLOW-ANCES in the previous chapter before calculating whether or not they can receive interest gross.

Non-taxpayers can register to receive interest gross by asking for form R85. It is available from banks and building societies. However, they must check that after totalling up all their income – including savings interest and investment income – they do not then earn more than their allowances.

**Ten per cent taxpayers**: Starting-rate taxpayers who pay the 10 per cent rate of income tax (which means their income including savings interest does not exceed their personal allowances plus the 10p starting-rate threshold of £1,920 for 2002/03) can claim back half the tax deducted.

A single taxpayer under 65 entitled to no other allowances than the basic personal allowance can earn up to £6,535 (the personal allowance of £4,615 for the 2002/03 tax year plus the £1,920 starting-rate tax band) and claim 10 per cent tax back. Those aged 65 and over can earn up to £8,020 and those aged 75 and over up to £8,290 in the 2002/03 tax year.

Some people may have higher allowances – for example, if they have a child living with them or are married – so they may be able to earn more, or in some cases less than these amounts and still reclaim tax.

---

### ✏ Tax tip

Even those whose income exceeds these levels may be entitled to some tax back. This will be the case if their income – excluding income from savings – is below the threshold and only exceeds the threshold once savings income is added. If this is the case, some of their savings income may escape tax or be taxed at 10 per cent rather than 20 per cent.

## Example

*Sid Saver had a pension income of £4,000 a year and savings interest of £2,500 in the 2001/02 tax year. His personal allowance for the 2001/02 tax year including the age-related allowance is £5,990. So his total income less his personal allowance is £6,500 – £5,990 = £510.*

*This is below the £1,880 starting-rate tax for the 2001/02 tax year so all of this income should be taxed at the 10% rate.*

*Tax due = 10% × £510 = £51*
*However, his bank has deducted 20% tax from his savings interest.*
*Tax paid = 20% × £2,500 = £500*
*Tax overpaid = £500 – £51 = £449*

*Although Sid cannot register to receive savings interest gross (his taxable income is not fully covered by his tax allowances) he can claim tax back. If his income was £510 lower, it would then be fully covered by his allowances and he could register to receive interest gross.*

In other cases, savings income can push the taxpayer into the basic-rate tax band.

## Example

*Tina Thrift had an income from a part-time job of £5,000 and savings income of £2,500.*

*Her personal allowance was £4,535. She could therefore pay the 10 per cent rate of tax on some of her savings.*

*£7,500 (her total income) – £4,535 (her personal allowance) = £2,965*
*Of this £1,880 was taxed at 10%*
*And £1,085 (£2,965 – £1,880) was taxed at the basic rate*

*Her salary used up the 10% rate first. So £465 of her pay (£5,000 – £4,535) was taxed at 10%.*

*The remainder of the starting-rate band, £1,415 (£1,880 – £465), was used to reduce the tax on her savings.*

*10% × £1,415 = £141.50 tax due at the starting rate*

*The rest of her savings interest £1,085 (£2,500 – £1,415) was taxed at 20%.*

*20% × £1,085 = £217 tax due at the basic rate*

*The total tax she should pay on her savings is therefore:*

*£141.50 + £217 = £358.50*

*However, her bank had deducted 20% tax on the entire amount.*

*20% × £2,500 = £500*

*So she is due tax back totalling £500 – £385.50 = £114.50.*

To claim tax back, savers should contact their tax office, if they know which one deals with their affairs, and ask for form R40. In some cases savers may be sent a Repayment Claim Form R40 or a tax return without needing to request one.

Form R40 – along with guidance notes on how to complete it – is also available at any Inland Revenue Enquiry Centre or Tax Office. There are different forms for different tax years, so specify for which year tax is being reclaimed.

For help in claiming back tax deducted on savings income, savers can call the Taxback Helpline run by the Inland Revenue on 0845 077 6543.

For help in registering to receive interest gross call the Inland Revenue Registration Helpline on 0845 980 0645.

**Note:** Those who register to receive interest gross and who then start paying tax as their income increases should write to their bank or building society straight away and ask them to start deducting tax from their interest. Savers can remain registered to receive interest gross only so long as their taxable income is fully covered by their tax allowances.

Once a saver has registered, the registration continues unless cancelled, so savers should not have to complete forms each tax year.

---

### ✎ Tax tips

Savers have five years and ten months to claim tax back (six years for the 1994/1995 and 1995/1996 tax years). So if a saver has paid more tax than needed for the tax year 1997/1998, he has until 31 January 2004 to claim this tax back.

The starting rate of 10 per cent did not apply to savings interest until April 1999 so starting-rate taxpayers cannot claim that they have over-paid tax as the minimum tax rate on savings was 20 per cent until that date.

When savers register to receive interest gross, the bank or building society may pay back tax already deducted from interest during that tax year. This will usually be the case if savers register before the end of the tax year. If the tax is not refunded it can then be claimed from the Inland Revenue by filling in the Repayment Claim Form R40 (available from any Inland Revenue Enquiry Centre or Tax Office).

Parents and guardians can claim back tax paid by a minor. Most children's accounts pay interest gross; however, if this has not been the case do not overlook any savings held in a child's name when checking if any tax has been overpaid. Where the child is under 16 enter the child's name as the saver on the form R85. A child who is 16 before the next 6 April can sign their own form.

If an account is held in more than one name, and only one account holder is a non-taxpayer then the bank or building society may not allow the non-taxpayer to fill in form R85 to receive interest gross. However, some will allow both net- and gross-account holders on the account.

Higher-rate taxpayers should receive a tax return for them to declare this savings income. The extra tax may be collected through their PAYE tax code. (See CHAPTER 9 for details on how this works.)

## Children and Tax

Yes – children are liable for tax too. As with an adult, children are entitled to the annual personal allowance which means they can earn up to £4,615 (£4,535 for the 2001/02 tax year) before paying tax.

Once their income – from savings, investments or even earnings (if they are a child model, for example) – exceeds this threshold, it is liable for tax. As most children do not have such high earnings they can earn savings interest free of tax. When opening a children's savings account check that the interest will be paid gross.

> ✎ **Tax tip**
>
> Parents reading that their children have a tax allowance too, may be tempted to put savings into their offspring's name to escape tax. The

Inland Revenue is wise to this possibility. If parents invest money in a savings account for their child and that account pays more than £100 in gross interest in any tax year, then the parents could find that they are liable to pay tax on the whole savings income (not just the proportion above £100). To get round this potential problem ask grandparents and other relatives to make investments or consider the Children's Bonus Bond (see below under National Savings).

**Note:** Accounts which include gifts from a parent which, either alone or when added to all other gifts from the same parent, produce more than £100 income a year cannot be registered to receive interest gross.

# TAX-FREE SAVINGS

Tax-free savings schemes include the ISA and its predecessor the TESSA and around half of the National Savings schemes.

## Cash Individual Savings Account (ISAs)

The ISA was introduced on 6 April 1999 to replace two existing tax-efficient savings schemes – PEPs and TESSAs.

Designed to encourage people to save more, ISAs enable savers to put their money into cash (savings), share-based investments and life insurance company investments (not to be confused with life insurance policies). The latter two are dealt with later in this chapter.

The ISA tax breaks are that they are:

• Free of income tax – savings interest is paid gross and is not liable to tax.

• Free of CGT – although this will not apply to the savings element of the ISA as there is no capital growth.

ISA investments do not have to be declared on tax returns.

## The Rules

As with any tax break, the government limits its generosity. It is important that savers stick to the rules so that they do not lose the tax-free status of their investment.

The rules state that investors:

- Must be aged 18 or over.

- Must be resident in the United Kingdom for tax purposes (or a Crown employee currently working overseas and treated as resident).

- Cannot hold an ISA jointly with anyone else (so couples cannot have a joint account) or hold one on behalf of another person (so grandparents or parents cannot open an account on behalf of their grandchildren/children).

## How Much can be Invested?

Up to £3,000 in each tax year (the tax year runs from 6 April to 5 April) in a cash ISA. This limit applies until April 2006 when it could be reviewed. The total that can be invested in an ISA is £7,000 with £3,000 of this in savings. The investment limits for the other types of investments (shares and life insurance investments) are covered later in this chapter.

It is possible to open an ISA with as little as £1. Further investments can be made at any time – either in lump sums or regular payments. Cash ISAs are offered by banks, building societies and National Savings.

The ISA rules are further complicated by the fact that there are three types of investment and three types of ISA.

The three types of ISA are:

- maxi

- mini

- TESSA-only

For those wanting an ISA for cash savings only, there is little difference between a maxi and a mini ISA in terms of the rules. The maximum investment in savings is £3,000 regardless of which type of ISA is purchased. However, for savings only, investors are advised to buy a cash mini ISA.

If investors wish to invest in stocks and shares (unit trusts, investment trusts, Open Ended Investment Companies (OEICs see later in this chapter) or shares) as well as cash savings through their ISA, they are advised to read the section on stocks and shares ISAs later in this chapter. They will generally be advised to opt for a maxi ISA.

TESSA-only ISAs are also covered in detail later in this chapter.

To ensure that investors are not being seduced by a tax break at the expense of their savings, the government introduced what is known as the CAT standard. This stands for fair Charges, easy Access and decent Terms and conditions. It is voluntary. The rules vary depending on the type of ISA.

For the cash element of an ISA to be CAT marked the ISA provider must:

- Make no charges.

- Have a minimum transfer/investment of £10.

- Allow withdrawals within seven working days or less.

- Not pay interest that is more than 2 per cent less than the bank base rate.

However, opting for a cash ISA that meets the CAT standard is no guarantee that it is the best deal for an individual saver. Some cash ISAs do not meet the CAT standard because they have notice periods and minimum investments of £3,000, but these non-CAT standard cash ISAs often pay the highest rates of interest.

### ✎ Tax tip

Don't put rainy day savings into a cash ISA if you feel you will need them in the near future. Once savers withdraw money from an ISA, that's it. The tax break is lost. The money withdrawn cannot be reinvested. And remember, the tax breaks do not just apply to this tax year, savings will continue to grow free of tax for years to come. Although the tax savings may only be £30 this year, these savings will mount up to £150 over five years.

## Example

*Anne Spender liked the interest rate offered by the cash ISA from her bank so she put her £3,000 savings – the maximum allowed – into the account.*

*However, two months later her central heating boiler blew up and she needed some of the money to pay for a new one. She withdrew £2,000. Within a couple of months she had saved £800 and wanted to put this into her ISA to escape tax on the savings interest.*

*She was disappointed to find that this was not allowed. Even though she only had £1,000 in her cash ISA account, because she had already invested £3,000 in that tax year, she could not top up her savings, so she lost out on the chance to shelter £2,000 of savings from tax for years to come.*

### ✎ Tax tips

It may still be worthwhile to invest in a cash ISA even if savers know they will withdraw the cash later in the tax year. If a saver knows he will not have sufficient to reinvest in the ISA (even if he were allowed) then at least he will have benefited from the ISA tax break for some of the year. Remember, the golden rule with the ISA allowance is 'use it, don't lose it'. In addition, ISA rates are often far more competitive than ordinary savings accounts (even after the tax breaks are discounted), so an ISA may still provide a better home for savings – even for the shorter term – than the average savings account.

Investors who are not happy with the performance of their ISA – whether it is a cash or shares ISA – can switch to another ISA provider. However, only the same components can be switched. An investor cannot move a cash deposit into a share ISA or vice versa.

Transfers must be made directly from one ISA provider to another – investors cannot cash in their investment and then reinvest this money with a different provider.

Each individual can invest £3,000 a year in a cash ISA. That means a couple can shelter £6,000 a year between them. It is important that partners each use their allowance (remember, joint ISA accounts are not permitted) even if one spouse is a non-taxpayer. By opening an account for the non-taxpayer, a taxpaying spouse can reduce the couple's total tax bill.

ISAs are ideal savings vehicles for those investing for their children or grandchildren's future. There is only one snag. ISA accounts cannot be opened in a child's name. That means the parents or grandparents have to use up their own ISA allowances. They may therefore prefer alternative investments for children. These are covered later in this chapter.

## Tax Exempt Special Savings Account (TESSAs)

Although the TESSA was withdrawn from sale on 6 April 1999 and replaced by the ISA, that does not mean investors lost their tax breaks. Any money invested in a TESSA can continue to grow tax free and investors with TESSAs taken out before 6 April 1999 can continue to invest regular amounts (up to set limits) until their TESSA matures at the end of five years.

### The Rules

TESSAs are a five-year investment.

- The maximum that can be invested over the five-year term is £9,000 (existing TESSA savers can invest up to £1,800 each tax year until the five-year term is reached).

Once the TESSA matures, investors have these options:

- Take all the proceeds.

- Place the capital (not any interest earned) of the maturing TESSA into a TESSA-only ISA.

- Transfer the capital proceeds up to a maximum of £3,000 into the cash component of a maxi or mini ISA.

Transfers into cash ISA or TESSA-only ISAs must be done within six months of the TESSA maturing.

---

**✎ Tax tips**

Savers who are unhappy with the performance of their TESSA (rates can be poor), should not cash in their account. Once they close their TESSA, the tax breaks these schemes offer are lost for ever. Instead, they should consider transferring their TESSA to another provider. However, check first if there are any penalties charged and that providers paying better rates accept transfers (not all do).

When a TESSA matures (they have a five-year term), do not cash it in or all tax breaks will be lost. TESSA investors get an extra tax break – an additional £9,000 ISA allowance in the year a TESSA matures. Known as TESSA-only ISAs, these are specially designed for savers with maturing TESSAs.

---

## TESSA-only ISAs

Over two million savers had £21 billion in TESSAs maturing in 2001. The most tax-efficient option for these savers is to transfer these savings (the capital only) into a TESSA-only ISA (which should be done within six months of the TESSA maturing).

TESSA-only ISA limits are in addition to normal ISA investment limits. So, investors with the maximum £9,000 of capital allowed in a TESSA can invest £12,000 of savings from the maturing TESSA-only ISA and £3,000 in a cash ISA – in the year their TESSA matures or, if they wish to invest in stocks and shares a total of £16,000 – £9,000 in a TESSA-only ISA and £7,000 in a stocks and shares maxi ISA.

---

### ✎ Tax tip

To maximize tax breaks and minimize tax, transfer a maturing TESSA into a TESSA-only ISA rather than a cash ISA. That way, up to £9,000 of savings (the maximum capital that could be invested in a TESSA), can be sheltered from tax compared to just £3,000 in a cash ISA (the maximum investment limit for these schemes).

## National Savings

National Savings has several schemes that are tax free. However, savers should not be seduced by the tax breaks because some accounts pay very poor rates of interest. In some cases the total return can be beaten by investing in an alternative savings account even where the interest paid is subject to tax.

In addition to offering a cash ISA, National Savings has the following tax-free schemes:

### *National Savings Certificates*

Both the index-linked and fixed-interest savings certificates are tax free. The minimum investment is £100 and the maximum in any one issue is £10,000. However, as new issues are made relatively frequently, investors have the opportunity to invest further amounts in each one. There is also no limit on reinvesting the proceeds of matured certificates.

Fixed-interest certificates pay a guaranteed income over five years – hence, the term 'fixed'. Index-linked certificates, as the name implies, pay interest at a fixed percentage above the annual rate of inflation (the retail price index).

---

✏ **Tax tip**

The rates on saving certificates may seem poor compared to other savings accounts. However, for higher-rate taxpayers the rate will be competitive. For example, if the savings certificate is paying 3 per cent interest, for a higher-rate taxpayer this is equivalent to 5 per cent in a taxable savings account.

---

**Note:** Savers who withdraw their money before the term of the account is up (two years or five years depending on the certificate) will suffer because reduced interest is paid or, in some cases, no interest. No amount of tax breaks will make up for this. Savers need to be sure that they can hold their certificate for the required number of years.

## *Children's Bonus Bonds*

These are bought by adults for children, so they are not children's savings accounts (accounts for children to operate themselves are run by banks and building societies).

Anyone over 16 can invest in a bond for a child aged under 16. The investment limits are quite low. They are sold in units of £25 and the maximum that can be held in any one issue is £1,000 a child. However, this limit applies to each issue so children can hold up to £1,000 in earlier or future issues.

They are called bonus bonds because they pay a bonus if held for five years. However, they can be cashed in with one month's notice – but this will mean a loss of the bonus. Although they need to be held for five years to qualify for the bonus, they do not have to be encashed at the end of this term. After they mature, they can be reinvested until the holder's 21st birthday. After that time no further returns are earned.

---

✏ **Tax tip**

Parents who invest on behalf of their children can find that they are liable to tax on income if this exceeds £100 gross in any tax year. Children's Bonus Bonds do not affect the parents' tax liability

---

even if they pay for the bonds. So they are one of the few ways for parents to give their children savings without creating a potential liability for tax.

## Ordinary Account

The first £70 of interest (£140 with joint accounts) is tax free. Unfortunately, as the rate of interest paid on the ordinary account is so low (currently well below 2 per cent), investors are usually better off investing in an account that is taxable – even after paying tax they will be better off.

However, there are some benefits to the ordinary account. It offers instant access from any post office for small withdrawals; handy for those who do not have a cash machine nearby but do have a post office.

## Premium Bonds

These are not savings accounts and they do not pay interest, so technically they are not tax-free savings schemes. However, the prizes paid are equivalent to a competitive rate of interest and all winnings are free of income tax and CGT. Bonds are included in the monthly prize draw once they have been held for one complete calendar month following the month they are purchased and they can be cashed in at the face value at any time.

The minimum investment is £100 and they can be purchased by parents, grandparents and guardians on behalf of children.

# All-in-one Accounts

These are not tax-free savings accounts but they do offer the same benefits – and more.

Rather than paying tax on savings interest, why not save interest and save tax?

This is how all-in-one accounts work: they combine borrowings with savings, so instead of earning interest on savings, any cash in a current account or savings account 'offsets' what is borrowed on the mortgage or overdraft. At the end of each day when interest is calculated, the savings offset or reduce the amount of the debt and, because the debt is lower, less interest is charged. To work effectively, interest must be calculated on a daily basis known as 'daily rests'. That way every penny works for the borrower every day.

Savings and current account balances can either be held in separate accounts or combined in an all-in-one account, known as a current account mortgage.

Whatever the set-up, the effects are the same. Credit balances (money in savings or the current account) earn the equivalent of the mortgage rate of interest. This is generally up to 1 per cent higher than the best savings rates. However, savers effectively earn a better rate because interest is not actually earned – it is saved – no tax is paid.

Assuming the mortgage rate is 6 per cent, then higher-rate taxpayers with one of these accounts will earn the equivalent of 10 per cent interest on their savings – because of the interest rate they would have to earn to clear 6 per cent after tax.

### Example

*Brenda Borrower has a £100,000 mortgage on which she pays £500 in interest a month at 6 per cent.*

*She also has £10,000 in savings. This is in a savings account which pays 5 per cent gross but as she is a basic-rate taxpayer she only earns 4 per cent net. This gives her just £33.33 in interest a month.*

*If she opted for an offset or all-in-one account she would be charged interest on only £90,000 of mortgage debt. Her interest bill would then be £450 a month. So she would be £16.67 a month better off – or £200 better off over the year.*

Although savings are combined with borrowings in these types of account, borrowers still get access to their cash. With all-in-one accounts, there is usually one overall credit limit and borrowers can withdraw money up to this limit at any time. So if they are saving for a particular reason, they can have access to this cash just as with any other savings account.

In the example above, the savings are minimal. To make the most of these types of accounts, savers need to pay in their salary. That way, at the start of the month, when they have just been paid, the total amount they owe is reduced giving the greatest benefits. As they spend throughout the month, their debt will be increased but it will still be lower than if they kept their current account and mortgage separate.

For example, paying in an annual salary of £35,000 each month and spending this evenly throughout the month would cut seven months off the mortgage terms (of 25 years) and save over £3,300 in interest (assuming the rate was 5.2 per cent). If £50 of salary was unspent each month and left in the account, according to Virgin One the loan would be repaid over five years early and save more than £14,000 in interest.

---

| ✎ Tax tip |
|---|

The average earner will pay in excess of £1 million into their current account over a 30-year working life but earn less than £40 in interest. That is because many interest-bearing current accounts pay pitiful rates of just 0.1 per cent gross – and then the tax man takes 20 per cent (or 40 per cent for higher-rate taxpayers) of this tiny amount. Combining a current account with a mortgage – so that all income automatically reduces debt – can improve this return to over £4,000 according to Virgin One.

## TAXABLE SAVINGS

As stated at the start of this chapter, most savings are taxable with tax deducted at source from savings interest at the rate of 20 per cent.

However, some types of savings earn interest that is paid gross –

without tax deducted. These include the following National Savings products: Capital Bonds, Income Bonds, the Investment Account and Pensioners' Bonds.

This does not mean that these accounts are tax free. Savers should still declare the interest and pay tax on it, unless they are non-taxpayers.

Why mention taxable savings in a book about ways to pay less tax? Well, the fact that interest is earned gross can be useful when it comes to tax planning.

# National Savings Accounts

## *Pensioners Bond*

For savers aged 60 and over, this bond pays a fixed rate of interest. There are several series of bonds with investors given a choice of a one-, two- and a five-year term. Interest is paid monthly – something that will be particularly useful for the retired who need to live off their savings. The minimum investment is £500 and the maximum £1 million.

The fact that the interest rate is fixed gives savers certainty – particularly if savings rates are likely to fall.

---

### ✎ Tax tip

Interest is paid gross but that does not mean it is tax free. It is liable to tax and must be declared. However, there are advantages to receiving gross interest. Non-taxpayers need not go to the bother of registering to receive interest gross. Starting-rate taxpayers who need only pay tax at 10 per cent but would otherwise suffer a 20 per cent tax deduction (this is the rate of tax deducted from interest paid net), do not have to go through the bother of reclaiming this tax and as a result they are better off. This is because they do not have to suffer a delay between when a tax is deducted and when they receive tax back.

**Note:** Early access to savings in these fixed-rate, fixed-term accounts leads to a loss of interest. So savers should ensure that they do not need the savings locked up in these accounts.

## Capital Bond

This is another fixed-rate National Savings product. It has a five-year term with the rates rising each year to give a competitive rate of interest over the total five years.

No interest is paid if the bond is cashed in within the first year. The minimum investment is £100 and the maximum in all series of Capital Bonds is £250,000.

Once again, interest is paid gross but liable to tax and must be declared.

---

### ✎ Tax tips

Even taxpayers can benefit from earning interest gross. This is because there is a delay of up to 21 months between earning interest and having to pay tax on it. However, taxpayers who regularly earn gross interest will usually find that their PAYE tax code is adjusted so that the tax owed is deducted monthly from their salary.

Interest is credited to the Capital Bond gross – which means that investors earn interest on their interest at a higher rate.

---

## Ordinary Account

This is an instant access account that pays a very low rate of interest. Interest is paid gross with the first £70 (£140 if a joint account) of annual interest paid free of income tax. The minimum investment to earn interest is £10.

---

### ✎ Tax tip

As the rate of interest on this account is so low (well under 2 per cent) many investors will find that they do not need to pay tax – so it is effectively a tax-free savings scheme. A higher rate can be earned if the saver keeps the account open for a year and maintains a balance of £500 plus.

## Investment Account

This one-month notice account pays a more competitive rate of interest, which is tiered, so the more investors save the higher the rate. The minimum investment is £20. Savers lose 30 days interest if they want instant access to their money.

## Income Bonds

This three-month notice account also pays interest gross. The rate is variable and unlike Pensioners Bonds which also pay a regular monthly income, these bonds are not restricted to those aged 60 and over. Once again early access to savings within the notice period will lead to penalties. The minimum withdrawal is £500 with no penalty, provided three months notice is given but there is a 90-day loss of interest if savers want instant access.

The minimum first purchase is £500 and further bonds can be bought (subject to this £500 minimum) up to a total value of £1 million.

> ### ✎ Tax tip
>
> Savers will be sent a statement each year showing how much interest they have earned. This will help them when filling in their tax returns if they need to declare any interest earned gross.

# Offshore Accounts

The term 'offshore account' sums up images of exotic island tax havens where dubious characters launder dirty money and the seriously rich hide their wealth from tax authorities.

The reality is often far more down to earth. Most of the big banks and building societies (Abbey National, Barclays, Halifax, NatWest etc.) have subsidiaries in the Channel Islands or the Isle of Man. All investors need is a few hundred pounds – and it doesn't even have to be in used notes – to open an offshore savings account which they can do by sending off a cheque (so no need to fly out with a suitcase full of money). Interest on these accounts is paid gross. However, this does not mean it is tax free. UK residents should declare this income on their tax return using the special pages for foreign income.

---

### ✎ Tax tips

Savers may be liable for tax on interest earned abroad whether they bring it into the UK or not. Simply leaving interest in an account off-shore does not mean that it does not have to be declared.

However, savers can delay paying tax on interest earned, they have up to 21 months from earning interest to paying tax owed on it because of the time lag between the start of the tax year and the deadline for filling in the tax return for that tax year and paying any taxed owed. In the meantime, they can earn interest on their interest. However, after doing this for one year the Inland Revenue will then usually ask savers to pay tax on account (in instalments) so it will only be a short-term gain. This tax may also be collected through the PAYE tax code of employees and those in receipt of a company pension.

Some offshore investments do allow investors to delay their tax liability until they become a lower or non-taxpayer. These are covered in the section on investments.

# INVESTMENTS

## How Investments are Taxed

Shares and share-based investments are taxed differently to savings. Income from investments that pay dividend distributions – including individual shares, investment trusts, unit trusts and open-ended investment companies – is treated as being paid net of tax at 10 per cent. This is known as a tax credit and it should be shown on the dividend or distribution voucher.

Only higher-rate taxpayers need pay more tax, and are required to pay a further 32.5 per cent.

Note, however, that some unit trusts or OEICs may pay interest distributions rather than dividend distributions. This will be the case if they invest in gilts (see later in this chapter), UK or overseas bonds, money market instruments or bank deposits. In these cases the income is classed as interest and, as such, tax is deducted at source at 20 per cent.

## ✎ Tax tips

While the tax deducted at source from interest (at the rate of 20 per cent) can be reclaimed by non-taxpayers, tax deducted from dividends from UK shares and distributions from unit trusts and OEICs (treated as being paid net of tax at 10 per cent) cannot be reclaimed.

Invest in stocks and shares via an ISA and there will be no worries about tax.

Investors are also potentially liable for CGT on the gains (or profits) they make on any investment. See CHAPTER 4: CAPITAL GAINS. Share investments are also liable to stamp duty which is levied at the rate of 0.5 per cent on all share purchases and adds to the cost of investing.

## ✎ Tax tips

Investors cannot escape being liable for income tax on any income from a share-based investment by asking the fund manager to reinvest the income in the scheme. This is treated as though the investor received the income in their hands even though they did not actually receive any money.

Investors who receive equalization payments (which adjust for the fact that investors may have paid more for their unit trust or OEIC because the price reflected income that had accumulated in the fund) do not have to declare these on their tax return. They are treated as returns of capital and as such are not taxable. When calculating a CGT liability, they should be deducted from the initial investment.

# TAX-FREE INVESTMENTS

## Stocks and Shares Individual Savings Accounts (ISAs)

ISAs enable savers to put their money into three different types of investment:

- Cash deposits: these are savings accounts offered by banks, building societies and other savings institutions. Some accounts may be more complex than others in that they may have tiered rates (a higher rate of interest is given, the more is invested) and notice periods (so investors cannot get access to their cash instantly without incurring an interest penalty).

- Stock-market based investments: these can include unit trusts, investment trusts, OEICs, government bonds (see later in this chapter) or gilts, corporate bonds and individual shares.

- Life insurance investments: there is no life cover as part of these investments, instead they are investment funds run by life insurance companies.

ISAs are free of income tax and CGT and ISA investments do not have to be declared on tax returns.

### The Rules

The income tax rules are:

- Interest on cash deposits (savings) is free of tax.

- Dividends from UK equities receive a 10 per cent tax credit for the period to 5 April 2004 and higher-rate taxpayers will have no further liability to tax.

- Corporate bonds (fixed interest distributions) receive interest gross of tax at 20 per cent.

The ISA provider will claim back all the income tax for investors, who do not have to do a thing.

However, after 5 April 2004 ISA investments that earn dividends will attract tax on these dividends which the ISA provider will pay. There will, however, still be no personal liability to income tax or CGT for ISA investors.

The CGT rules are:

- All gains from any investment sold within an ISA are free of CGT.

- Investors cannot offset any losses on ISA investments against gains made elsewhere.

The investment requirements are that:

- Investors must be aged 18 or over.

- Investors must be resident in the United Kingdom for tax purposes (or a Crown employee currently working overseas and treated as resident).

Investors cannot hold an ISA jointly with anyone else (so couples cannot have a joint account) or hold one on behalf of another person (so grandparents or parents cannot open an account on behalf of their grandchildren/children).

## How Much can be Invested?

Each individual can invest up to £7,000 in each tax year (the tax year runs from 6 April to 5 April). This limit applies until April 2006 when it could be reviewed.

Within this overall limit there are restrictions on the amount that can be held in each type of investment depending on the type of ISA that investors choose.

Investors who do not have the full £7,000 need not worry. It is possible to open an ISA with as little as £1. Further investments can be made at any time – either in lump sums or by regular payments.

---

### ✎ Tax tips

The £7,000 limit applies to each tax year. Investors have a new tax allowance each year.

Married couples each have an ISA allowance of £7,000 a year. That means a total of £14,000 can be sheltered from tax in each tax year by a couple.

---

The amount that can be invested in an ISA (within the £7,000 overall limit) depends on the type of investment and the type of ISA. There are three different types of ISA:

- maxi

- mini

- TESSA-only

For details of TESSA-only ISAs see page 96 earlier in this chapter.

## Maxi ISAs

These allow investors to invest the maximum ISA allowance of £7,000 with just one ISA provider. Investors cannot shop around for the best rates on savings and buy these from one provider and then find the most suitable investment fund and buy it from another provider. They have to buy all their investments from the same company. (There is an exception to this – see fund supermarkets, later in this chapter.)

If investors buy a maxi ISA they cannot also have a mini ISA. However, they can also have a TESSA-only ISA.

Within the overall £7,000 limit, maxi ISA investors can invest:

- up to £7,000 in stocks and share-based investments

- up to £3,000 in cash savings

- up to £1,000 in life insurance investments

So an investor wanting to invest £2,000 in savings and £5,000 in share-based investments can do so with a maxi ISA as this does not exceed the £7,000 overall investment limit.

Alternatively, the investor can put the whole £7,000 into stocks and shares.

## Mini ISAs

Investors can have up to three mini ISAs provided each invests in a different type of allowable investment, so that could be one cash ISA, one share-based ISA and one life-insurance ISA. It is not possible to have two cash ISAs – even if the investor does not exceed the overall £7,000 ISA investment limit, and if an investor has a mini ISA, he cannot have a maxi ISA.

The maximum that can be invested in each type of investment through a mini ISA is:

- up to £3,000 in cash savings

- up to £3,000 in stocks and shares

- up to £1,000 in life insurance investments

## Which Type of ISA is the Most Tax Efficient?

Both types of ISA – maxi and mini – are free of income and CGT, so there are no differences in the tax breaks. However, the different investment limits for each type of ISA mean that investors can invest more free of tax if they make a wiser choice.

## Example

*John Cash has £1,000 in savings with another £10,000 set aside to invest in the near future. He expects to dip into his savings to pay for a holiday, but wants to keep his share-based investments for the long term as he believes that they will perform better over five to ten years than money saved with a bank or building society.*

*He wants to take out an ISA and was considering putting his savings into a cash mini ISA as he suffers 40 per cent tax on interest, he then planned to put some of his investment cash into a stocks and shares ISA.*

*So what are his options?*

*With mini ISAs he could invest:*

*£1,000 in cash*
*£3,000 in stocks and shares*
*Giving a total of £4,000*

*With a maxi ISA he could invest:*

*£1,000 in cash*
*£6,000 in stocks and shares*
*Giving a total of £7,000*

*By selecting a maxi ISA he could boost the amount of savings sheltered from tax by £3,000. However, he would be better off picking a maxi ISA and investing the full £7,000 in stocks and shares. It would mean that he suffered tax on his savings as they would not be invested in an ISA, but, as he plans to withdraw some of this cash to pay for a holiday, it would be a waste of his ISA allowance anyway. Remember, once money is withdrawn from an ISA, it cannot then be reinvested.*

### ✎ Tax tips

Investors who want to shelter more than £3,000 in a stocks and shares ISA should opt for a maxi ISA. Those who mainly want to invest in a cash savings ISA should look primarily at mini cash ISAs.

Share-based investments are not short-term investments. Advisers recommend that investors plan to hold the Investment for at least three to five years to cover the costs of investing and to allow for rises and falls in the stock market. Even so, ISA investments can be cashed in at any time if money is needed in a hurry. However, investors should remember that once they withdraw money from an ISA, that's it. The tax break is lost. The money withdrawn cannot be reinvested. Investors should also remember that the tax breaks do not just apply to this tax year, savings will continue to grow free of tax for years to come.

## Maximizing the Investment Potential

The tax breaks of an ISA may be very appealing, but investors should not let the tax tail wag the investment dog.

There is no point investing in a tax-free savings account which pays 4 per cent interest if there is a taxable one paying 6 per cent and the investor is a basic-rate taxpayer.

To ensure that investors are not being seduced by a tax break at the expense of their savings, the government introduced what is known as the CAT standard (see CASH ISA in Chapter 1). For stocks and shares ISAs to be CAT-marked the charges cannot total more than 1 per cent of the investment and the minimum saving must be no more than £500 in a lump sum per year or £50 per month.

For life insurance ISAs to be CAT-marked the charges must be no more than 3 per cent of the investment, there must be no penalty when the ISA is cashed in and investors must get back at least all the premiums that they have paid in the three years or more before the date when the life insurance investment is cashed in.

---

### ✎ Investment tips

CAT standards are only a guide. Some ISAs with low charges that meet the CAT standard have poorer performance than those with high charged and not so correct. It to be the fund a 20 per cent return on the investment year-on-year and suffer a 3 per cent initial charge and a 1.5 per cent annual charge than to get a 5 per cent return with charges totalling just 1 per cent a year.

Investors who are not happy with the performance of their ISA should not be tempted to cash in their investment because they will lose the tax break. Instead, they should consider switching to another fund or another ISA provider. However, only the same components of an ISA can be switched. An investor cannot move a stocks and shares ISA into a cash ISA or vice versa. Transfers must be made directly from one ISA provider to another – investors cannot cash in their investment and then reinvest this money with a different provider.

## Self-select ISAs

Investors who believe they can produce better returns than a fund manager can make their investment decisions themselves. Self-select ISAs allow the investor to choose individual shares or even a combination of shares, investment trusts, unit trusts, open-ended investment companies, gilts and bonds.

## Fund Supermarkets

Although investors with a maxi ISA are restricted to buying all their investments from their ISA provider, there is a way for investors to purchase a range of different funds from different fund managers. Fund supermarkets allow investors to mix and match. So instead of being restricted to the choice of funds from XYZ fund manager, the investor can select two or three from various fund managers from a choice of hundreds and hold these within one ISA account. The added advantage is that fund supermarkets usually sell unit trust funds at a discount – rebating some of the commission they would otherwise have earned from the fund management company. However, this comes at a price: individual investment advice is not given, although most have lists of recommended funds. As a result these supermarket services tend to cater for the more sophisticated investor.

> ### ✏ Tax tip
>
> It is vital that investors understand which type of ISA they are purchasing. A significant number have unwittingly flouted the investment rules by buying both mini and maxi ISAs and consequently risk losing the tax-free status of their savings and investments.

## Personal Equity Plans (PEPs)

Although PEPs were withdrawn from sale on 6 April 1999, when ISAs were launched, they did not cease to exist. Any PEP investments made before that date can continue to grow free of tax. However, no additional investment in the fund can now be made.

PEP investments are restricted to stocks and share-based investments. In that sense they are similar to stocks and shares ISAs. They were available for a decade and attracted £70 billion of investors' money – far more than is invested in ISAs. So it is vital that investors do not forget about any money tied up in a PEP and review their investments regularly to ensure they are performing well.

> ### ✏ Tax tips
>
> Do not cash in a PEP investment unless there are no other options. Once a PEP is sold, the tax breaks offered by these schemes are lost for ever. Remember, PEP investments are in addition to any ISA investments – so they increase the amount that can be invested free of tax.
>
> Investors who are unhappy with the performance of the PEP should not cash it in to reinvest the proceeds in another investment or an ISA. Instead they should consider switching their PEP to another company. Transfers are allowed. All investors need to do is check there are no penalties or charges for switching and to check that the manager to whom they want to transfer their holdings is willing to accept the transfer.

---

✐ **Investment tip**

Investments held in a PEP should be reviewed regularly. A fund that was a strong performer two or three years ago may now be performing badly. Most fund managers allow investors to switch their investments from one fund to another often for very little cost.

---

# Life Insurance Policies

Although life insurance policies are included in this section on tax-free investments, they are not technically tax free.

The proceeds from most 'qualifying' life insurance policies are usually tax free. However, while the investor need pay no tax, the life company has already paid tax on the underlying investment. This tax is equivalent to the basic rate of tax and cannot be reclaimed.

To be a qualifying policy the investment must last ten years or more. Most regular premium policies such as endowment policies are qualifying. Investors must keep their policy for at least ten years or for three quarters of the term if they are to escape paying tax on the proceeds.

Compared to unit trusts, investment trusts and OEICs, life insurance investments tend to be inflexible (there are fixed investment terms and penalties for early encashment of the policy), expensive (charges are usually far higher than for many other forms of investment) and complicated.

So, readers may wonder why they should bother with any form of life insurance investment particularly in light of the recent headlines about the poor performance of endowment policies.

There is one good reason why – tax. As the proceeds of a maturing life assurance policy are usually tax free to the investor, life assurance investments are particularly tax efficient for higher-rate taxpayers.

**Note:** Life insurance investments which do not have an element of life insurance – which include with-profits bonds, guaranteed income bonds, unit-linked bonds and maximum investment plans – are non-qualifying and the proceeds are liable to CGT. Even these non-qualifying policies have tax advantages. In terms of income tax, it is the life office that pays the tax on the investment funds, not the investor, and no further tax is due from basic-rate taxpayers. However, higher-rate taxpayers must pay extra tax on any income. These investments – including with-profits bonds and distribution bonds – are covered in more detail later in this chapter. Non-qualifying life insurance policies can be tax free if they are held in an ISA. Each year an investor is allowed to invest up to £1,000 tax free either through a mini or maxi ISA.

Life insurance investments split into three types:

- With-profits – where the investor shares in the profits of the life fund by receiving bonuses. These types of investment are designed to smooth out rises and falls in the stock markets by keeping money back in good years to fund bonuses in years when performance is less strong.

- Unit-linked – where the investor's money is used to buy units in the fund (these units are of equal value) and the value of the units rises and falls in line with the value in underlying investments. They can therefore be more risky.

- Unitized with-profits – these are a mixture of the two in that investors purchase units but also receive bonuses.

The tax treatment is the same regardless of the type of policy.

---

### ✎ Tax tip

Although most investors think of endowments as being 25-year policies sold to pay off mortgages, they can also be purchased as stand-alone investments running over ten, 15 and 20 years. Higher-rate taxpayers looking for long-term, relatively safe, investments should therefore consider life-insurance based plans – for example, to invest for school fees. However, they should note that not all of their money is invested, some pays for life cover. Also charges can be high, and they must keep up their regular monthly premiums if they want a maximum return because the penalties for cashing in a policy early can be high.

---

## *Traded Endowment Policies (TEPs)*

It may seem that investors to invest in an endowment policy at a time when hundreds of thousands of investors in these types of investment are finding that they will not produce the returns required to pay off the mortgages to which they are linked. However, second-hand endowment policies can be worthwhile investments.

Instead of cashing in the policy – known as surrendering it – the policyholder can sell it or auction it through what is known as the traded endowment policy market. Surrender values are often very poor and do not reflect the value of the policy should premiums be invested until the policy matures. Selling the policy can usually give a better deal to the policyholder while still being attractive to investors. The new owner pays the premiums and is guaranteed clear title on the policy.

The only types of endowment that can be traded are with-profits policies, which have a guaranteed sum assured onto which are added bonuses each year. These are known as reversionary bonuses and, once allocated, they cannot be removed or reduced. Additionally, these policies have a terminal bonus, which is paid on maturity but is not guaranteed.

Although performance of these endowments has been poor compared to what was forecast at the time they were sold to homebuyers (80 per cent of home loans sold in the 1980s were endowment mortgages), the current performance still compares well with other types of relatively safe investment.

As with many long-term investments sold by life insurance companies, the premiums in the early years are used principally to pay the expenses of setting up the policy. With a traded endowment policy many of these charges have already been covered. As a result, more of the premiums paid by the new owner of the policy go towards investment.

A TEP investor inherits all the bonuses accrued by the previous owner. In some cases these bonuses and the guaranteed sum assured can exceed the actual purchase price.

However, unlike other life insurance investments, the proceeds on maturity are not tax free. These policies are subject to CGT on maturity.

---

> ✏ **Tax tip**
>
> Couples can consider purchasing the policy in joint names so that they can both maximize their CGT allowance and reduce – or eliminate – any CGT liability. When calculating CGT, premiums paid into the policy are treated as part of the original purchase price.

# Friendly Societies

Savers could salvage £55 million through friendly society savings schemes according to IFA Promotion. Friendly societies are similar to building societies in that they are mutual organizations set up to benefit their members (rather than being owned by shareholders) but offer similar products to life insurance companies. There are over 300 societies with some £13 billion of funds under management and six million members with the biggest including Liverpool Victoria. However, as investors are restricted to paying small premiums, costs are disproportionately high and the investment rules make these investments very inflexible.

Friendly society life policies qualify for tax relief, which means that in addition to any ISAs they may hold, savers can invest up to £25 per month (a total of £300 a year) or £270 as an annual premium in a friendly society and receive a tax-free lump sum when the plan matures.

Only one plan is allowed per saver. Premiums must be paid for seven and a half years on a 10-year term policy or for ten years on any longer-term policy to be tax free.

Unlike other insurance policies, the society pays no tax on the underlying investment.

**Warning:** Investors who fear they may not be able to keep up regular payments to a friendly society investment should think twice before investing. Early encashment penalties are often hefty and there is no guarantee that investors will get back what they have paid in, particularly in the early years of the

> ✎ **Tax tips**

Many investors will not miss £25 a month diverted to a friendly society investment. As such, they are worth considering particularly for higher-rate taxpayers, provided the investor is happy to leave their money invested for ten years.

The long-term, tax-efficient nature of these schemes makes them ideal investment vehicles for parents, grandparents or anyone setting aside money for young children as they grow up. In fact, many friendly societies market their plans to people investing for children.

# Spread Betting

Betting? Surely that is not an investment? Well, yes . . . and no. Spread betting is increasingly being seen as an alternative to futures investing. Instead of buying a FTSE 100 future, those who like to punt on stock market movements might spread bet on how much the FTSE 100 might rise – or fall – in the future. They can also bet on individual share-price movements. Most stock market investments are a bit of a gamble, spread betting is just a far higher-risk gamble.

The reason why spread betting is included in this book is that there are tax advantages. Because spread-betting profits are in fact gambling winnings, there is no CGT to pay, and, as they are bets, there is no stamp duty to pay unlike on other stock market investments.

Spread betting is not like conventional gambling. Unlike fixed-odds betting (where punters multiply their stake by the odds at which they win), spread betting has no odds – the more correct the gambler is, the more he makes and conversely the more incorrect he is, the more he stands to lose. That means gamblers stand to lose more than their stake . . . far more.

According to the IG Index, the longest established spread-betting firm, the average stake is just £15 and the average loss/winnings around £200. So although some punters lose tens of thousands of pounds, most place much smaller bets.

Gamblers place a bet on whether a figure (a share price, stock market index or even the difference between the closing price on the FTSE and Wall Street, for example) will be above or below the price (which is given as a spread) quoted by the spread-betting company (which acts like a bookmaker) at a future date (prices tend to be quoted quarterly). So it is possible to bet on the closing price of a share next December, for example. However, gamblers do not have to wait until then. They can take their profits – or cut their losses – at any time.

The spread refers to the difference between the selling price and the buying price. Investors placing a bet on the movement of a share may be given a spread of 512–520. In this case, the selling price (for those who want to go low – or bet the price will fall) is 512 and the buying price (for those who want to go high – or bet the price will rise) is 520.

If a gambler bet £10 per point that the price will fall and then the spread price moved down to 492–500 he could buy back his down bet at 500 (the fall or sell is always measured from the lower end of the spread, in this case 512, and punters always buy at the higher end, in this case 500). He would take a profit on the difference between 500 and 512 or a total of 12 points. As he had bet £10 a point that would give a profit of £120.

---

**🖉 Tax tip**

No tax on profits and no stamp duty make spread betting a tempting investment. However, investors need to know what they are doing because it is possible to lose far, far more than the original stake.

## Annuities

Although most annuities are purchased on retirement from the proceeds of a pension fund to provide an income for life (known as compulsory purchase annuities), annuities can be purchased as a means of providing investment income. An annuity is a lump-sum investment that gives a guaranteed income for life.

While the income from compulsory purchase annuities is subject to tax – and is usually paid net of tax – those who buy an annuity with non-pension capital (or even from the lump-sum proceeds of their pension fund – the bit that does not have to be used to buy a compulsory annuity) pay less tax. This is because part of the income from the annuity is treated as a refund of the initial investment and is therefore free of tax.

Several life offices have now developed long-term-care annuity products because they recognize the suitability of an annuity in meeting the ongoing cost of long-term care. The government has allowed better tax concessions for these products and in some instances the long-term-care annuity can be paid gross with no tax deducted.

As retirees who enter into long-term care are generally elderly, their life expectancy is relevantly short, which means that the annuity income they receive is usually quite high. These retirees are also likely to qualify for an impaired life annuity, which will again lead to an improved annuity income.

---

### ✎ Tax tip

Don't be fooled by the fact that part of the income from the annuity is tax free. Investors should be aware that this is paid from their capital. However, as many of the elderly are capital rich and income poor, they may be prepared to sacrifice capital in exchange for a guaranteed income for life.

---

## Save As You Earn (SAYE)

The SAYE accounts are tax free. They are a way for employees to save up to purchase shares in their employer's company. However, the employee does not have to purchase the shares. If the price of the share is not attractive, the employee can, instead, take the proceeds of the account – including any bonuses – tax free.

These schemes are covered in greater depth in Chapter 1 in the section on TAX SAVINGS FOR EMPLOYEES.

## Pensions

These investments are tax free – the pension fund grows free of tax – and contributions also attract tax relief.

Pensions are covered in CHAPTER 3: INVESTING FOR RETIREMENT.

# INVESTMENTS THAT ATTRACT TAX RELIEF

In addition to pension contributions, the following investments attract tax relief:

## Venture Capital Trusts (VCTs)

One industry expert put it like this: 'Venture capital trusts offer the most generous cocktail of tax reliefs available to the private investor.' As a means of getting tax back from the Inland Revenue they should not be overlooked by investors.

These trusts invest in smaller companies which usually have a potential for strong growth.

**Warning:** Investing for tax reasons alone can be a recipe for disaster. Experts recommend that no more than 25 per cent of an individual's investable assets should be committed to UK smaller companies.

Tax relief is given as compensation for some of the requirements placed on investors and the risks involved. There is a three year minimum holding period for investments and there is poor liquidity in the secondary market (often making it hard to sell an investment). In addition, investors will find that there are higher charges than with a conventional investment trust.

VCTs will therefore only appeal to higher-rate taxpayers, because they should see the benefits of the tax relief outweighing the disadvantages listed above, but there are no guarantees.

Risks can be reduced by investing in a VCT that has a good management team and a diversified range of investments – at least 20 holdings. The investment remit of the VCT can also indicate the level of risk investors face. Many are AIM (Alternative Investment Market) specialists, who invest in companies listed on the junior stock exchange while others focus on higher-risk sectors such as technology. Spreading risks by investing across several VCTs can not only provide access to different investment policies, but can also reduce risk.

Once a VCT has been selected, time investments carefully. Each VCT share issue is of a finite size and closing dates are only indicative. If the offer is fully subscribed before this date, then the offer will close.

However, while careful selection of a VCT may reduce the risks of the investment performing badly, it can still not eliminate the risk of poor liquidity. Investors who want to sell may have to accept a poor price, although the share buyback provisions of most trusts should prevent this. VCT shares are fully listed on the London Stock Exchange but as there is very little buying and selling (because most shareholders face a tax penalty by selling), in most cases the VCT has the power to repurchase the shares.

The VCT rules are:

- Shares must be held for at least three years (this was reduced from five years in the 2000 Budget) – however, as these are risky investments, many advisers recommend that investors look at VCTs as minimum five-year investments.

- The maximum total investment per person in any number of VCTs in any one tax year is £100,000.

Minimum investments vary from £1,000 to £5,000 and costs typically include a 5 per cent initial charge and an annual management fee of between 2.5 per cent and 3.75 per cent.

## Income Tax

There is no income tax to pay on dividends on VCT ordinary shares, therefore there is no need to declare dividend income on tax returns or to pay higher-rate tax.

## Income Tax Relief

Income tax relief of 20 per cent is given on the amount invested. This is claimed by sending off the certificate issued by the VCT (it should be sent to investors shortly after subscribing) to the individual investor's tax office.

If investors receive the certificate after the end of the tax year, they should send it with their tax return. If they receive it during the tax year, they may be able to obtain a coding change (change to their PAYE tax code if they are employees) by sending it to their tax office before the end of the tax year.

In order to receive the full tax rebate the investor must have paid at least that amount of income tax in that tax year.

### Example

*Mr Risk wants to invest £100,000 in a VCT. However, he must have paid at least 20 per cent of that amount 20% × £100,000 = £20,000 = in tax in the tax year of investment.*

Investors cannot claim tax relief on tax they have not paid.

## Capital Gains Tax (CGT)

There is no liability to CGT on any growth in value of the VCT shares.

One of the main tax benefits of VCT investments, other than income tax relief, is that investors can use these schemes to defer CGT. This means that investors with a large capital gain can shelter much or all of the CGT liability in a venture capital trust.

There is a popular misconception that CGT can only be deferred in the current tax year. Investors can get up to 40 per cent tax relief from CGT deferral in respect of any gains realized in the period from 12 months before the allotment of the VCT shares and up to 12 months after the allotment. If an investor realized a gain in February 2002, he can defer that gain by investing in a VCT no later than February 2003. Likewise, if he realized a gain in June 2001, he has until June 2002 to invest in a VCT if he wants to defer this CGT liability.

Investors should check the share allotment date of their selected VCT to ensure that they will be able to invest within the required time limit. VCTs have a minimum funding target. If the trust fails to raise this money then the trust will not go ahead. They also have a maximum funding target. If this is reached quickly then the trust will be closed to additional funds before the advertised closing date.

---

### ✎ Tax tips

Investors who need to meet a deadline should check when their chosen VCT next plans to make a share allotment. Some will do so on demand.

When the VCT shares are sold (after at least three years) the original gain is recrystallized, even if the VCT shares are eventually sold for a loss.

Investors do not have to make a VCT investment in the same tax year as a disposal that leads to a capital gain which they then want to shelter (defer). It must, however, be within 12 months. So investors who discover they have a large CGT liability have time to decide how to defer this. Any capital gains can be deferred. The reliefs are not restricted to just capital gains from shares, for instance.

---

**Note:** Most VCTs only have a provisional tax clearance, but this does not mean they should be avoided. They have three years in which to meet the qualifying provisions. These require that a minimum of 70 per cent of net assets are in qualifying companies within three years. While investments are being selected and made, the Inland Revenue grants provisional relief. At the time of writing no VCT had yet failed to meet the requirements.

Tax relief is claimed by filling in box 15.4 on the main tax return. Investors should ask for the Inland Revenue leaflet Venture Capital Trusts (VCTs), a Brief Guide.

# Enterprise Investment Scheme (EIS)

The EIS is similar to VCTs, but is generally regarded as riskier. Once again, investors qualify for tax relief at 20 per cent.

Whereas VCTs are trusts investing in a range of smaller companies to spread the risks of investing, investors in EIS invest in single companies. Some are quite glamorous – theatre productions as well as film projects.

The EIS rules are:

- Shares must be held for at least three years (this was reduced from five years in the 2000 Budget) – however, as these are risky investments, many advisers recommend that investors look at EISs as minimum five-year investments. The three years applies to EIS companies carrying on a qualifying trade at the time of issue. For EIS companies which are preparing to trade at the time of issue, the minimum holding period will end when the company has been carrying on its qualifying trade for three years.

- The maximum total investment per person in any number of EIS schemes is £150,000 – higher than the £100,000 limit set under the VCT scheme.

## Income Tax Relief

Tax relief of 20 per cent is given against income tax in the current tax year. As with VCTs, investors must have paid enough tax in order to get tax relief. If they invest £10,000 then they must have paid at least 20 per cent of that amount – £2,000 – in tax in the current tax year.

## Capital Gains Tax (CGT)

EIS investments are exempt from CGT. In addition, investors can defer capital gains by investing in an EIS. This means that investors with a large capital gain can shelter much or all of the CGT liability getting up to 40 per cent tax relief from CGT deferral.

---

✎ **Tax tip**

The EIS may be a better bet than VCTs as EIS investments can be used to shelter gains made up to three years earlier rather than gains made within the last 12 months as is the requirement for VCTs.

---

EIS investments should be considered long-term and it is not always easy to cash them in. Increasingly EIS companies are seeking an early listing of their shares on the Ofex dealing facility (the share trading market for unlisted and unquoted securities), so that investors can track their value.

If an EIS company fails – as some do – investors do not necessarily lose tax relief. In the case of a bona fide liquidation or receivership (not voluntary receivership) then the EIS will continue to qualify for tax relief.

---

✎ **Tax tip**

Even if an EIS investment turns out to be a disaster, all is not lost. The shares may fall in value, but tax relief has still been received at 20 per cent of the original investment. In addition, relief is given for any losses on the shares against either income or chargeable gains.

---

Investors claim tax relief by filling in box 15.5 on the main tax return. They should ask for Inland Revenue Help Sheet IR341: Enterprise Investment Scheme – Income Tax Relief. A separate Help Sheet – IR297 – deals with CGT.

## Community Investment Tax Credit

Those investing in enterprises in disadvantaged communities will be able to claim the tax credit which will be set against their tax liabilities when it is introduced shortly. The credit will be worth 25 per cent of the investment, spread evenly over five years.

# TAXABLE INVESTMENTS

## Shares

Shares are a way for individual investors to share in the success of a company. Investors benefit in two ways – through growth in the share price and through a share in the profits in the form of dividend distributions.

A share is simply a legal document that gives the person who holds it part-ownership of the company that issues the share. Companies issue shares to raise finance. Most shares owned by private investors are ordinary shares, however there are different types of share each of which gives the shareholder different rights (see the section on INVESTMENT TRUSTS later in this chapter).

Shares are 'quoted' on the stock market. Large companies – known as blue-chips – tend to make up the FTSE 100, known as the Footsie, which is the index of the 100 leading shares by market value. Other indices are the FTSE 250 (the 250 largest by share value) and the All Share Index (all companies listed on the UK stock market). There is also a junior stock market – the Alternative Investment Market (AIM) – where companies hoping to get a full listing on the main stock market can float initially (a flotation is when a company joins the stock market and starts to sell its shares).

The main way to make money from shares is to buy them and then sell them at a higher price than originally paid. Not all of the difference will be profit, though – investors do have to pay dealing costs, stamp duty and, sometimes, tax.

## How They are Taxed

Investors in individual shares can be taxed in two ways:

- On the dividend distribution – this is a tax on income earned from shares.

- On the profits on sale – this is CGT.

In addition, when shares are purchased investors must pay stamp duty of 0.5 per cent on the purchase price. This is payable regardless of whether or not the individual investor is a taxpayer.

The Inland Revenue treats dividends from UK shares as being paid net of tax at 10 per cent. When investors receive their dividend voucher this will detail the amount of tax deducted which is known as a tax credit. Starting-rate and basic-rate taxpayers have no more tax to pay. However, higher-rate taxpayers pay a further 32.5 per cent – even though the higher rate of tax is 40 per cent. However, they are no better or worse off than under the old rules when they did pay tax at 40 per cent. Before 6 April 1999, an £80 cash dividend came with a tax credit of 20/80 or £20, which brought the total taxable income up to £100. Higher-rate tax of 40 per cent or £40 left the investor with an after-tax income of £60. Since April 1999 when the tax credit was cut to 10/90 an £80 cash dividend now comes with an £8.89 tax credit. This brings the taxable income up to £88.89. Tax of 32.5 per cent on this amount totals £28.89 leaving the investor with £60 after tax – the same as under the old system when the tax rate was 40 per cent.

---

### ✎ Tax tips

Buy individual shares through an ISA (self-select ISAs enable investors to purchase individual shares) and there will be no income tax or CGT liability.

Non-taxpayers may not see the benefits of buying shares through an ISA. However, as the tax deducted on dividends cannot be reclaimed by the individual there is a tax advantage. This is because the ISA manager can reclaim the tax on dividends (but only until 5 April 2004).

Existing shareholders who want to shelter their share investments in an ISA will need to sell them and repurchase them through an ISA provider (there are exceptions for employee shares – see TAX SAVINGS FOR EMPLOYEES in Chapter 1). Before doing so, they should check that they do not create a taxable gain.

Investors who pay income tax (and higher-rate taxpayers in particular) and who do not use up their CGT allowance, should consider investing in shares that are likely to provide strong capital growth but little income. Smaller (and therefore riskier) companies are likely to fall into this category. These companies tend to reinvest their profits to finance growth rather than paying out large sums to shareholders in the form of dividends. As the bulk of the returns on these shares is in the form of a capital gain, and shares can be sold in a year when the investor has not already used up his CGT allowance – or has some allowance to spare – much of the profits will be tax free.

The growth of electronic trading (trading without share certificates) means that investors increasingly are asked to have their shares held in a nominee account by a stock broker. Although the shareholder does not have the shares held in his name, that does not mean he can escape tax. The nominee account means that the investor is the actual owner of the shares and receives the dividends earned by those shares, but does not appear on the company's register of shareholders.

Some companies offer extra incentives to encourage their shareholders to become customers and to promote loyalty. These perks can include discount vouchers or invitations to shareholder-only sales. The number of shares that an investor needs to purchase to qualify for the perk varies.

If an investor regularly uses a particular company or its products, he may want to buy some shares to get those products or that service at a discount. For example, those who regularly eat in a particular chain of restaurants may find that by buying just a few shares they may be able to benefit from a free meal once a year or receive money-off vouchers. These perks are tax free. However, it is only worth buying shares if the perk is so good that it outweighs any losses you might make on the shares. For example, if an investor is planning an expensive long-haul trip and the holiday company offers 10 per cent discounts to shareholders, then the perk could be worth more than the cost of the shares.

# Unit Trusts

These are collective or pooled investments that invest in shares. The advantage is that whereas an individual investor would need thousands of pounds to buy a spread of shares – and therefore spread the risks of investing – he can buy into a portfolio of investments for as little as £50 a month or £500 as a lump sum.

Unit trusts work by pooling together the money of hundreds – if not thousands – of investors and then investing it on their behalf. The unit trust fund is split into units of equal value, which investors can buy – and sell – at any time. The value of these units rises and falls in line with the value of the underlying investments.

There are over 1,000 unit trusts to choose from – some with a very general investment remit, such as UK growth funds, and some with more specific investment remit such as technology funds.

The fund manager levies two types of charges: initial and annual. In some cases there are no initial charges, but usually the charges range from 3–5 per cent. Annual management charges are around 1–1.75 per cent.

Although these charges may seem high, if the investor wanted to purchase a spread of shares (some unit trusts will hold 100 or more), the costs would be far greater.

---

### ✐ Investment tip

It is possible to cut the costs of investing by purchasing unit trusts from a discount broker who will rebate some of the commission that would usually be earned by those selling unit trusts. Fund supermar-

kets, which enable investors to buy a range of unit trusts from different
fund managers, also usually discount the costs of investing.

## How They are Taxed

Unit trusts are taxed in the same way as UK shares. Income
distributions are taxed in the same way as dividends with payments
treated as being paid net of tax at 10 per cent. The amount of tax
deducted – the tax credit – should be shown on the statements sent
out by the fund management company.

The tax that has been deducted cannot be reclaimed by non-
taxpayers. Basic-rate taxpayers have no further tax liability; however, higher-rate taxpayers need to pay a further 32.5 per cent. This
needs to be declared on the tax return.

When investors come to sell their units they may be liable to pay
CGT if their total chargeable gains made within the tax year, offset
by any capital losses, total more than the current allowances.

---

### ✏ Tax tips

Purchase a unit trust through an ISA and there will be no income tax
or CGT to pay. Note that ISA fund managers can reclaim the tax on
dividends but only until 5 April 2004. After that dividends will attract
tax. However, this will not be paid by the individual – the ISA provider
must pay it.

Buying a unit trust through an ISA can work out cheaper because
many discount brokers and fund supermarkets cut the costs of
investing by rebating some of the commission they would have
otherwise earned. Even without the reduction in charges, ISA providers do not make an additional charge for holding a unit trust in an ISA
– so the tax break does not cost a penny.

Investors who have used up their annual ISA allowance and still want
to invest in a unit trust should, if they do not require the income, invest
in units that offer a high capital gain but low income. That way they
can sell their unit trust holdings in years when they have not used up

their CGT allowance. As a result, the profits on investing will be largely tax free.

Unit trusts pay a regular income (in the same way as shares) with distributions usually paid twice a year. Although investors can ask for all income to be reinvested, they are still liable for tax on this income – even though they do not receive a cheque or see the money. However, only higher-rate taxpayers are liable for any additional tax.

# Open Ended Investment Companies (OEICs)

As financial acronyms go, OEICs – pronounced oiks – do not exactly sound enticing. However, thousands of investors now hold them because unit trusts are being switched into OEICs to make them simpler to understand and, in some cases, to cut the costs of investing.

The key difference between OEICs and unit trusts is that an OEIC is a company rather than a trust and investors purchase shares in this company rather than units in a fund. In addition, OEICs have single pricing. Whereas units have a buying or offer price and a selling or bid price with a spread of around 5 per cent between the two, OEICs have just one price. As a result, when a unit trust is converted into an OEIC some investors can expect a small increase in the value of their assets. Single pricing should also make it easier to calculate the value of their holdings.

In addition to having more transparent pricing, OEICs should also have lower overheads. Costs can be cut by turning an OEIC into an umbrella covering many different unit trust funds. However, this does not necessarily lead to lower charges.

## How They are Taxed

OEICs are taxed in the same way as UK shares and unit trusts with income distributions treated as being paid net of tax at 10 per cent.

The amount of tax deducted – the tax credit – should be shown on the statements sent out by the fund management company.

Although investors purchase shares in OEICs, as with unit trusts, there is no 0.5 per cent stamp duty to pay.

For tax tips see UNIT TRUSTS, above.

# Investment Trusts

Investment trusts are similar to unit trusts, in that they are a collective or pooled investment. However, like OEICs they are companies. Investment trusts are quoted on the stock market and, rather than buying units in the investment fund as in the case of unit trusts, investors purchase shares in the company – as they would any other share of a UK quoted company.

The difference is that instead of the company making a product or selling a service, investment trusts use their shareholders' money to invest primarily in the shares of other companies. Each trust has a portfolio of investments run by professional fund managers and supervised by an independent board of directors. They offer an easy way into the stock market. If an investor wanted to buy a spread of investments, then he would need substantial capital to cover the costs but with an investment trust, the investor still purchases a range of shares but from just £40 a month through an investment trust savings scheme.

## How They are Taxed

Investors receive dividends just as if they were a shareholder in any company. These come together with a tax credit (remember, share dividends are paid net of tax at 10 per cent). Basic-rate taxpayers have no further income tax to pay on these dividends. Non-taxpayers cannot reclaim the tax on these dividends. Higher-rate taxpayers will have additional tax to pay.

When they also come to sell their shares they may be liable to pay CGT if their total chargeable gains made within the tax year, offset by any capital losses, total more than the current allowances.

However, when the trust manager sells shares, the individual does not have to worry about CGT. This is another advantage buying a pooled or collective investment has over an individual buying his own portfolio of shares.

In addition there is 0.5 per cent stamp duty to pay – as there is on the purchase of all shares.

---

### ✎ Tax tip

Buy investment trust shares through an ISA and there will be no income tax or CGT to worry about.

As with unit trusts there can be two charges: an initial charge and an annual management charge. These tend to be far lower than for unit trusts at around 0.5 per cent a year.

---

## Split Capital Trusts

Investment-trust shares may appear to be like any other share, but certain types of trust – known as split capital trusts – offer different types of shares, which are unique to these types of investment.

These different classes of share appeal to different types of investor and to different types of taxpayer.

By buying the right mix of shares, investors can reduce – or eliminate – their tax liability on their investments.

## Zeros

Zeros are a type of investment-trust share that pays no income. Their full name is zero dividend preference shares and, as their name suggests, they are not entitled to any dividends. So how do investors make money? At the redemption date investors receive a set price which is equivalent to earning a set percentage a year on their investment (usually more than they would earn in a savings account).

They are relatively low-risk investments as these shares usually rank before all other classes of share if an investment trust is wound up (although some split-capital trusts issing zeros have recently run into difficulties).

Until zeros are redeemed they are traded on the London Stock Exchange and therefore investors can sell their investment before the wind-up date. Although no income is paid on the shares, a profit is possible as, like other shares, their prices are subject to the normal forces of demand and supply. As a zero gets nearer to its maturity date, it is more likely to trade closer to its redemption price.

The fact that zeros have specified dates and prices at which they will be redeemed means their returns are predictable. This makes them ideal for school fees and retirement planning.

Although zeros are low-risk investments, they are not no risk. However, no zero has ever defaulted and investors can check that the investment trust is likely to meet its payments by looking at the 'hurdle rate'. This is an estimate of the extent to which the assets would have to fall in value before maturity before the trust could not meet the redemption price.

Like any share, zeros can be bought and sold almost immediately. They are flexible investments with no exit penalties for early encashment (unlike some life-assurance-based products).

Advisers recommend investing at least £5,000 per zero with a minimum portfolio of at least four to ensure a good spread of investment and to lower the risk. Investors can, of course, invest less. Those with smaller amounts are often advised to buy a unit trust fund that invests in a wide variety of individual zeros in order to minimize the risks and to be more cost effective.

As with other shares, investors must pay stockbroking commission and stamp duty. Commission starts at around 1 per cent. If bought through a unit trust, there will be an initial and an annual management charge although some discount brokers reduce this so that investors may only have to pay 1 per cent as an annual management

✎ Tax tips

Investors can use zeros for future tax planning. The shares have a fixed life and wind-up price. By investing in a zero that is redeemed in, for example, four years time, an older investor can time the capital gain for when he retires or is likely to have no other capital gains.

No income means no income tax. Higher-rate taxpayers looking for a relatively safe investment should consider zeros. The same applies to those who have used up their ISA allowance.

Investors should take care when buying a zero and pick a year when it is unlikely that they will have other capital gains – or when they are likely to be a lower- or basic-rate taxpayer – if returns are likely to be subject to CGT.

By buying a combination of zeros designed to mature in different tax years, investors can make use of their annual CGT allowances. As zeros have a fixed redemption price, investors know in advance what gain they are likely to make ensuring that this falls below their annual CGT allowance thus creating a tax-free portfolio.

## Capital Shares

These are another type of investment-trust share. Like zeros, capital shares are a way for investors to earn a return without suffering income tax. However, these are higher risk than zeros as capital shareholders are only entitled to the remaining assets of an investment trust once every other class of share has received their entitlement in the event that the investment trust is wound up.

They receive no dividends and any return is counted for CGT purposes rather than income tax.

✎ Tax tip

Higher-rate taxpayers who have used up their annual ISA allowance and who do not need an income from their investments should consider capital shares as a means of investing for growth potentially tax free. However, it is essential that they time the sale of their investments carefully so that they do not create a taxable gain that exceeds their CGT allowance.

# Life Insurance Investments

While pay-outs on maturity from 'qualifying' life insurance policies (regular premium policies such as endowments that include an element of life insurance as well as being investments) are tax free, non-qualifying policies are less tax efficient.

However, these non-qualifying policies – generally single premium investment bonds – can still be used for tax-planning purposes.

As with other life insurance policies, life insurance investments invest in a life company fund or funds, which in turn invest in a broad range of shares, bonds and other investments. These funds can be of two main types:

- Unit-linked in which the investor buys units in a fund and these units rise and fall in line with the rises and falls in the underlying assets held by the fund.

- With-profits – these investors share in the profits of the fund but the rises and falls in stock markets are smoothed out.

In addition, life companies offer unitized with-profits policies which are a combination of the two.

Unit-linked life funds are split into different sectors (as are unit trust funds) ranging from general funds such as 'balanced managed' to more specific funds such as property or gilt funds.

## *How They are Taxed*

The life insurance company pays tax on the underlying investments in non-qualifying life policies. This covers the investor's liability to basic-rate tax.

Higher-rate taxpayers, however, must pay 18 per cent more tax. This is the difference between the basic- and higher-rate tax.

This additional tax is due when they cash in the policy or if they withdraw more than 5 per cent of the original investment in a tax year.

---

### ✎ Tax tip

Even those who do not pay higher-rate tax on their main earnings may find that they are liable for higher-rate tax on their investments. This is because other income – such as savings income – is added to earnings to determine an individual's top rate of tax. This additional income can push the investor into a higher-rate tax band. In the case of non-qualifying policies any income which exceeds the basic-rate tax limit will be liable to the difference between basic- and higher-rate tax. However, as income is often reinvested and paid out as a lump sum when the policy matures, this may often push investors into a higher tax band because ten years' income will be paid in just one year (when the policy matures). So that this is not an issue, the income is divided by the number of years the policy ran to ascertain if the investor is pushed into the higher-rate tax band.

---

Life insurance investments cover many types of product: with-profits bonds, unit-linked or investment bonds, maximum investment plans and distribution bonds as well as guaranteed equity bonds and guaranteed growth bonds. The most popular are explained in more detail below.

## With-profits Bonds

These are a popular type of life insurance investment. These policies, issued by life assurance companies, enable investors to share in the investment growth of a fund in the form of regular bonus payments. Investors, known as policyholders, do not see their investment rise and fall in value in line with stock market movements – as they do with unit trusts, investment trusts or OEICs. Instead, with profits bonds smooth out the rises and falls in the stock market by declaring annual bonuses, called reversionary bonuses, so that in years when the performance is good money is held back in reserve to fund bonuses in years when performance is poor. When added to the policy, the bonuses increase the price of the units. So a 5 per cent bonus added to a 100p unit will bring the new price to 105p.

In addition to reversionary bonuses, investors may also qualify for a terminal bonus when they cash in the policy. They usually need to have held the policy for at least five years to qualify.

The life company invests in a wide variety of assets including shares, fixed-interest securities and profits. Typically around 70 per cent is invested in equities, 15 per cent in gilts, 10 per cent in property and 5 per cent in cash.

---

### 🖊 Tax tip

Most with-profits bonds allow the investor to make regular withdrawals. Each year up to 5 per cent may be withdrawn as a return of capital and is therefore tax exempt. Any amount in excess of 5 per cent is a withdrawal of capital, but is considered to have had basic-rate tax deducted. Normally withdrawals are capped at 7.5 per cent, above which any withdrawals are deemed to be a partial surrender. This will lead to early encashment penalties within the first five years.

---

**Warning:** Cash in a with-profits bond before five years are up, and there could be a hefty exit penalty to pay. If the stock market is falling (as was the case following 11 September 2001) the life company can introduce a market value adjuster (MVA), which means it will not pay out the full value of declared reversionary bonuses. Charges can also be high and include a bid–offer spread (the difference between the buying and selling price of units), annual expense costs and allocation rates.

> ✎ **Tax tips**

There is no personal CGT liability from these bonds and they are therefore attractive for basic-rate taxpayers who are already using their CGT allowances.

Basic-rate taxpayers who have used up their full ISA allowances should consider with-profits bonds for the tax advantages – the ability to withdraw 5 per cent a year tax exempt and the fact that basic-rate tax is already paid by the fund.

Life companies pay basic-rate tax on the fund but this cannot be reclaimed. This makes with-profits bonds unsuitable for non-taxpayers.

Higher-rate taxpayers will have to pay additional tax as only basic-rate tax is deducted by the life company. However, they may still find with-profits bonds attractive if they expect to be basic-rate taxpayers in future years of the policy (for example, if they will be retiring shortly). They can also make use of the 5 per cent per annum tax-exempt withdrawal facility.

## Distribution Bonds

These are similar to with-profits bonds in that they are run by life insurance companies and invest in equities and fixed-interest investments. However, while a with-profits bond will increase in value, the value of a distribution bond can fall as well as rise. To compensate for the additional risk of a distribution bond, there is additional growth potential.

The investment is structured so that the capital growth and income can be separated from each other. Income can either be paid out or distributed – hence the name of these bonds – or reinvested to purchase extra units.

As with other life insurance investments the returns on a distribution bond are paid net of basic-rate tax so only higher-rate taxpayers have any tax liability on encashment or regular withdrawals.

Distribution bond funds have a maximum equity content of 60 per cent and pay a before-tax income above that earned by the stock market as a whole.

---

✎ **Tax tips**

Interest paid on these bonds – as is the case with other income-generating bonds such as guaranteed income and guaranteed growth bonds – is paid net and cannot be reclaimed even by non-taxpayers. If investors want to earn income gross from a life insurance company income bond they should consider offshore bonds (see below).

On encashment, the profit made on the capital element of the bond is divided by the number of years that the bond has been in operation to ascertain if the investor is pushed into higher rates of tax. Only higher-rate taxpayers need pay any additional tax.

---

## Offshore Funds

Just because an investment is held offshore does not mean it can escape the UK tax authorities. Anyone who is a UK resident is liable to tax on investments regardless of whether they are invested in the UK or in a tax haven.

However, that does not mean there are no tax advantages to holding investments offshore. It is possible to use some offshore investments to delay a tax liability and is a good way to save tax for those who expect to be lower-rate or non-taxpayers in the next few years. Why suffer 40 per cent tax when they can earn the income tax free in a couple of years' time?

---

✎ **Tax tip**

Investors planning to retire in the near future or even take a career break, should consider investing on one of these tax-delaying schemes.

## *Roll-up Funds*

Offshore roll-up funds, which have a minimum investment starting at between £1,000 and £5,000 are like unit trusts and accumulate any income and reinvest it. Investors do not have to declare these earnings until they cash in the scheme. However, as the charges of these funds are often much higher than for ordinary unit trusts, the tax breaks may only be worthwhile for higher-rate taxpayers – provided when they come to cash in the scheme (when the earnings must be declared) they no longer pay tax at the higher rate.

## *Insurance Bonds*

Offshore insurance bonds work on the same basis, with the added advantage that investors can take out 5 per cent of their investment each year without having to pay any tax until they cash in the bond – usually after five to ten years. Insurance bonds are offered by most of the major UK life companies.

Another advantage of investing in an offshore life fund is that the insurance company does not have to pay capital gains or income tax on its investments. On-shore life insurance investments have basic-rate tax deducted (which cannot be reclaimed by non-taxpayers).

> ### ✎ Tax tip
>
> Investment advisers recommend that investors use up all their tax-free investment allowances in the UK first including ISAs and National Savings before considering an offshore investment because of the charges involved.

# Bonds and Gilts

There are many different types of bond. What they have in common is that they pay fixed interest. Bonds include British Government securities known as gilts, corporate bonds and permanent interest bearing shares. While shares are a way of owning a part of a company and sharing in its success through dividends and growth in the value of the share, bonds or gilts are loans made to companies or to the government. Gilts are issued by the UK government periodically at varying rates of interest (the predetermined rate of interest known as the coupon depends on the economic situation at the time) and with different maturity dates (although investors can buy and sell gilts at any time they are fixed-term investments which run for 15 years or more).

As with a savings account, an investor in a bond receives regular interest and the repayment of their initial investment. However, while most savings accounts pay a variable rate of interest, the interest paid on a bond will be fixed. This is why they are known as fixed-interest or fixed-income investments.

Because these bonds have a fixed rate of interest, if investors hold them until maturity, they will receive back their initial investment in full and will have earned the set rate of interest with usually little risk to their capital. However, bonds are usually traded. This means that investors do not buy them at their face value – known as the nominal value. Instead the value rises and falls depending on demand for the bond, which is usually linked to what is happening with interest rates.

Income from bonds is taxed at a different rate to income from dividends. This is because the income earned is classed as interest and is usually paid with 20 per cent tax deducted (dividends and distributions from shares, unit trusts and investment trusts are paid net of tax at 10 per cent). However, this tax can be reclaimed by non-taxpayers unlike the tax deducted on dividends.

---

### ✎ Tax tip

Non-taxpayers will find that bonds and gilts are more tax efficient than share-based investments (because they can reclaim the tax deducted) unless they invest through an ISA.

However, returns from bonds and gilts are not always as high as returns from stock market based investments (other than in recent times when shares have fallen in value). The tax breaks need to be balanced against potential investment returns and the risk to capital.

### The Accrued Income Scheme

When investors buy or sell a bond, including a gilt, they may come within this scheme. Part of the price received on sale may be taxable as the equivalent of interest, because it will reflect the amount of interest accrued (due to the investor) by the bond. Purchasers may receive tax relief on their first interest payment because interest accrued was reflected in the price they paid. However, the scheme only applies if the face value (the nominal value not the price paid or received) exceeds £5,000.

## Corporate Bonds

Corporate bonds tend to pay interest of around 0.5–1.5 per cent more than gilts as there is a higher risk (the chances of the government defaulting on its loans are very slim compared to a company defaulting on its loan). The higher the risk of the bond, the higher the rate offered in an attempt to attract investors. Those companies with lower credit ratings need to pay around 3–5 per cent more than gilts to attract funds.

Most investors buy corporate bonds through a bond fund. These unit trusts spread the risks of investing by pooling investors' money and buying a broad spread of corporate bonds. However, the level of income paid by these bond funds is not guaranteed and the value of the investors' capital can fluctuate.

---

### ✎ Tax tips

Corporate bonds may pay a higher rate of income compared to many other income-generating investments, but this income is taxable. Invest in a corporate bond fund through an ISA and this income will be tax free.

Those in need of an income from their investments should use their ISA allowance on high-income generating investments rather than safe savings accounts. This is because the ISA allowance does not restrict the amount of income that can be earned free of tax – the only restriction is on the initial amount invested. It is far better to earn an 8 per cent return free of tax than a 5 per cent return – the tax savings will be greater.

Those who want to invest in bonds for the high, fixed rate of interest and the lower risk compared to many share-based investments, but who do not need to take the income today, should consider zero dividend preference shares. Although these 'earn' a fixed rate of interest, it is not paid out in the form of a dividend but added to the total repaid on redemption. There is therefore no income tax to pay. See the section on INVESTMENT TRUSTS earlier in this chapter for more information on zeros.

# Gilts

Gilts are government bonds – basically an IOU issued by the government in the form of a bond. In return for lending the government money, the holder of a gilt gets a fixed income stream called the coupon which lasts until the bond's redemption date, when the original loan, measured in units of £100, is repaid by the government.

Although gilts have a nominal price of £100, in practice, most investors do not pay this amount. Gilts are traded and the price depends on how attractive the fixed income from the gilts is in relation to prevailing interest rates. When interest rates are set to rise, then gilt prices usually fall because the rate of income they pay becomes less competitive compared to savings accounts. When interest rates are falling, gilt prices usually rise. For example, a gilt called Treasury 5% 2004 will pay out £5 on every £100 of stock held until 2004. However, the gilt could be traded at £80 or £120 depending on whether it is demand or not.

The value is also determined by the length of time there is to run before the loan is due to be repaid. The closer to the redemption date, the nearer the gilt will be to its par value, i.e. the value on the original loan, usually £100.

Some gilts are index-linked, which means both the interest rate and the capital repayment on redemption are adjusted in line with inflation.

Gilts can be bought via the Bank of England Brokerage Service simply by picking up a form at a post office. Or they can be purchased via a stockbroker. Some stockbrokers offer cheap advisory services (to help investors select the best gilts) with costs from 1 per cent including dealing commission. They can also be purchased via a collective investment such as a unit trust.

## How They are Taxed

Private investors pay no tax on capital gains from gilts but tax is payable on income, at the highest rate.

Profits or losses made when an investor buys or sells gilts are not taxable and do not have to be included in the investor's tax return (either as income or capital gains). The inflation uplift (in effect its increase in value) component of the capital amount of index-linked gilts is therefore tax free.

Gilts bought since 6 April 1998 pay interest gross (without tax deducted); however, investors can ask to be paid net of tax by applying to the Bank of England Registrar's Department. There are no real financial advantages to having interest paid net. Gilts purchased before that date pay interest net, unless investors choose to be paid gross.

Gilts may come under the accrued income scheme (see page 145 earlier in this section).

No stamp duty is payable on purchases of gilts.

---

&#x270F; **Tax tips**

The fact that interest is now paid gross on gilts is particularly useful for non-taxpayers who would otherwise have to go to the trouble of reclaiming the tax deducted.

Gross interest is good news for taxpayers. They have the full use of their income and do not have to pay tax on it for up to 21 months because of the delay between the start of a tax year and paying the tax due for that year.

---

## Strips

The gilt strips market is relatively new (launched in the late 1990s). It allows the income stream from a gilt to be separated out or stripped – hence the name – from the capital element. The income stream and capital are then sold as separate units: as income for a given year or as capital on redemption.

Zero dividend gilts trade at a discount to their eventual redemption value and the investor's return comes in the form of the capital uplift between issue and redemption. In other words, the investor buys the zero-coupon strip at a discount and on maturity receives its nominal value.

However, while gilts are exempt from CGT (there is no income tax or CGT on the uplift in the capital component of the gilt), the whole of the capital gain on a strip is taxed as income and taxed on an annual basis. That means the investor is deemed to have sold and repurchased the strip at the end of each tax year and is taxed accordingly – even if he is buying to hold on to it until maturity.

Investors who hold gilt strips on 5 April in any year of assessment will be treated as having transferred and reacquired the strip at market value on 5 and 6 April of the relevant year and may be taxed on any increase in that value over the previous year.

## Traded Options and Financial Futures

Derivatives – the generic name for futures and options – are securities that are derived from (hence the term) other securities such as shares, foreign exchange or government bonds. The underlying instruments can be almost anything that is actively traded in a market – equities or commodities, for example.

There are two categories of derivatives. Forwards are contracts that set a price for something to be delivered or purchased at a future date and are known as futures. Options are contracts that give the option – but do not require – their purchase under certain conditions. Both can be traded over the counter.

Those who think, for example, that a particular share will rise in future can purchase an equity call option on the shares. (Call options are for investors who think the price will rise, put options for investors who think it will fall). This entitles them to buy a certain number of common shares once they reach a certain agreed price, although they do not actually own the shares – or receive any dividends – unless they exercise that option. So, for a premium (which is not refundable), they have the right, but not the obligation to buy the shares at a future date at a set price. If the shares rise the investor buys them at the agreed price – which he will only do if the market value is higher than that agreed price. He can then sell them at an instant profit. If the price of the shares falls, then he does not have to buy the shares and all he loses is the option price.

Futures are more risky. Futures are delivery contracts. Investors only need pay a percentage of the contract price (for example, 10 per cent) when buying a future. So they can 'buy' £100,000 of gold/shares/wheat or whatever for only £10,000. If the value of the commodity or share rises to say £110,000, they can sell at an instant profit without ever having to part with £100,000. As they only invested £10,000 to start with, this £10,000 profit means they have doubled their money. However, if the value falls to £90,000 they lose £10,000 on top of their original investment. So investors can lose more than they invest.

*How They are Taxed*

There is no stamp duty to pay – as there is if an investor purchases the shares rather than buying an option to purchase the shares.

Profits are potentially subject to CGT and losses can be offset against gains to reduce the investor's CGT liability.

By timing the exercising of an option, investors can ensure any capital gains remain within their CGT threshold. Alternatively a loss generated when a futures contract is sold could be used to offset other capital gains and reduce any CGT liability.

## Contracts for Differences (CFD)

These are similar to futures contracts on a stock market index. They allow investors to take a position on a particular stock without having to actually buy or sell that stock.

The profit or loss is the difference between the contract's price when it is bought and the contract's price when it is sold (hence the term contracts for differences – and they are contracts because investors do not actually own the shares but instead borrow money to speculate on their future value and agree to pay the price quoted when the contract ends or when they sell).

There are two main reasons to buy a CFD rather than a share. Investors can trade on margin – which means they do not have to part with the full cost of the shares they are trading – and they can go short, which means they can profit from a falling share price, something investors cannot do with shares themselves. Even though investors are not actually buying the underlying shares they are trading, they still receive dividends.

*How They are Taxed*

As investors are not actually buying the shares they are trading they do not have to pay stamp duty of 0.5 per cent which they would have to pay if they bought shares.

Investors are potentially liable for CGT on any profits and can offset losses against other capital gains or to reduce their overall tax liability.

## Alternative Investments

Wine, antiques, classic cars . . . racehorses. These can all be classed as alternative investments. Whether they prove to be wise investments is another matter.

Depending on the investment – and how well it performs – there can be tax advantages to looking at alternatives to the stock market.

For many people, their first step into alternative investments is through a hobby such as antique collecting. They then sell the antique at a profit and thus begins the start of an investment strategy. The added advantage of turning an investment into a hobby is that it is less important for the investment to perform well. Someone who furnishes his house with antiques he loves will own a beautiful item of furniture to admire even if it does not rise in value.

However, if the hobby turns into a business then they will be liable for income tax or corporation tax on their profits.

### *How They are Taxed*

Investors are generally liable for CGT on the gains (profits) made when they sell (dispose of) any asset. So an investor in antiques or art will potentially face a CGT bill. As alternative investments do not tend to earn an income, there is no income tax liability. The exceptions could be rental incomes from an overseas home, for example.

---

✎ **Tax tip**

Most alternative investments are not subject to income tax and investors need only worry about CGT. By timing investments and

sales carefully, investors can therefore ensure that they pay no tax. By
ensuring that any gains fall within their CGT allowances in any one tax
year, these investments will be tax free.

There are exceptions to the CGT rules.

Private motor cars are not subject to CGT. So if an individual
purchases a second-hand classic car that then rises in value and
later sells it at a profit, there is no tax to pay.

Some second-hand goods sold for less than £6,000 are also tax
exempt. The Inland Revenue defines these as 'chattels' – a legal
term meaning an item of tangible moveable property. Many day-to-
day items are chattels including:

- Items of household furniture.

- Paintings, antiques, items of crockery and china, plate and
  silverware.

- Motor cars, lorries, motor cycles.

- Items of plant and machinery not permanently fixed to a
  building.

Although private motor cars are exempt from CGT, if any other
chattel is disposed of, the investor may be liable to CGT.

However, investors only need to include on their tax return any
gain on the disposal of a chattel where the disposal proceeds are
more than £6,000.

---

### ✎ Tax tips

If a chattel has a predictable life of 50 years or less, then it is deemed
to be a wasting asset and as such is exempt from CGT. However, as
a wasting asset is presumed to become less valuable over its predictable life, in most cases there will be little or no gain.

If investors make a loss on the sale of a chattel, then this loss can be
used to offset any profits. However, the amount that can be claimed
depends on the amount of the disposal. If the disposal proceeds are

less than £6,000, then the loss is restricted. Investors can only claim the full loss if the proceeds are £6,000 or more.

**Warning:** Investors can find that their profits are taxed as business profits – even if they escape CGT.

## Example

*Johnny Car bought an old Bentley which he lovingly restored over several years. However, when he was offered a spectacular price for the vehicle at a classic car rally he decided to part with his labour of love – the price was very tempting. He then bought another car to restore. His profits (gains) on the sale of the car should be free of CGT.*

*However, had Johnny then decided to restore several cars at one go with the aim of selling these at a profit, the Inland Revenue would probably decide that he was in fact running a business. He would then have to register as self-employed or form a company and pay tax on these profits.*

The Inland Revenue uses 'badges of trade' to determine whether someone is trading rather than investing or doing something as a hobby. These are:

• Frequency or number of similar transactions by the same person – so if someone buys and sells similar items with the aim of making a profit and does so frequently they will generally be regarded as running a business and therefore will be taxed as self-employed.

• Buying and selling within a short period of time.

• Supplementary work – the owner alters or improves items so they can make more money when they sell them.

• Motive – the motive for buying and selling is to make a profit.

• Subject matter of sale – if the item was bought for personal use (an antique desk, for example) then the seller may not be classed as trading.

# INVESTING FOR CHILDREN

## Savings

The most tax-efficient way to save for a child's future is to open a savings account in the child's name. Most banks and building societies offer special children's accounts (which often have the added attraction of perks such as free gifts or membership of a club).

However, children pay tax too. Although unlikely in most cases, if the child's income exceeds the basic personal allowance (£4,615 for 2002/03) then any income exceeding this threshold is subject to income tax.

**Warning:** Parents who put savings into their children's names to avoid paying tax, will find that the Inland Revenue is wise to this. If interest exceeds £100, then the entire amount of interest is treated as being earned by the parent and, as such, is taxable at the parent's highest rate of tax.

---

### ✎ Tax tips

Get round the fact that parents can be taxed on their children's savings interest by asking grandparents, godparents, other relatives and friends to give children cheques as presents which can then be invested in a savings account in the child's name and therefore earn interest gross (free of tax).

Parents concerned that they may be taxed on interest earned by their children can consider investing in the National Savings Children's Bond as this is exempt from this rule (as it is a tax-free investment product).

## Investments

Over the longer term stock market based investments, such as unit trusts, have historically produced higher returns than savings accounts, making them ideal as investments for a child's future. However, they will be taxable unless purchased via an ISA. That means the parent's ISA allowance is used up in part or in full to invest for their children.

## How They are Taxed

Nobody under the age of 18 can enter into a legally binding contract, which means that they cannot normally buy or hold investments.

> ### ✎ Tax tip
>
> It is not possible for parents to avoid paying tax on shares or share-based investments purchased for their child's future by putting the investment in their child's name, and tax credits deducted from dividends cannot be reclaimed. Parents should therefore consider alternatives to individual shares when investing for their children's future (unless they are prepared to use up their ISA allowance).

**Note:** Children do not have an ISA allowance of their own.

# Unit Trusts

Some unit trust companies do allow children aged 14 to 18 to hold investments in their own name, provided that all income is rein-vested and there are no redemptions (the investment is not cashed in even in part) until the child reaches the age of 18. This is relatively rare, however, as most fund mangers required the holding to be registered in the name of the adult buying the investments.

Most fund managers do allow the opening of a designated account which is an informal way of recording the fact that the investment has been bought for, and is held on behalf of, another person. However, once again, the adult is taxed on the investment.

# Bare Trusts

It is possible to set up a bare trust which is a simple type of legally binding trust document, where an individual holds assets, such as units in a unit trust, or shares, on behalf of someone else, but does not control them or any income arising from them. It is a formal way of recording that an investment has been made on behalf of another person.

If the Inland Revenue recognizes the investments as being held in a bare trust, then the tax treatment of income from the investments will depend on what relationship the person who makes the investment has to the child. If the trust was set up by a parent, any income is taxed as the parent's income if it is more than £100. If the total income is less than £100, it will be treated as the child's income.

Where a bare trust is set up, the capital and any income arising from the trust's investments must be accumulated. It must not be paid to, or spent on behalf of, the child.

---

### ✎ Tax tip

For tax purposes, bare trusts are normally treated as if the child holds the assets in their own name. Therefore the child – not the adult making the investment – is liable for tax. As most children do not pay tax, then these investments will be tax free. However, note that the tax deducted on dividends (at the rate of 10 per cent) is not reclaimable – even by non-taxpayers.

---

To make a declaration of trust and draw up a trust deed, investors will need to write to their tax office to tell them that they have made an investment on someone else's behalf and get the trust deeds drawn up by a professional adviser such as a solicitor.

See the section on trusts in CHAPTER 5: INHERITANCE TAX for more information.

Also note that a bare trust may not be ideal if the investment is for school fees as the money cannot be withdrawn from the trust to pay for education and instead must be accumulated.

## Friendly Societies

One other tax-free way to invest is in a Friendly Society children's or baby bond. These are inflexible investments with the investor committed to making regular payments every month for a number of years – usually at least ten. There are often hefty penalties if the investor ceases to make contributions or requests early encashment of the plan.

However, these relatively safe investments have no restriction on who can take out a plan for a child. The maximum monthly investment is low, only £25.

## Life Company Investments

Another tax-efficient investment is a with-profits endowment policy from a life insurance company. Once the policy matures the pay-out is tax free. However, the fund itself is taxed and, once again investors are committed to the long term and penalties can be high for early encashment.

# 3 Investing for Retirement

Investing in a pension plan is one of the most tax-efficient ways to save and invest. Not only does money in a pension fund grow free of tax, in addition, tax relief is given on contributions (at the highest rate the individual pays) and a tax-free lump sum can be taken on retirement.

Sounds too good to be true? Well, the government is not *that* generous. There are restrictions on how much can be paid into a pension fund and how much can be taken out. And once an individual retires, the bulk of the fund must be used to provide an income – and that income is taxable

## OCCUPATIONAL PENSION SCHEMES

There are two main pension choices – join an employer's occupational scheme or make private provision using a stakeholder or personal pension or some other savings or investment scheme.

The benefits of an employer's scheme are that:

- The employer usually makes contributions – employer contributions are not taxed so employees are effectively getting extra pay, tax free. The only drawback is that it has to be invested in their pension fund and cannot be withdrawn until they retire.

- The employer pays the costs of setting up the pension fund – with a personal pension these costs fall on the individual (and can be expensive, particularly with older types of plans).

- Life insurance is usually provided as part of the scheme.

Employees also usually contribute an average of 3–6 per cent of their salary. If the scheme does not require an employee contribution it is known as a non-contributory scheme.

## Tax Relief

Employee contributions to an employer's company pension scheme are taken out of the employee's salary before calculating tax. Contributions are therefore made from gross (untaxed) income, effectively giving tax relief at source, so no tax relief needs to be claimed.

However, this tax benefit is not unlimited. Employees can only contribute up to 15 per cent of their annual earnings which is defined as annual salary, bonuses, commissions and the taxable value of most benefits in kind such as company cars. Contributions can only be made out of earnings up to the earnings cap of £97,200 (for the 2002/03 tax year).

So the maximum possible contribution for the current tax year was 15% × £97,200 = £14,500.

---

### ✎ Tax tips

Barely 1 per cent of people retire on the maximum pension allowed and very few contribute the maximum allowed (£14,500 is a sizeable sum). This is because they fail to contribute the maximum possible to their pension. When calculating how much can be paid in, employees should not forget that their employee perks add to their earnings.

Employer's contributions do not count towards the 15 per cent of earnings contribution limit and are not taxable as a benefit in kind.

---

Money paid into the company pension scheme continues to grow tax free and on retirement employees can take some of their pension as a tax-free lump sum. However, the income paid by the scheme on retirement is taxable.

> ### ✎ Tax tip
>
> The tax rules have always stated that an individual cannot contribute
> to a company pension scheme and a personal pension at the same
> time – unless he has additional earnings other than from his main
> employment. Even then, contributions made out of these additional
> earnings are subject to maximum contribution limits (ranging from
> 17.5–40 per cent). So if an employee who was a member of an
> occupational pension scheme earned an extra £1,000 a year from
> part-time lecturing or working in a bar at weekends, the maximum
> that could be paid into a personal pension ranged from £175 to £400
> a year. However, the new stakeholder pension allows employees to
> get round this rule. They can be a member of an occupational scheme
> and contribute to a stakeholder plan but only if they earn less than
> £30,000 and/or are not controlling directors.

Outlined below are the various occupational schemes.

## Final Salary Schemes

These pay a pension based on a proportion of earnings at or near to
retirement. Although the majority of employees are members of
these types of scheme, the costs of running them mean that employers are increasingly closing these schemes to new members.

As the pension on retirement depends on final salary, it is not
dependent on investment performance which is why these schemes
are often known as defined benefit schemes.

Employees receive a fraction of their salary – usually 1/60th
of final pay – for each year they have been a member of the
scheme, so after 20 years will receive 20/60ths or one third of their
final pay.

The maximum pension they can receive is two-thirds or 40/60ths
of their final salary which is defined as either:

- Remuneration in any of the five years preceding retirement
  (leaving service or death), together with the average of any
  fluctuating payments such as bonuses and commissions,

averaged from at least three consecutive years ending with the year of retirement.

- Or, the highest average of the total pay, bonuses, commissions etc. from the employer, from any period of three consecutive years ending within ten years before retirement, leaving service or death.

The maximum rate at which pension benefits can accrue is one-thirtieth of final salary for each year of service giving the maximum two-thirds of final salary after just 20 years of complete service.

When calculating final salary the maximum amount that may be taken into account is subject to the same earnings cap as contributions to other pension schemes. It is £97,200 and for the 2001/02 tax year it was £95,400. However, those who joined schemes before 1990 may not be subject to this earnings cap because when it was introduced in the 1989 Budget existing schemes could continue to benefit from the old rules. It is important that scheme members check with their pension trustees as to which rules apply.

---

### ✏ Tax tips

Members of schemes that are not subject to the earnings cap (introduced in the 1989 Budget) should think twice before moving jobs or schemes as they could potentially miss out on the chance to receive a far higher pension (if they earn in excess of the earnings cap) as a result.

Boosting pay at or near retirement will boost the pension of those who are members of final salary schemes. While commissions and bonuses can help boost the final pay figure, any income or gains from shares and options acquired through share option, share incentive or profit-sharing schemes cannot be included and neither can golden handshakes – payments on termination of employment.

Those earning in excess of the earnings cap can still receive benefits on earnings in excess of this cap if their employer offers an 'unapproved' scheme. These schemes can also be used to provide benefits in excess of two-thirds of final salary or to provide greater benefits for those with less than 20 years' service. See the section below on UNAPPROVED SCHEMES.

Although there is a cap on the maximum pension that can be paid out (two-thirds of final pay), few employees retire with such a generous pension. It is sometimes possible to top up and boost this pension by 'buying' extra years of pension contributions. As the pension is dependent on length of service, this boosts the pension. Employees make additional voluntary contributions (AVCs) and receive tax relief at their highest rate. See the section on AVCs later in this chapter.

Employees can usually take up to one and a half times final salary on retirement as a tax-free lump sum. However, this will reduce their pension income. This lump sum is calculated as three-eightieths of final salary for each year of service up to a maximum of 40 years' service or 2.25 times the pension available before commutation (taking the lump sum), if this is greater.

Final salary schemes can provide for lump-sum payments of up to four times the employee's final remuneration on death in service and for a return of the employees' contributions in certain cases. This free life insurance cover is very valuable. When employees switch jobs they should bear in mind that they may have to buy their own life insurance cover in future.

Tax is deducted automatically on pension payments: they are treated in the same way as salaries with tax deducted through the PAYE system. It should be more tax efficient to take the maximum tax-free lump sum allowed out of the pension scheme and to invest this in schemes that are tax free – such as ISAs and certain National Savings products. Not only will the income from these schemes be tax free (unlike the remainder of the income paid by the company pension scheme), but the rate of return could be higher too.

# Money Purchase Schemes

These schemes pay a pension based on:

- The amount of contributions – money paid in by both the employer and employee.

- How well these contributions are invested.

- The charges of the fund.

- Annuity rates when the individual retires (an annuity, which is a policy that provides an income/pension for life must be purchased with the bulk of the proceeds of the pension fund. (See ANNUITIES, later in this chapter).

It is difficult for employees to know what level of pension they will receive on retirement. If the stock market slumps for the last few years before retirement or annuity rates fall, they could be worse off than colleagues who retire a few years earlier or later.

While final salary schemes are known as defined benefit schemes, money purchase schemes are known as defined contribution schemes.

> ### ✏ Tax tips
>
> As the pension paid out of these schemes is largely dependent on what was paid in, it will pay to maximize contributions. Tax relief will be given at the highest rate payable by the employee (provided contributions do not exceed 15 per cent of earnings up to the earnings cap of £97,200 – £95,400 for the 2001/02 tax year).
>
> If employees are given the choice of joining a final salary scheme or a money purchase scheme, they will generally be better off in the former. This is because these schemes guarantee a set level of pension and because employers tend to contribute less to money purchase schemes.

## Group Personal Pensions

These were the main option for smaller employers who did not have an occupational scheme but wanted to offer an employer pension to staff – that was, until the stakeholder scheme was launched (see the section later in this chapter).

The benefit of a group personal pension (compared to an individual employee investing in his own personal pension) is that the employer makes a contribution. Also, as the employer may collect the contributions from all employees, lower charges can usually be negotiated. However, charges are still usually higher than for the new stakeholder pension and the employee has no choice of pension provider.

Group personal pension plans must:

- Be available to all employees who should have access to a stakeholder scheme (see below).

- Have an employer contribution equal to at least 3 per cent of the employee's basic pay.

- Have contributions deducted directly from pay and sent to the personal pension provider – if the employee asks the employer to do so.

In all other respects, group personal pensions have the same investment limits and tax benefits as individual personal pensions. These are detailed later in this chapter.

---

### ✎ Tax tip

The main benefit of a group personal pension over an individual personal pension is that the employer makes a contribution. It will usually be worth sacrificing choice of pension provider in return for this extra contribution. However, if employees want to set up their own pension then they will usually be better off with a stakeholder pension (see below).

## Stakeholder Schemes Run by Employers

As from October 2001, all employers with more than five employees must offer access to a stakeholder pension scheme unless:

- The employer already has an occupational pension scheme (that all staff can join within a year of starting work with that employer).

- Or already offers a group personal pension scheme.

Company or group stakeholder pension schemes work in the same way as group personal pension schemes except that there is no requirement on the employer to contribute.

In addition to the fact that there may be no employer contributions, employees get no choice – the employer is only obliged to offer access to one stakeholder pension.

Some employees do not come under these requirements, including employees:

- Who have worked for the employer for less than three months in a row.

- Who are members of the employer's occupational pension scheme.

- Who cannot join the occupational pension scheme because its rules do not admit employees aged under 18 .

- Who cannot join the occupational pension scheme because its rules do not admit those within five years of the scheme's normal retirement/pension age.

- Who could have joined the employer's occupational scheme but chose not to.

- Whose earnings have not reached the National Insurance lower earnings limit (£75 a week for the 2002/03 tax year) for at least three months in a row.

- Who cannot join a stakeholder pension scheme because they live abroad or fail to meet another Inland Revenue requirement for membership of a stakeholder pension.

---

✎ **Tax tip**

Employees who are given the choice of joining an occupational scheme or a group stakeholder scheme, will generally be better off with the first type of scheme. This is because employers tend to make larger contributions to occupational schemes (there is no requirement for contributions to group stakeholder schemes) and those who could have joined an employer's occupational scheme but chose not to do so, do not have to be offered access to the group stakeholder scheme.

---

Stakeholder pensions are flexible, have low charges and offer better value than most personal pensions. For details see stakeholder pensions in the section on INDIVIDUAL PENSIONS later in this chapter.

## Additional Voluntary Contributions (AVCs) and Top-up Plans

Employees can boost their occupational pension – and the amount of tax relief they receive – by investing in a top-up plan.

These are unnecessary with a money purchase scheme as employees can usually simply ask to increase their contributions.

However, with a final salary scheme they may be able to 'buy' extra years of service to boost their benefits or invest in a top-up money purchase pension. Although all occupational pension schemes must offer an AVC, not all enable employees to buy extra years of service – some simply boost the pension.

There is only one drawback. AVCs cannot be used to boost the tax free lump sum taken on retirement, they can only be used to increase the amount of pension (and this is taxable).

---

✎ **Tax tip**

This rule does not apply to schemes started before 8 April 1987, so members of these older schemes have a significant tax advantage – they can take some of the pension built up by their AVCs as a tax-free lump sum instead of having to take it as a taxable pension.

---

Contributions to employee schemes and AVCs cannot exceed 15 per cent of the employee's remuneration in any one tax year.

---

✎ **Tax tip**

With final salary schemes there is no limit on how much can be paid in by the employer (some can be very generous). However, there is a limit on how much can be taken out. The maximum benefits are usually two-thirds of final salary. If, as a result of AVC contributions, these limits are exceeded, the contributions will be refunded with tax deducted. This refund is treated as being paid net of basic-rate tax. So a higher-rate taxpayer will have further tax to pay.

---

In most cases employees will be better off contributing to the AVC scheme offered by their employer. However, they do have a choice. They can buy an AVC from a life company. These are known as Free Standing AVCs (FSAVCs).

---

✎ **Tax tip**

FSAVCs tend to have higher charges than AVCs and do not neces-sarily offer better investment performance. However, they were widely sold – something that led to a second pension misselling scandal with the offer of compensation to employees who were pressured or misled into buying these plans (which earned the salesmen lucrative commis-sion). Those who feel they were wrongly advised to take out an FSAVC can apply for compensation from the Financial Services Authority (call 0845 6061234 for a factsheet or see www.fsa.gov.uk).

Tax relief on these contributions is given automatically at the basic rate. Higher-rate taxpayers will have to claim higher rate relief and will either receive this through their PAYE coding or at the end of the year after filling in the tax return.

As with AVCs, the FSAVC can only provide a pension, not a tax-free cash lump sum.

---

🖉 **Tax tip**

Although the pension built up in an AVC/FSAVC cannot be taken as a tax-free lump sum, the amount accumulated can be used when calculating how much can be taken as a tax-free lump sum – 2.25 times the pension available. AVCs can therefore enhance the tax-free lump sum. However, check that the rules of the scheme allow this.

---

Like other occupational pensions, the pension from an AVC is paid net of basic-rate tax under the PAYE system.

---

🖉 **Tax tip**

AVCs/FSAVCs may become largely redundant. From April 2001 it has been possible to invest in a stakeholder instead. Until then employees could not be members of company schemes and have a personal pension (unless they had additional earnings other than from their main employment from which to fund these personal pension contributions). However, those earning less than £30,000 a year and who are not controlling directors can, instead of putting AVCs into a pension scheme, pay the contributions into a stakeholder fund. The advantages are that they can take part of their stakeholder fund as a tax-free lump sum.

---

## Unapproved Schemes

These are schemes that enable companies to provide additional benefits to employees who:

- Have earnings in excess of the salary cap (£97,200 for the 2002/03 tax year).

- Want a pension in excess of the normal maximum of two-thirds of final pay.

- Have less than 20 years' service so cannot build up the maximum pension.

Schemes can either be funded (with contributions paid in to fund the benefits) known as FURBS or unfunded with the benefits paid out of company funds. Although there is no limit on contributions by the employer (unless they are excessive) and, as with other pension contributions the employer gets tax relief, the same tax breaks do not apply to the employee.

Employees are taxed on contributions paid by the employer as if they were salary. Employee contributions are not usually made as the employee receives no tax relief. Neither does the pension scheme grow tax free and tax is payable at 20 per cent or 22 per cent depending on the type of income.

In addition, CGT of 34 per cent (the rate for trusts) has to be paid. Finally, pensions paid are subject to income tax – as are other pensions.

---

✎ **Tax tip**

Although unapproved schemes do not have the same tax breaks as other pensions and the employee is taxed on both the contributions made by the employer and the pension paid out, they may still be worth having as the costs are borne by the employer, and if the contributions were paid as salary instead, they would still be subject to the same amount of tax. Funded schemes can also pay a tax-free lump sum on retirement. This is tax free if it does not exceed the amount of the contributions on which the employee was taxed.

# INDIVIDUAL PENSIONS

Those who do not have the option of joining an occupational scheme or who do not want to join one perhaps because they are planning to move jobs in the near future, need to make their own pension provision, as do the self-employed. The basic state pension is not called basic for nothing!

The main options for individuals are personal pensions and stakeholder pensions (these terms are explained later in this chapter).

Both benefit from generous tax breaks – tax relief at the individuals' highest rate on any contributions and the ability to take a tax-free lump sum on retirement.

---

> ### 🖉 Tax tip
>
> Given the choice, most employees will be better off joining an occu-
> pational scheme as the employer usually makes a generous contribu-
> tion to the scheme and pays for the costs of running the scheme.

---

## *Maximum Contributions*

There are two options:

1. For those wanting to make a maximum contribution of up to £3,600 payments can be made out of any income, or savings, or can be paid by another person. So non-earners, non-working wives and even children can now have a pension plan and receive tax relief. Individuals make contributions net, which means they only need pay £2,808 if they want to make the maximum contribution of £3,600. The remaining £792 is tax relief at the basic rate of 22 per cent (22% × £3,600 = £792).
2. Contributions over £3,600 can be made, but in this case the contributions cannot exceed a maximum percentage of 'net relevant earnings' up to an earnings cap of £97,200 (£95,400 for

the 2001/02 tax year). For employees, 'net relevant earnings' will usually be salary plus bonuses minus any expenses or payroll donations. For the self-employed (and those in partnership), 'net relevant earnings' are usually the taxable profits of the business. So non-earners and low earners cannot contribute more than £3,600 a year to their pension because they do not have sufficient/any 'net relevant earnings'.

---

### ✎ Tax tip

Even those with little or no earnings may be able to get round this rule as contributions over £3,600 can continue to be made for up to five years after an individual's earnings have ceased.

---

The rules are different for pensions taken out before personal pensions were launched in the late 1980s. Old-style pensions (taken out before July 1988) are known as retirement annuity contracts and have lower contribution limits and the maximum lump sum that can be taken tax-free on retirement is different.

## Contribution Limits

| Age at start of tax year | Max contribution as % of net relevant earnings | (Limits for retirement annuity contracts taken out before July 1988) |
| --- | --- | --- |
| Up to 35 | 17.5% | (17.5%) |
| 36 to 45 | 20% | (17.5%) |
| 46 to 50 | 25% | (17.5%) |
| 51 to 55 | 30% | (20%) |
| 56 to 60 | 35% | (22.5%) |
| 61 to 74 | 40% | (27.5%) |
| 75 and over | nil | nil |

---

### ✎ Tax tips

Even those who have no income at all and pay no tax at all can still get tax relief on pension contributions. Husbands can make contributions for non-earning wives, and parents for their children. However, they can only do so on contributions up to £3,600 gross a year. To make contributions of more than this, an individual needs to have earnings.

Higher-rate taxpayers can claim higher-rate tax relief on contributions. While contributions are made net of basic-rate tax (with the pension provider claiming the basic rate of tax as tax relief), higher-rate tax relief of 18 per cent (the difference between the higher rate of 40 per cent and the 22 per cent basic rate) needs to be claimed – either by filling in form PP120, or when filling in the tax return.

Employees usually receive higher-rate tax relief on their personal-pension and stakeholder-pension contributions by an adjustment in their PAYE tax codes – that way they receive tax relief when they make the contribution and do not have to wait until the end of the tax year to claim this tax back.

It pays to make additional contributions in years when the individual is a higher-rate taxpayer – to maximize tax relief. If a higher-rate taxpayer has missed out on a chance to make the most of this higher-rate relief, all is not lost. Carry back rules allow the individual to backdate contributions. See the section on CARRY BACK later in this chapter.

## *Tax-free Lump Sums*

Up to 25 per cent of the stakeholder or pension plan fund can be taken as a tax-free lump sum on retirement. With retirement annuity contracts the maximum is three times the annual annuity pensions payable (after the lump sum has been taken) but contracts taken out on or after 17 March 1987 are subject to a maximum of £150,000.

The remainder of the fund must be used to purchase what is known as a compulsory purchase annuity. This is an investment plan, which provides the retiree with an income for life. For the rules on when these must be purchased, see the section on ANNU-ITIES later in this chapter.

---

| ✏ Tax tip |
| --- |

Retirees will often be better off taking the maximum tax-free lump sum on retirement, rather than foregoing this and opting for a larger pension. Note that the larger the tax-free lump sum, the smaller the annual pension. However, because pension income is taxable, if the tax-free lump sum is invested in tax-free investments such as ISAs and certain National Savings products, the income can be earned tax free. Retirees should also be able to ensure that the income they earn is higher than the income that would be paid out by an annuity. For a guide to tax-free investments see CHAPTER 2: SAVINGS AND INVESTMENTS.

## Retirement Rules

Personal and stakeholder pensions can be taken at any time between the ages of 50 and 75 (although certain classes of worker such as jockeys and athletes can retire earlier). However, benefits can be drawn even if the individual does not retire – or can be taken well after retirement.

This gives great flexibility. Someone planning to retire early, can build up a decent pension without their employer knowing of their intentions. Someone who has built up an inadequate pension can continue to contribute after retirement or leave their pension fund to grow, so that when they do take their pension it is enhanced.

On retirement up to 25 per cent of the total fund can be taken as a tax-free lump sum. The remainder must be used to purchase an annuity to provide an income for life. See the section on ANNUI-TIES later in this chapter.

## Stakeholder Pensions

Although stakeholder pensions and personal pensions have the same tax regime (the same contribution limits and tax reliefs) there are differences between the two types of pension. Generally, stakeholder pensions are cheaper and more flexible. To qualify as a stakeholder, the plan must meet certain conditions:

- Charges must be a set percentage of the pension fund to make them easy to compare (that means no separate policy fees or penalties).

- The maximum charge is 1 per cent of the fund a year (personal pension fund charges usually have charges of 1.5 per cent).

- Low charges may mean no advice. If investors want detailed advice, the plan provider can charge extra. Most do, however, offer very good basic guides so detailed advice may not be needed.

- No charges can be made for transfers in or out of the scheme.

- Transfers should be accepted from other schemes.

- Minimum contributions must be no more than £20.

- There can be no penalties for stopping and starting contributions.

Designed to appeal to those on lower incomes who would otherwise not have any private pension provision, stakeholder pensions have proved a valuable tax break for higher earners.

Until they were launched only people with earnings could take out a pension plan and get tax relief on their contributions. Employees who were members of occupational schemes were generally barred from also having a personal pension. Provided they earn no more than £30,000 (and are not controlling directors) they can now have a stakeholder and pay in up to £3,600 a year and receive tax relief on these contributions as well as having a company scheme.

# Personal Pension Plans

When personal pension plans were introduced in 1988, they were widely missold to millions of employees who would have been better off joining or remaining in their employer's schemes. The selling of these schemes has since been more stringently regulated. However, a second wave of pensions misselling could occur if individuals are recommended to take out a personal pension plan rather than a stakeholder scheme. This is because personal pension plans are usually far less flexible and have higher charges than the new stakeholder pensions.

Those who have already invested in personal pension plans should not, however, switch to the new stakeholder schemes because many personal pension plans impose penalties on plan-holders who wish to transfer their pension plan to a different provider. This can mean that even though the value of the pension plan may be several thousand pounds, the transfer value may only be a few hundred pounds.

---

### ✎ Tax tip

Those unhappy with the performance or charges of their personal pension plan should think twice before transferring to a stakeholder pension because of the penalties. Instead they can consider leaving their personal pension where it is and then setting up a new stakeholder pension in addition to their existing plan.

Some pension providers will enable their customers with personal pensions to switch to their new stakeholder scheme at little or no cost. If an investor wants to switch, they should check with their existing pension provider if they will be better off doing so. If investors decide to leave their personal pension where it is, they should find out what charges will be deducted as these could eat into their fund.

## Life Insurance Contributions

Anyone contributing to a personal pension or stakeholder pension can divert some of their contributions to pay for life insurance. For policies started before 6 April 2001, the maximum that can be used to buy life insurance is 5 per cent of contributions. For policies started on or after that date it is 10 per cent.

---

**✐ Tax tip**

Buying life insurance through a personal or stakeholder pension is very cost effective because plan holders can get tax relief on their life insurance premiums – a big saving, particularly for higher-rate taxpayers.

---

## Annuities Purchase

A compulsory purchase annuity is an investment policy purchased on or after retirement, which provides an income for the rest of the policyholder's life. Retirees can take a maximum of 25 per cent of their pension fund on retirement as a tax-free lump sum. The remainder must be used to purchase an annuity.

Only those people in final salary schemes (where the pension is dependent on pay near retirement) need not purchase an annuity. People with personal pensions, stakeholder pensions, retirement annuity contracts and money purchase occupational schemes and group personal pensions all need to buy an annuity on retirement.

The level of income paid by the annuity depends on how long an individual is expected to live. Younger, healthier retirees will receive less, as do women who tend to live longer than men. Those with impaired lives (a history of illness, heavy smokers etc.) receive a higher income.

The income paid by an annuity is taxable.

**Tip**

Retirees should always shop around for the best annuity rate. Once an annuity is purchased it is purchased for life – it is not possible to switch to another company. However, only one in three people bother to ensure they are buying the best annuity. The difference between the best and worst annuity rates can vary by as much as 30 per cent.

It is possible to defer investing in an annuity until age 75 and, in the meantime, invest the pension fund (in the hope of getting a better return) with the option of withdrawing an income equivalent to that which would have been paid should an annuity have been purchased on retirement.

## Maximizing Tax Relief

We waste, as a nation, some £977 million a year by failing to optimize the tax reliefs offered by company, personal and stakeholder pensions and AVCs.

The most obvious way to maximize tax relief – i.e. get some money back from the Inland Revenue for a change – is to contribute more. The only snag is that investors cannot get their hands on this money until they reach 50 (with a personal pension or stakeholder pension) or until they retire (if they are members of a company pension scheme).

**Tax tips**

Higher-rate tax relief is not given automatically – it needs to be claimed. If the taxpayer receives an annual tax return, then he can claim tax relief by filling this in. Alternatively contact your tax office for form PP120.

Employees contributing to personal pensions and stakeholder pensions can receive tax relief through their PAYE tax codes. This is a valuable tax benefit. Instead of waiting for up to 21 months (from the start of one tax year until the deadline for submitting tax returns) for tax relief, they will receive it instantly.

## Carry Back

Anyone contributing to a personal or stakeholder pension or to a retirement annuity contract can ask for all or part of the amount they contribute to their pension to be treated for tax purposes as if they had made the contribution in the previous year. This can only be done if they have sufficient unused relief in that year, in other words they had not contributed the maximum allowed (for details, see the table earlier in this chapter).

---

### ✎ Tax tip

Anyone who was a higher-rate taxpayer last year but is now a basic-rate taxpayer should consider carrying back contributions to last year to receive tax relief at the higher rate.

---

### Example

*Sally Stakeholder has left work to have a baby. As she does not intend to work for a few years she wants to boost her pension now, so that when she retires she does not suffer too much. She wants to pay in £3,000 – which is well within the maximum contributions allowed both for this year and last.*

*If she treated this contribution as being made in this tax year when she is a basic-rate taxpayer she would receive the following tax relief:*

$$£3,000 \div 78 \times 100 \text{ (to gross it up)} = £3,846 - £3,000 = £846$$

*If she backdated the contribution to the previous tax year when she was a higher-rate taxpayer her total tax relief would be:*

$$£3,000 \div 60 \times 100 \text{ (to gross it up)} = £5,000 - £3,000 = £2,000$$

*So she will be £1,154 (£2,000 – £846) better off by backdating her contribution.*

**Note:** The facility to carry forward unused personal pension contribution allowances for six previous years and then claim income tax relief ended in the 2000/01 tax year.

Investors only have until 31 January following the year in which they want to carry back contributions to elect to carry them back. Investors who later realize they have missed out on a valuable tax break and want to claim tax relief cannot do so. The option to use the carry-back facility must be made either before or at the time the contribution is paid.

---

#### ✏ Tax tip

To carry back a contribution to the last tax year, a new contribution must be made (it is not possible to decide to carry back after the event) and it must be made by 31 January 2003 for it to apply for the 2001/02 tax year.

---

The rules for retirement annuity contracts are slightly different. To carry back a contribution for the 2001/02 tax year, the contribution must be paid by 5 April 2003. However, unlike with personal pensions and stakeholder pensions, the decision to carry back can be made after the event. Investors then have until 31 January 2004 to decide if they want to carry the contribution back. Carry-back claims are only allowed once the tax for the year to which contributions are being carried back has been calculated and paid. Inland Revenue form PP43 can be used to carry back contributions.

## Switching Jobs

Employees generally need to have 40 years of continuous service with the same employer to build up the maximum pension allowed by the Inland Revenue. However, jobs for life are a thing of the past and most workers have between five and nine jobs during their

working lives, which means they may never build up a decent
pension.

---

| ✎ **Tax tip** |
| --- |

The solution is to also have a stakeholder pension, which they can
keep for their entire working lives (and contribute up to £3,600 a year
even if they are also members of occupational schemes). They will
then get the benefits of an employer scheme and the chance to build
up a decent pension.

When switching employment, there are several options:

- Leave the pension behind where it will continue to grow.

- Take a transfer and switch the pension to a new scheme (but
  watch out for any transfer penalties).

- Or, in the case of personal and stakeholder pensions, continue
  with the same pension and suffer no penalties.

There are no tax advantages to opting for one particular option
over another.

## Pension Alternatives

Workers who do not want to wait until they are 50 to get their
hands on their pensions, or who want more flexible investments,
should consider tax-free savings plans such as ISAs. However, they
should note that no tax relief is given on these schemes – it is only
given on approved pension plans. They will have to contribute £100
to invest £100, whereas with a pension they only need pay in £78
(as a basic-rate taxpayer) or £60 (as a higher-rate taxpayer) for £100
to be invested in their pension.

However, with an investment such as an ISA, no annuity needs
to be purchased so the entire sum can be taken tax free on retire-

ment. As annuity rates are less generous for younger retirees (in their early 50s), ISAs could produce a better rate of income.

# State Pensions

## Basic State Pension

The basic state pension is a contributory scheme that individuals pay for out of their National Insurance Contributions. Contrary to popular belief not everyone is entitled to the full basic state pension. To receive the full amount individuals generally have to pay – or have been credited with – National Insurance contributions for about 90 per cent of their working lives. The basic state pension is taxable as income.

---

| ✎ Tip |
| --- |

It is possible to increase the amount of pension paid by postponing it for up to five years.

---

## State Earnings Related Pension Scheme (SERPS)

SERPS is also based on NICs. Contributions made by employers and employees on earnings between the lower and upper earnings limits (known as band earnings which are £89 and £585 per week respectively for 2002/03) count towards SERPS.

SERPS provides a pension at state retirement age as a percentage of band earnings. At the moment this is 25 per cent and will drop to 20 per cent for those retiring in 2009/2010 or later. Band earnings are based on the average over the individual's entire working life.

The self-employed do not contribute towards SERPS or benefit from it. Those in contracted out (opted out) company pension schemes (most schemes) do not contribute to SERPS either, instead they pay reduced NICs.

Individuals can contract out of SERPS with a rebate paid into a personal or stakeholder pension plan. The rebated NICs must be used to fund a pension and are known as 'protected rights contributions'. Rebates depend on age and range from 3.8–9 per cent for the 2001/02 tax year. Both the employee and employer continue to

# 4 Capital Gains Tax (CGT)

CGT is the tax on gains made when an asset is sold. While income is subject to income tax, profits are subject to CGT.

However, the tax is a little more complex than this. A potential CGT liability can occur when an asset is disposed of which can include being given away. In addition, if a loss is made on disposal of an asset, this loss can often be used to offset any gains to reduce a CGT bill.

As with the income tax personal allowance, everyone is entitled to a personal CGT allowance each year which is the amount that can be earned before paying tax. For the 2002/03 tax year it is £7,700 (£7,500 for 2001/02), which means everyone can make this amount of gains without suffering any capital gains liability. The allowance, which usually increases each year following the Budget, applies each tax year. Any unused allowance cannot be carried forward to future years. However, losses made in this tax year can be carried forward to be offset against gains made in future years.

---

## ✎ Tax tips

Millions of investors fail to use up their CGT allowance each year and, as a result, they are missing out on a valuable tax break. By selling assets each year to create a gain that is below the annual allowance, investors can ensure they do not build up a substantial CGT liability in future years.

The CGT allowance is much higher than the basic personal allowance for income tax and is therefore more valuable. Therefore it is worth considering investments that create a capital gain rather than ones that generate income.

CGT is fairly simple to avoid (as this chapter will detail). As a result, fewer than 100,000 taxpayers actually pay the tax each year.

Assets given away on death are not subject to CGT and instead may be liable to inheritance tax (see CHAPTER 5: INHERITANCE TAX). However, when an inheritance is sold, the inheritor can be liable for CGT on any profits made while they have owned the inheritance.

# WHAT IS SUBJECT TO CGT?

The gain on the disposal of any asset is potentially liable to CGT (apart from those which are tax exempt).

The assets most likely to be subject to CGT include:

• shares, unit trusts and other investments

• businesses or business assets

• second homes, land and property

• antiques and works of art

• most assets held for personal or investment purposes (unless they are chattels, see section later in this chapter) – basically any asset that is not exempt

# WHICH GAINS ARE TAX FREE?

Certain assets are exempt from CGT. These include:

• Private cars.

• A main home (principal private residence) provided it has not been let out or used for business and also any grounds if they are sold with the property.

• Gifts between husband and wife.

- Personal possessions or chattels with a predicted useful life of 50 years or less when they are first acquired (see the CHATTELS section later in this chapter).

- ISAs – and also PEPs and TESSAs. For more details see CHAPTER 2: SAVINGS AND INVESTMENTS.

- National Savings products.

- Betting, lottery or pools winnings.

- Gilts (government stocks) and corporate bonds.

- Enterprise Investment Scheme (EIS) and Venture Capital Trust (VCT) shares. For more details see CHAPTER 2: SAVINGS AND INVESTMENTS.

- The proceeds of most life insurance policies (but not those bought from a third party known as second-hand or traded endowments).

- Compensation – for personal injury, for missold personal pension plans – and damages including those for defamation.

- Foreign currency for personal use.

- Gifts to charities and certain national institutions/heritage bodies.

- Most cashbacks.

- Money or assets which are taxable as part of income or would be subject to income tax.

---

### ✏ Tax tip

When a gift is made to charity – or shares transferred to that charity – this does not lead to a capital gain. So those facing a large tax liability could instead donate their shares to a charity and give to a good cause rather than the Inland Revenue.

# WHEN IS A GAIN MADE?

A gain is made when an asset is disposed of. This generally means that it is sold. However, disposals can also be made when an asset is:

- given away

- destroyed and an insurance company pays out

- sold for less than its market value

- exchanged for another asset

    The date taken for the disposal is the date of:

- sale

- when the gift was made

- when a capital sum was received (such as an insurance payment)

# HOW THE TAX IS CALCULATED

The tax is based on how much an asset has increased in value during the time the taxpayer has owned it, minus certain allowable expenses. In other words this is how much it was sold for (or its value on disposal) minus the initial value when it was bought (or acquired). Investors can then subtract any allowable expenses when calculating the profit.

    Allowable expenses include:

- Costs incurred in buying and selling, including valuer's/ surveyor's fees and auction fees as well as advertising costs – but it is not possible to claim the costs/interest on a loan used to purchase the asset.

- The cost of legal advice.

- Stamp duty.

- Stockbrokers' fees (if only part of an asset is sold, such as part of a block of shares, you can claim a proportion of the costs).

- Costs of enhancing the value of the asset – restoration etc., but not maintenance or repairs.

- Inflation (only if the asset was acquired before 1 April 1998). See the section on the INDEXATION ALLOWANCE later in this chapter.

If an asset is given away, valuation costs needed to work out a chargeable gain can be deducted. It is possible to make a capital gain even if an asset is not sold, for example if the asset is given away or exchanged, or the investor sells the rights to it or even receives insurance money for it if it is lost or destroyed – this is classed as a disposal for CGT purposes. The date an asset is disposed of – not necessarily the date it is paid for – is the date that must be used when calculating the gain.

Once the gain has been calculated any losses made on the disposal of other assets can be deducted to arrive at the total chargeable gain for the tax year. This is then reduced the longer the asset is held, using taper relief (see the section later in this chapter).

It can sometimes be difficult to get an accurate valuation for an asset (for example, if it is not sold but is destroyed). Those who want the Inland Revenue to check their CGT valuations can ask for form CG34. All they need to do is complete the form and return it to their tax office with any supporting information and documents.

## How Much Tax Must be Paid?

Taxable gains are taxed at the highest rate of income tax an individual pays. The taxable gains are treated as the top slice of an individual's income, which means that the rate depends on which tax band the individual falls into once taxable gains are added to other taxable income.

As with income tax, CGT is charged at three rates:

- 10% starting rate – only if taxable income (income exceeding personal tax allowances) and taxable gains (exceeding the CGT threshold) when added together do not exceed £1,920, the basic-rate threshold for 2002/03 (£1,880 for 2001/02).

- 20% basic rate – if total taxable income and gains fall in the basic-rate tax band of between £1,921 and £29,900 for the 2002/03 tax year (£1,881 and £29,400 for 2001/02).

- 40% higher rate – for gains that fall into the higher-rate band of over £29,900 for the 2002/03 tax year (£29,400 for 2001/02).

**Note:** A chargeable gain is the amount of gain before applying the tax-free allowance, losses and any taper relief, whereas a taxable gain applies after taking into account these items.

### Example

*Annie Investor had earnings of £33,000 in the 2001/02 tax year and made £2,500 of taxable gains. As a single woman with no children she was entitled to the basic personal allowance of £4,535 a year.*

*The amount of her income subject to income tax was:*

*£33,000 – £4,535 = £28,465*

*This was below the higher-rate threshold, which started at £29,400 during the 2001/02 tax year. So she was not liable to any higher-rate tax.*

*She paid the basic rate of 20% on the amount of gains that fell into the basic-rate tax band (not all of this was used up by her income):*

*£29,400 (the higher-rate threshold) – £28,465 (income subject to income tax) = £935. And she paid the higher rate of tax on the remainder of her gains.*

*£2,500 – £935 (taxed at the basic rate) = £1,565*
*So her CGT bill was:*

*£935 @ 20% =        £187*
*£1,565 @ 40% =      £626*

*TOTAL               £813*

> ✎ **Tax tip**
>
> Investors tempted to sell assets for less than their market value should note that the final value is usually taken as the market value even if an item is sold at a discount. Assets cannot be given away to escape CGT. Once again it is the market value that is used in calculations.

# Losses

If any losses are made on the disposal of an asset, they can be used to offset or reduce the profits made on the disposal of other assets.

> ✎ **Tax tip**
>
> Investors who face a hefty CGT liability may want to consider divesting themselves of any assets that are proving poor investments. By creating a loss on the sale of one asset they can reduce the CGT liability on another.

The rules require that:

- Losses must be offset against any gains made in the same year.

- If, after using current year losses, there are still taxable gains above the tax threshold, losses made in any previous years must be used to reduce gains to the level of the tax-free amount.

**Note:** It is not possible to use losses that are exempt from CGT to offset gains on assets that are liable to CGT. That means investors cannot offset losses on sales of ISA or PEPs or transfers between a husband and wife. The exceptions are losses on shares in an Enterprise Investment Scheme (EIS) company and certain loans made to businesses.

Unused losses that have not been used against gains (for example, if there are no gains in that particular tax year or gains are less than losses) can be carried forward indefinitely.

## Example

*Amelia Asset decided to sell her share portfolio. Some shares have done well and others very badly and as a result she made total chargeable gains of £12,000 and allowable losses of £10,000 in the 2001/02 tax year.*

*She deducts all the allowable losses leaving her with a chargeable gain of £2,000. This was below the annual exempt amount (£7,500 for the 2001/02 tax year) so she will not have to pay any CGT.*

*However, she has wasted her CGT allowance. It would have been far better to only realize losses of £4,500 reducing her gains to £7,500. That way she would have made the most of the exempt amount. Even if she does not use her full allowance, she cannot carry this allowance forward to the next tax year. The only way she could carry forward an unused loss would be if her losses exceeded her gains.*

*If her chargeable gains were £12,000 and her allowable losses £15,000 she would be able to carry forward £3,000 of losses to future tax years.*

### ✐ Tax tips

It is vital that losses are reported to the tax office – they will not be allowable unless the Inland Revenue has been informed that the taxpayer has made a loss. This must be done within five years and ten months of the end of the tax year in which the loss arose.

Investors who made a CGT loss that they cannot use to offset gains and who want to carry this forward to use in future tax years must notify their tax office of their intention. However, they have up to six years from the end of the tax year in which the loss is made to do this. Any investors who have only just realized that they have unused CGT losses for past years have plenty of time in which to make use of this tax-saving tip. Note that losses made before 6 April 1996 do not have to be notified to the Inland Revenue within a certain time limit.

There is no time limit within which losses brought forward must be used.

## Example

*Graham Gain suffered badly on a poor investment when he sold it in the 1997–1998 tax year. As he had no chargeable gains in that tax year, he carried forward this loss of £8,000. In the 2001/02 tax year, Graham sells a more lucrative investment making a chargeable gain of £10,000. Another investment results in an allowable loss of £1,000.*

*He deducts the losses brought forward to reduce the chargeable gains (after losses have been deducted) to the level of the annual exempt amount.*

*£10,000 – £1,000 = £9,000 chargeable gain for 2001/02*

*Less the annual exempt amount £9,000 – £7,500 = £1,500*

*So he uses up £1,500 of the losses he brought forward*

*£8,000 – £1,500 = £6,500*

*This leaves him £6,500 of losses to carry forward again.*

*And as his chargeable gains after losses do not exceed the annual exempt amount, Graham has no CGT to pay.*

**Note:** Taper relief (the relief that reduces the amount of CGT an individual has to pay the longer an asset is held, for a full explanation see TAPER RELIEF later in the chapter) is calculated after all other reliefs and allowable losses have been deducted from the chargeable gain. Losses are not tapered, so they are applied to untapered chargeable gains. If the chargeable gain is below the annual CGT threshold there is no need to calculate taper relief.

### ✎ Tax tips

Investors who make a loss on shares in a trading company (one that is not quoted on the stock exchange) can offset these losses against their income to reduce their income tax rather than against their capital gains – but only if they subscribed for new shares.

Investors can claim as a loss anything that is destroyed or no longer has any value (or negligible value) including shares in companies that have gone into liquidation.

It is possible to claim losses from a business against a CGT liability to reduce the amount of tax to be paid. Losses from some rented pro-perties (only those classed as furnished holiday lettings) can also be used to offset a CGT liability.

Those making a loss on the sale of an asset must use it to reduce their CGT liability for the same tax year in which the loss was made. However, they should not reduce their gain to less than the CGT threshold of £7,700 for the 2002/03 tax year. Additional losses can be offset against other income or capital gains in future years.

Losses cannot normally be carried back to earlier tax years. However, there is an exception – when someone dies. Their personal representative can carry back any unused allowable losses arising in the tax year in which they die and deduct them from total chargeable gains of the three preceding tax years.

# Chattels

The word chattel is a legal term meaning an item of tangible, movable property and can cover a range of everyday items including:

- household furniture
- paintings
- crockery and china
- antiques
- first editions of books
- silver

Taxpayers only need to include gains on their tax return if the chattel was sold for more than £6,000 even though the CGT threshold is £7,700. (Taxpayers only have to fill in the CGT pages of the tax return if their gains exceed this threshold or they disposed of chargeable assets worth more than twice the threshold.) So, for example, if a table was sold for £8,000 then it would exceed this £6,000 limit. Even if the gain was only £200, the same limit applies.

Special rules for calculating chargeable gains then apply. The gain is the amount by which the disposal proceeds exceed £6,000 divided by 5/3.

## Example

*Paul Portrait sold a painting he acquired for just £2,000 in July 1988 at a large profit in September 2001 when he auctioned it and received £7,500.*
   *He calculates the amount by which the disposal proceeds exceed £6,000.*

*£7,500 – £6,000 = £1,500*

*Then he multiplies this by 5/3 (£1,500 × 5/3) = £2,500*
   *This is his maximum chargeable gain before taper relief. If he had no other gains, he would not need to do any further calculations as he has not exceeded the £7,500 CGT allowance for the 2001/02 tax year.*
   *However, assuming he has other gains he then needs to work out the actual gain before taper relief to see if this is lower. To do this calculation he deducts certain costs:*

| | | |
|---|---|---|
| *Disposal proceeds* | | *£7,500* |
| *Less   Cost of purchase* | *£2,000* | |
| *Expenses (auction fees)* | *£   200* | |
| | | |
| *TOTAL* | *£2,200* | |
| | | |
| *Actual gain* | | *£5,300* |

*If the painting had been purchased before April 1998 he could also have deducted indexation (the allowance for inflation).*
   *His actual gain of £5,300 is higher than the maximum chargeable gain using the calculation that allows him to deduct £6,000 and multiply by 5/3 which gave him a maximum chargeable gain of £2,500. He therefore uses the lower figure of £2,500 in his calculation and when deducting taper relief.*
   *If, when using the £6,000 calculation, a loss is created, then different rules apply. The £6,000 figure must be used as the sale or disposal price. If an item was sold for £4,000, it has to be assumed that it was, in fact, sold for £6,000. This will limit the amount of losses. These losses can still be offset against any gains to reduce the total amount of CGT liability.*

---

**🖊 Tax tip**

Do not try to get round these rules by selling sets of items separately so that each is sold for less than £6,000. The rules require that if, for example, a set of four dining chairs were sold separately for £3,000 each, the proceeds should be taken as being £12,000 and would therefore exceed the £6,000 threshold. If they are sold one at a time to the same person, they are regarded as a single asset – even though the sales may have taken place at different times.

# TAPER RELIEF

Taper relief reduces the amount of capital gain that is charged to tax on the disposal of an asset. The longer the asset has been held after 5 April 1998, the larger the reduction.

Introduced in the Finance Act 1998, taper relief applies to the capital gains of individuals, trusts and the personal representatives of deceased persons, but not to the capital gains of companies.

Different tapers apply to business assets and non-business assets.

The taper reduces the effective CGT rates for a higher-rate CGT payer from 40 per cent to 10 per cent for business assets and from 40 per cent to 24 per cent for non-business assets.

**Note:** Taxpayers only need to work out taper relief if their chargeable gains after allowable losses have been deducted are more than the annual exempt amount of £7,700 for the 2002/03 tax year.

---

**🖊 Tax tips**

Taper relief cuts the chargeable gain the longer the asset is owned (after 5 April 1998). So it pays to hold on to assets for longer periods as the proportion of any gain on which tax is payable reduces.

It is not possible to apply taper relief and then deduct any CGT losses, which could lead to substantial tax savings. Instead, losses from the current tax year and any unused losses from previous tax years must be offset against gains before applying taper relief.

Offset or allocate any losses to gains that qualify for the least amount
of taper relief before using them to reduce gains that qualify for greater
amounts of taper relief. This maximizes the taper relief and reduces
the CGT bill.

As stated above, losses made in the current tax year must be offset
against gains before any losses are brought forward from previous
years. If a chargeable gain remains, unused losses must be applied
to the gain (they cannot be carried forward) but only to bring the
gain down to the level of the tax-free allowance of £7,700 for the
2002/03 tax year. Taper relief only applies if the remaining gain is
greater than the tax-free allowance.

## How Taper Relief Reduces the Equivalent CGT Rate

Gains on non-business assets:

| Complete years after 5 April 1998 the asset was held | Percentage of gain chargeable (this is the taper) | Equivalent CGT rate | |
|---|---|---|---|
| | | basic-rate taxpayers | higher-rate taxpayers |
| 0 | 100 | 20 | 40 |
| 1 | 100 | 20 | 40 |
| 2 | 100 | 20 | 40 |
| 3 | 95 | 19 | 38 |
| 4 | 90 | 18 | 36 |
| 5 | 85 | 17 | 34 |
| 6 | 80 | 16 | 32 |
| 7 | 75 | 15 | 30 |
| 8 | 70 | 14 | 28 |
| 9 | 65 | 13 | 26 |
| 10+ | 60 | 12 | 24 |

A whole year refers to any continuous period of 12 months – it does
not have to coincide with a tax year. Fractions of a year are ignored.

---

### ✎ Tax tip

Investors must own a non-business asset for at least three years before taper relief reduces their tax bill. However, non-business assets held before 17 March 1998 have an extra year added to the period of ownership that qualifies for taper relief.

## Example

*Susan Shareholder purchased 10,000 shares in the Big Profits Company in September 1987. She sold them in November 2001 for a profit of £12,500 calculating her gain after deducting the costs of buying/selling the shares and the indexation allowance up to April 1998. She had no allowable losses in the 2001/02 tax year.*

*As her gain exceeded the CGT threshold of £7,500 for the 2001/02 tax year, she needs to calculate taper relief.*

*The complete number of years she had held the shares after 5 April 1998 were three (remember, fractions of years are ignored). However, as she owned the shares before 17 March 1998 an extra year is added.*

*Percentage of gain chargeable for non-business assets held for four years = 90%*
*Net chargeable gain is 90% of £12,500 = £11,250*
*Only now does she deduct the £7,500 CGT threshold to reduce her tapered gain*
*£11,250 − £7,500 = £3,750 which is her CGT liability.*

**Note:** When calculating the amount of gains chargeable to CGT, losses are deducted from gains first and then, if this amount exceeds the annual threshold of £7,700 for the 2002/03 tax year, the gain is tapered and only then is the annual exempt amount deducted.

## Example

| | |
|---|---|
| *Chargeable gain on asset owned for 6 complete years* | £9,000 |
| *Less  Taper relief 80% of chargeable gain (80% × £9,000)* | £7,200 |
| *Annual exempt amount* | £7,500 |
| *Amount chargeable to CGT* | *nil* |

# Business Assets

These are any assets that are used to carry out a trade. The following shareholdings also count as business assets:

- Shares owned by employees and officers in an unquoted trading company where they work as well as unquoted non-trading companies (these include property and investment companies) provided they do not hold more than 10 per cent interest in the company.

- Shares in unlisted trading companies.

- Shares in listed (stock market quoted) trading companies provided that the individual controls not less than 5 per cent of the voting rights.

Taper relief is more generous for business assets. Once the asset has been owned for just one tax year (after 5 April 1998), taper relief reduces the CGT tax bill on these assets.

## How Taper Relief Reduces the Equivalent CGT Rate

Gains on business assets from 6 April 2002 (pre 6 April 2002 rates in brackets):

| Complete years after 5 April 1998 the asset was held | Percentage of gain chargeable (this is the taper) | Equivalent CGT rate | |
|---|---|---|---|
| | | basic-rate taxpayers | higher-rate taxpayers |
| 0 | 100 (100) | 20 (20) | 40 (40) |
| 1 | 50 (87.5) | 10 (17.5) | 20 (35) |
| 2 | 25 (75) | 5 (15) | 10 (30) |
| 3 | 25 (50) | 5 (10) | 10 (20) |
| 4+ | 25 (25) | 5 (5) | 10 (10) |

For more information on taper relief see Inland Revenue Help Sheet IR279: Taper Relief.

# Indexation Allowance

The indexation allowance, which enables those disposing of assets to deduct the effects of inflation so they do not pay tax on gains that are purely due to inflationary price increases, was abolished in 1998.

Only assets acquired before 1 April 1998 – and from March 1982 onward – come under this scheme. The initial value and allowable expenses are linked to the retail price index (RPI) which measures inflation. They will increase in line with this index.

---

### ✎ Tax tips

The indexation allowance can either reduce or eliminate a taxable gain, however it cannot be used to create or increase a loss. The inflation factor can only reduce profits, not create losses.

The indexation allowance can also be applied to costs in buying an asset and the cost of enhancing an asset.

---

When calculating the indexation allowance only costs and expenses incurred after 31 March 1982 can be indexed – even if the asset was owned before that date. The Inland Revenue supplies tables of the retail prices index to help individuals calculate the indexation allowance.

## Rebasing

When calculating gains/losses, individuals only need to take into account the rise in value of any assets since 31 March 1982. Assets held before that date can have the gain calculated assuming the market value on 31 March 1982. So any appreciation/profit made before that date will not be taxed. This can make life simpler – and can lead to substantial tax savings.

In order for assets to have the March 1982 value taken as the initial value, it is necessary to make an election to 'rebase' them.

However, once an election is made to rebase assets, it is final – the individual cannot change his mind – and it will cover all assets. In addition, no expenses incurred before 31 March 1982 can be deducted when calculating a taxable gain.

---

### ✎ Tax tip

Those unsure as to whether they will be better off rebasing or not, should not make an election to rebase and they can then treat each asset differently. They will have the flexibility to use the calculation that will result in the lowest CGT liability for each asset.

---

If no election to rebase is made, two calculations must be performed:

1. Calculate the gain using the market value on 31 March 1982.
2. Calculate the gain using the original acquisition cost (in this case expenses incurred before 31 March 1982 can be claimed).

As indexation (the factor that adjusts for inflation) did not start until March 1982 it can be included in both calculations.

- If both calculations show a gain, the smaller of the gains is the chargeable gain.

- If both calculations show a loss, the smaller of the losses is the allowable loss.

- If one calculation shows a gain and the other shows a loss, there is neither a chargeable gain nor an allowable loss.

---

### ✎ Tax tip

Anyone wanting to rebase their assets should let their tax office know by the second 31 January after the end of the tax year in which they first dispose of the asset.

---

Inland Revenue Help Sheet IR280 Rebasing – Assets Held at 31 March 1982 has further guidance.

# Calculating a Capital Gains Tax (CGT) Liability

Now that the terms have been explained, this is how a CGT calculation is worked out:

|  | Disposal proceeds |
|---|---|
| Less | Allowable costs |
| = | Gain before indexation (negative numbers mean a loss) |
| Less | Indexation allowance (for inflation up to April 1998) |
| = | Indexed gain |
| Less | Other reliefs (any reliefs that reduce or defer a gain) |
| = | Chargeable gain (for each asset individually) |
| SUM | Total chargeable gains (total of all of the chargeable gains in that tax year) |
| Less | Allowable losses (any losses in that tax year and any unused losses carried forward from earlier years) |
| = | Chargeable gains after losses |
| Less | Taper relief |
| = | Tapered chargeable gains |
| Less | Annual exempt amount of £7,700 (£7,500 for the 2001/02 tax year) |
| = | Amount chargeable to CGT |

### Example

*Archibald Antique is moving to a smaller property and recently sold a grandfather clock he bought for £6,000 in January 1987 for £25,000 in September 2001. He needs to calculate his chargeable gain.*

|  |  |  |  |
|---|---|---|---|
|  | Disposal proceeds |  | £25,000 |
| Less | Allowable costs |  | £ 8,200 |
|  | Cost of acquisition | £ 6,000 |  |
|  | Incidental costs of acquisition | nil |  |
|  | Enhancement costs |  |  |
|  | – restoration (Jan 1987) | £ 2,000 |  |
|  | Incidental disposal costs |  |  |
|  | – advertising | £  200 |  |

| | | |
|---|---|---|
| *Gain before indexation* | | £16,800 |
| *Less indexation allowance\** | | £ 3,360 |
| *cost of acquisition £6,000 × 0.42* | £ 2,520 | |
| *restoration £2,000 × 0.42* | £ 840 | |
| *Indexed gain* | | £13,440 |
| *Less Other reliefs* | *nil* | |
| *Chargeable gain* | | £13,440 |
| *Less Taper relief* | £13,440 × 90% | |
| *Tapered chargeable gain* | | £12,096 |
| *Less annual CGT allowance of* | £ 7,500 | |
| *Amount chargeable to CGT* | | £ 4,596 |

*\* Indexation is given from January 1987 to April 1998 and is based on RPI for the month of purchase/item of expenditure and the RPI in the month of the date of disposal.*

*If the asset was purchased before the start of this period and sold after this period ended the indexation would be given based on the RPI in March 1982 and the RPI in March 1998. The Inland Revenue produces tables giving these figures.*

# CGT AND SHARES

Special rules apply for:

- shares or securities of the same class in the same company

- units of the same class in the same unit trust

If there has been more than one purchase on more than one date, then special identification rules apply.

This is to stop investors selling shares and then buying them back on the same date to realize a capital gain without incurring a CGT liability (known as bed and breakfasting).

Until this loophole was closed, it was a valuable tax break. For example, if an investor had held 1,000 shares for ten years and faced a large CGT bill if the shares rose any further in value, he could sell them, make a gain below the CGT threshold, and then buy them back. Any future gains would be calculated on the price paid when he bought them back again not on the original purchase price. He could keep realizing these gains selling and buying back the same shares in future tax years and never face a CGT liability. Sadly, this is no longer possible.

The rules determine:

- Which shares, securities or units the individual is treated as having sold.

- What acquisition costs they can deduct when calculating their chargeable gain.

See SHARES IN THE SAME COMPANY section below.


## Pooling

Shares of the same type in the same company are, if they were acquired after 5 April 1982 and before 6 April 1998, pooled for tax purposes. This means that the average cost of acquiring the shares is taken as the original cost.

However, for shares and units in a unit trust purchased on or after 6 April 1998, each purchase has to be recorded separately.

The rules for pooling are explained in Inland Revenue Help Sheet IR284: Shares and Capital Gains Tax.


## Shares in the Same Company

Investors who own shares of the same type in the same company but purchased these at different times may be tempted when they sell shares to claim that the shares purchased earlier or later are in fact the ones being sold. They may do this to create a loss, reduce the CGT liability or to claim indexation allowances.

If an investor owns £10,000 of shares with half bought five years ago and the remainder last month, he cannot claim that the £5,000 of shares being sold now were in fact bought five years ago if it suits him for tax purposes.

So that investors cannot abuse the system, the Inland Revenue has rules for deciding what order the shares are disposed in. When calculating when a share is acquired the Inland Revenue requires that investors treat disposing of shares in the following order:

- Shares bought on the same day.

- Shares bought within 30 days of the date of disposal.

- Shares acquired after 5 April 1998 taking the last in, first out (LIFO) approach – so the most recent acquisitions are taken first.

- Shares bought between 6 April 1982 and 5 April 1998 – which are kept in a pool known as a section 104 holding.

- Shares acquired between 7 April 1965 and 5 April 1982 – kept in a pool called a 1982 holding.

- Shares held on 6 April 1965.

## Example

*Ian Investor bought 2,000 shares on 19 May 1998 at a cost of £4,000. He thinks the company is a good investment and decides to buy another 500 of the same shares for £1,500 on 20 September 1998.*

*Ian decides to cash in his investment on 1 March 2002, so he sells 1,200 of his shares for £3,600 (the net amount). Because the shares were acquired after 5 April 1998, he must use the last in, first out (LIFO) basis. So 500 of the shares he sells are identified with the 500 shares bought in September 1998. The remaining 700 of shares are identified with the shares bought in May 1998.*

*His gains/losses are calculated as follows:*

*Disposal of 500 of the 1,200 shares*

| | |
|---|---|
| Proceeds 500/1200 × £3,600 (the net disposal proceeds) = | £1,500 |
| Allowable costs | |
| (the net amount paid for 500 shares in September 1998) = | £1,500 |
| Gain | nil |

*Disposal of the remaining 700 shares*

| | |
|---|---|
| *Proceeds*   700/1200 × £3,600   = | £2,100 |
| *Allowable cost* | |
| *(net amount paid in May 1998)* 700/2000 × £4,000 = | £1,400 |
| *Gain* | £700 |

# Rights and Bonus Issues

These are classed as belonging to the original shares to which they relate. So they are treated as having the same acquisition date and purchase cost as the original shares if they are issued after 6 April 1998.

However, scrip dividends – dividends in the form of shares rather than cash – are treated as new acquisitions at the dividend date.

# Takeovers and Mergers

Exchanging shares for new shares in the event of a takeover or merger does not normally count as a disposable. However, if shareholders receive a mixture of new shares and cash they are deemed to have disposed of a proportion of their shares (the percentage of the exchange in cash).

Further information is available in Inland Revenue Help Sheet IR285: Share Reorganizations, Company Take-overs and Capital Gains Tax.

---

**✎ Tax tip**

Hold shares – or unit trusts, OEICs or investment trusts – in an ISA and they will not be liable for CGT.

# Employee Share Schemes

Many employee share schemes including SAYE Sharesave schemes are known as tax-free schemes. While investors do not suffer any tax when they purchase the shares (usually at a substantial discount), they may be liable to CGT when they sell their shares. They do not have to pay CGT when they exercise the share option and acquire the shares and may only be liable for CGT if they:

- sell the shares after they exercise the option

- sell the option rather than exercising it

For CGT calculations, the date the option was exercised is used when working out taper relief – not the date the option was granted. If employees acquire shares under different employee share schemes on one day and sell some of them, they can elect that the shares with a smaller capital gain are disposed of first.

---

### ✎ Tax tips

Once shares have been realized (the employee has bought the shares), there is a ninety-day window in which they can be transferred directly into an ISA. The maximum that can be transferred is £7,000. The advantage? Once in an ISA they can be sold free of tax. The disadvantage? The investor's ISA limit is then used up. However, if by transferring some of the shares into an ISA, the investor escapes a hefty CGT bill it will be worthwhile.

Investors do not have to realize their shares (purchase them) for up to six months after the maturity date comes up. They then have a further ninety days within which to transfer any shares into an ISA. This extra time can mean that a capital gain is deferred into a new tax year. Alternatively if an employee has used up this year's ISA allowance and faces a CGT bill, it may be possible to delay purchasing (realizing) the shares until they can be transferred into an ISA once the new tax year begins and investors are given a new ISA allowance.

Investors in SAYE schemes can realize options on shares at regular intervals rather than selling them all at once. This way they can use up their annual CGT allowance to make a tax-free profit but ensure that they do not exceed the annual allowance and face a hefty CGT bill.

Further information is available in Inland Revenue Help Sheet IR287: Employee Share Schemes and Capital Gains Tax.

## CGT AND COUPLES

Shares – and other assets – can be transferred between spouses without incurring a CGT liability, so both members of a couple can use their CGT allowance against shares originally owned by just one of them.

When calculating a capital gain on an asset given by a spouse, then the acquisition costs used in the calculation should be the price the partner originally paid for the asset together with his or her allowable costs and the indexation allowance and taper relief.

> ✎ **Tax tip**
>
> Couples can avoid or reduce a CGT bill by making the most of the allowance given to both the husband and the wife. If they make a profit of £15,000 on jointly held assets, by splitting this (putting half on the husband's tax return and half on the wife's) they will not have to pay CGT.

### Example
*Wendy Worker has been investing in her company SAYE scheme for several years and has seen the value of her shares soar making £13.50 a share profit on the option price. Now they are reaching their five-year maturity.*

*As a result of the success of the company, she will make a large capital gain if she sells her shares, which she wants to do to help pay for the family's move to a bigger house. Even after deducting her CGT allowance*

*(£7,500 for the 2001/02 tax year) and taking into account the price she paid for the shares, she is left with a £12,500 taxable gain.*

*As a higher-rate taxpayer her CGT bill will be £12,500 × 40% = £5,000.*

*A £5,000 CGT bill like this can be easily avoided.*
*Her options are:*

- *Sell the shares and pay all the CGT of £5,000.*

- *Give £7,500 of shares to her husband so that he can sell them. As they fall within his CGT allowance, he will pay no tax. Her taxable gain will then also fall to (£12,500 – £7,500) £5,000. So her CGT bill will be £5,000 × 40% her higher rate of tax = £2,000.*

- *Give £7,500 of shares to her husband, who does not have any capital gains in the current tax year, and transfer a further £5,000 into an ISA within the 90-day window allowed by the Inland Revenue. She then has no CGT liability.*

*In future years, she would be advised to realize the shares gradually over time so she uses up her CGT allowance each year and does not face a CGT bill.*

---

### ✎ Tax tips

If, even after splitting the ownership of assets, the couple still face a CGT bill they can transfer assets to make the most of a lower-tax rate paid by one partner. As CGT is charged at the taxpayer's top rate of tax, it pays to transfer the asset to the spouse who can then sell it, realize a gain and pay tax at only 10 or 22 per cent instead of 40 per cent.

It is important that couples each make the most of their annual CGT allowance of £7,700 (£7,500 for the 2001/02 tax year). If the allowance is not used in one year, it cannot be carried forward. This means a large gain in a future tax year may be subject to tax while in earlier tax years the allowance was wasted. If the couple had sold assets creating gains up to the allowance each year, they may have avoided

this CGT bill. In order to make full use of the allowance, assets should
be transferred between spouses so they both use up their allowance.

If an asset is jointly owned, each owner is treated as making a
separate disposal based on their share of the proceeds and the costs.
So only half of the disposal proceeds should be included on each
spouse's tax return (or what ever proportion the couple has agreed
with their tax office).

Alas, marriages do end in divorce, and the tax breaks also end.
Part of any settlement may mean a partner has to transfer assets to
a former spouse. However, transfers between spouses are only
exempt if they are still married and living together. Those in the
process of separating should make sure they take account of any
potential tax liability when reaching a divorce settlement.

## CGT and Families

If a gift is made to another member of the family (other than a
spouse) then the exception does not apply. The person making the
gift may be liable to CGT.

### Example
*Daniel Dad bought a property for his son and daughter to live in when
they moved to the same city to study. After a few years he realized that
this could lead to a large inheritance tax liability and decided to give the
home to his children.*

*If he survives another seven years the gift would be exempt from
inheritance tax. However, he was stung for CGT when he transferred the
home to his children as it was classed as a disposal for CGT purposes.*

*It was not his principal private residence so it did not qualify for
private residence relief and he had to pay CGT on the gain made since he
first bought the house using the market value when he made the gift.*

# CGT AND PROPERTY

The fact that a main home is exempt from CGT means that what is possibly the largest investment anyone makes is tax free. Even if the property owner spends money and time improving the home in order to make a profit and sells it shortly after purchasing it, then the profits are tax free. In this way, the owner can become a mini-property developer trading up the property ladder by making larger and larger profits on the sale of each home.

There are, however, drawbacks. The increasing rate of stamp duty on property purchases is an indirect way of taxing the profits made on property (although it is paid by the purchaser not the vendor). The extra costs of buying, as a result of the tax that has to be paid, means that profits are eroded. For more details see CHAPTER 7: LAND AND PROPERTY.

As with most tax rules, there are exemptions to this one on private residence relief.

If the property owner has sold some land, earned money from their home (for instance, by renting it out) or used their home for running a business, then the profits made on the sale of the home may be subject to CGT.

If, for example, someone purchased a home and converted it into self-contained flats, which were then sold off, they would be liable to CGT. The same applies if they built a second home in their garden.

If the property has been partially rented, they could be liable for tax on the area let for the period of the letting. So, if the home was let for only a few years, they will only pay tax on a proportion of the profits made over the total years of ownership of the property and only on the proportion of the home let.

---

> ✎ **Tax tips**
>
> Homeowners who rent out or let a property can often escape tax as the gains up to £40,000 are exempt (and even if the gains exceed

£40,000, individuals also have a CGT allowance of £7,700 enabling them to make gains of up to £47,700 free of tax.

The final 36 months of ownership of a main home always qualify as tax exempt (for private residence relief) regardless of whether the property was let out during this time.

Taking in a lodger does not jeopardize private residence relief – the home still qualifies as tax free. Only if the homeowner has more than one lodger could the property become liable to CGT.

A homeowner does not have to live in their property for it to qualify as their principal private residence provided they are not living in it because they have been employed outside the UK or have been forced to live elsewhere because of their job (but not for more than four years.

Property buyers who purchase a home but then cannot move into it because they are unable to sell their existing home (or still own their existing home because they cannot sell it) are allowed to own both homes for up to 12 months without being liable for CGT. In the meantime they can rent out one home and earn an income from it (although any profits on this income after allowable expenses will be subject to income tax).

On marriage, if both partners own existing properties and then move into one and sell the other neither will pay CGT on the profits on the sale of the property. However, they do not have to sell the second home immediately; provided it is sold within three years of marriage, they may not have to pay any CGT. If they do not need the capital, they can let out their second home to provide additional income and benefit from any capital appreciation in the value of the property with this gain being tax free.

Further information is contained in Inland Revenue Help Sheet IR283: Private Residence Relief.

# Working from Home

Increasing numbers use their home as their office. However, working from home – and claiming part of the costs of the home against tax – could mean that the profits made on the sale of the property are liable for CGT. Only the proportion of the home used for business will be liable for CGT. So if a home has four rooms (excluding kitchens and bathrooms) and one room is used exclusively for business, then one quarter of the profits could be subject to CGT.

---

✏ **Tax tip**

To get round this rule, those working from home can use a room almost exclusively for business. They will still be able to claim for some of the running costs such as heating, light and telephone bills. If the house has four rooms (excluding kitchens and bathrooms) and one is used mainly for business, instead of claiming a quarter (25%) of the running costs of the home as an allowable expense, the home worker can claim, say, 75% of this 25%. The self-employed should agree these proportions with their local tax office when starting to work from home.

---

## DEFERRING A CAPITAL GAIN

It is not always possible to eliminate a CGT liability. In these cases, there is another option – to defer it.

There are two investment schemes that enable investors to do this. The first is the Venture Capital Trust (VCT) and the second the Enterprise Investment Scheme (EIS). In order to defer a gain investors must invest in a VCT within 12 months of the capital gain taking place and within three years for an EIS.

These schemes are covered in depth in CHAPTER 2: SAVINGS AND INVESTMENTS.

In addition, tax relief can be given in the following circumstances:

- Business asset roll-over relief: this allows the gain to be deferred when one business asset is sold and another acquired.

- Business transfer relief: this defers the gain where the business is transferred to a company in return for shares.

- Retirement relief: this reduces the chargeable gain when an individual disposes of a business or shares in a trading company and they are aged 50 or over or are retiring before that age owing to ill-health. This relief is being phased out and will not apply to gains arising after 5 April 2003.

## CGT AND INHERITANCES

When someone dies and their assets are passed on, then this is not treated as a disposal for CGT purposes. So when the assets are sold to be distributed to the deceased's beneficiaries no CGT needs to be paid. However, the estate may be liable to inheritance tax.

Once the inherited assets are sold, however, they may be liable for CGT. For the CGT tax calculation the market value of the asset on the date of death is taken as the acquisition cost.

# 5 Inheritance Tax (IHT)

The UK wastes £1.1 billion through poor IHT planning according to research from IFA Promotion. In the tax year ending April 2001, 1.1 million people were expected to have shared inheritances totalling £25 billion, with £1.4 billion of this going straight to the tax man. Yet, with a little financial planning, much of this tax could easily have been avoided. In fact, some accountants call IHT the 'voluntary tax' because it is so easily avoided.

Soaring property values, especially in the south-east, mean that increasing numbers of people will find that their assets exceed the threshold for IHT. Even so, many believe – wrongly – that IHT planning is just for the rich. It is not. People who want to make sure that as much of their estate as possible goes to the people or charities of their choice, need to plan ahead for their inheritance. With effective advance planning, it may well be possible to pass on all assets free of tax to the next generation.

## WHO IS TAXED ON WHAT

Anyone living in the UK is subject to IHT on all their property owned worldwide even if they have no assets in the UK and have lived abroad. However, many estates fall within the nil-rate band of IHT which means no tax is payable if the value of the estate does not exceed £250,000 for the 2002/03 tax year.

IHT is paid on the value of the estate upon death. This includes:

- property
- bank and building society deposits
- shares and unit trusts

- investments – including tax-free investments such as ISAs

- cash

Gifts or transfers made within seven years of death are also potentially liable to IHT.

# WHAT IS EXEMPT FROM IHT

The following assets are exempt from IHT and not included when the value of the estate is assessed:

- all transfers between spouses

- normal expenditure out of income

- gifts made more than seven years before death

- pension fund savings

  In addition, the following gifts and transfers are exempt:

- £250 to any number of individuals as small gifts each tax year.

- £3,000 per year given to one individual in any tax year.

- Gifts on marriage to a maximum of £5,000 from each parent (£2,500 by each grandparent or other relative and £1,000 by anyone else). The gift must be made before the wedding day.

- Gifts to charities.

- Gifts for national purposes (for example, the gift of a work of art to a museum, gifts to colleges or universities, the National Trust, National Gallery or the British Museum).

- Gifts to political parties.

- Gifts to housing associations.

For those members of company or occupational pension schemes who 'die in service', the benefits may be tax free. Up to four times salary is allowed as death in service benefits. The rules state that these payments are only exempt from IHT where the pension trustees retain discretion about paying beneficiaries. However, in practice they follow the employee's statement of wishes.

> **✎ Tax tip**
>
> Company pension schemes are not only tax efficient in life (contributions qualify for tax relief, the pension fund grows free of tax and a tax-free lump sum can be taken on retirement), they can be tax efficient in death. Employees should ensure that they update their statement of wishes as circumstances change. After a divorce, they will probably not want their former spouse to receive the death benefit.

The death benefits from personal pensions and other life assurance policies can be 'written in trust' to exclude them from the policyholder's estate for the purposes of IHT.

## AT WHAT RATE IS IHT LEVIED?

IHT is levied at 40 per cent on all assets in excess of the nil-rate threshold (£250,000 for 2002/03). This nil-rate band threshold is increased each year in the Budget and is usually raised in line with inflation.

The full amount is not charged on gifts made within seven years of death, known as potentially exempt transfers (PETs). (Gifts made more than seven years before death escape IHT.) The reduced rates are:

| | |
|---|---|
| One to three years | 100% of the full charge at 40% |
| Three to four years | 80% of the full charge giving an effective rate of 32% |
| Four to five years | 60% of the full charge giving an effective rate of 24% |
| Five to six years | 40% of the full charge giving an effective rate of 16% |
| Six to seven years | 20% of the full charge giving an effective rate of 8% |

**Inheritance Tax (IHT)**

**Note:** Even those who are non-taxpayers or basic-rate taxpayers will suffer 40 per cent tax on their estate if it exceeds the nil-rate band.

There is no upper limit on the amount of IHT.

---

**✎ Tax tip**

Quick succession relief reduces the tax burden of someone who has recently inherited property and then dies. To prevent the full rate of IHT being paid twice, only 80 per cent of the tax due on the second death is paid if it is within two years of the first, dropping every year to 20 per cent if it is within five years.

---

## How Much Could it Cost?

As transfers between husband and wife are exempt, the tax is usually paid on the death of the second partner. Calculated below is the IHT liability that would be payable on the family home. Remember, the tax is only payable on the value of the estate above the nil-rate band – in the table the threshold for 2001/02 of £242,000 is used – and on sums above this IHT levied at 40 per cent.

INHERITANCE TAX LIABILITIES ON SECOND PARTNER'S DEATH

| Value of Home | IHT Bill |
| --- | --- |
| £300,000 | £23,200 |
| £400,000 | £63,200 |
| £500,000 | £103,200 |
| £600,000 | £143,200 |
| £700,000 | £183,200 |
| £800,000 | £223,200 |
| £900,000 | £263,200 |
| £1 million | £303,200 |

## Who Pays Inheritance Tax?

It is the estate that pays the tax. It is deducted from the assets and must be paid before probate is granted (before the will is officially recognized). Any tax liability must be agreed and paid before the beneficiaries receive any inheritance. The tax is due within six months of the end of the month in which death occurred. Interest is usually charged on late payment.

However, it is the recipient of a gift who pays the IHT on the PET which becomes liable for tax because the donor dies within seven years of making the gift.

---

### ✎ Tax tip

It may be difficult to pay the IHT within the time limit required, if, for example, a property needs to be sold and no buyer can be found within the time limit. In these cases it is possible to pay IHT in instalments, with the agreement of the Inland Revenue.

---

**Warning:** Because the Inland Revenue is paid first, this can mean that assets such as the family home may have to be sold to meet the tax liability even though there may be other ways to pay this bill once the assets are distributed to beneficiaries.

## HOW IHT IS CALCULATED

All of an individual's assets (other than those that are exempt) at the time of death are added up. Any liabilities, such as debts, a mortgage, bank overdrafts, are then deducted from this sum.

### Example

*Richard and Ruth Rich decide to sit down and work out whether their estate is likely to exceed the IHT nil-rate band. They work out their assets as follows:*

*Assets:*

| | |
|---|---|
| Market value of home | £210,000 |
| Household contents | |
|     Furniture | £ 12,000 |
|     Antiques | £ 5,000 |
|     Paintings | £ 2,500 |
|     Other items | £ 4,000 |
| Personal effects | |
|     Jewellery | £ 2,200 |
|     Other items | £ 1,300 |
| Car | £ 6,000 |
| Bank and building society savings | £ 3,000 |
| ✓ ISA | £ 9,000 |
| Stocks and shares | £ 1,500 |
| National Savings investments | £ 500 |
| Life insurance | £ 25,000 |
| Gifts made within the last 7 years | none |
| Pension fund lump sums | none (they have already retired and invested these) |
| Money owed to them | none |
| | |
| TOTAL ASSETS | £282,000 |

They found it difficult to put precise values on individual items and realized that if they left this up to their children, then their children would be faced with a massive task. As a result, they decided to do the work themselves. The added advantage was that they now had a complete list of assets for insurance purposes.

They also realized that their life insurance should be written under trust, to save tax, and that they had not made any gifts that would count as potentially exempt transfers. They had also failed to use up their annual £3,000 exemption on gifts.

Then they added up their liabilities:

| | |
|---|---|
| Mortgage outstanding | nil |
| Bank loans/overdraft | nil |

Credit cards                          £  200
Hire purchase agreements              nil
Funeral expenses                      £4,000 (estimate)

TOTAL LIABILITIES                     £4,200

So the total value of their estate – assets minus liabilities – is currently:

£282,000 – £4,200 = £277,800

The proportion of the estate liable to IHT is therefore:

£277,800 – £242,000 (the nil-rate band for 2001/02 when they undertook
the calculation) = £35,800

Their estimated potential IHT liability is:

£35,800 × 40% = £14,320

The Riches know that this tax liability is likely to increase as the value of
their home increases and that unless they take action when the second
spouse to die passes away (remember all transfers between husband and
wife are currently exempt) the estate will suffer an unnecessary IHT bill.
So they decide to:

- Make use of annual gift allowances.

- Agree to leave some liquid assets to their children in their individual
  wills so that on the death of the first spouse the value of the estate is
  reduced and the first spouse uses some of his/her nil-rate band.

- Write their life assurance policy in trust.

# HOW TO AVOID AN IHT LIABILITY

This so-called 'voluntary tax' is easily avoided. Just follow these tax
tips.

✎ **Tax tips**

Transfers between husband and wife during their lifetime, or on death, are totally free of IHT. However, this often lulls people into a false sense of security. If the surviving partner inherits everything, the deceased partner has not made use of the IHT threshold – the facility to leave up to £250,000 (for the 2002/03 tax year) tax free to their children, grandchildren or other beneficiaries. To ensure that this tax threshold is used to full advantage, any liquid assets such as savings, shares or mutual funds should be split between the two partners so that each can leave up to the £250,000 nil-rate band to their children or grandchildren. This, however, is only of use if the surviving spouse would have sufficient income left and is not suitable for those whose only or main asset is the family home.

Give it away. That is the easiest way to escape IHT. However, taxpayers should do this before they get too old. Only if the asset is given away more than seven years before death does it escape IHT and remain outside the estate on death. These are known as potentially exempt transfers or PETs. As a safeguard, those making gifts should insure their life for seven years for the amount of the IHT liability with a policy written in trust for the beneficiaries of the estate.

Some parents wrongly think that they can give away their family home to escape IHT while still living in it. This is called a 'gift with reservation' and it does not count as a potentially exempt transfer. However, it is possible for them to give the home to their children, provided they pay a commercial rent to remain in the home. The main drawback with this is that few retired people can afford such a level of rent.

Make use of the annual gift allowances. The annual exemption allows £3,000 to be gifted each year by an individual and if this has not been used up in one tax year, this allowance can be carried forward to the next.

If a taxpayer has not used up this year's exemption they can carry it forward to the next. In addition, it is possible to make gifts of £250 to any number of people free of tax. However, if the value of gifts to one person exceeds £250 then all of the gifts to that person must be deducted from the £3,000 annual exemption. So consider passing on wealth to children and grandchildren in smaller amounts each year.

Both husbands and wives have an annual exemption which means a couple can give away £6,000 between them – £12,000 if they carry forward any unused exemption from one year to the next.

Regular gifts from income which do not reduce the individual's standard of living are exempt from IHT. There is no maximum limit on the value of this. However, these gifts cannot be made out of capital such as savings or investments and cannot be funded by the sale of assets.

Parents who help pay for a child's wedding should ensure that their financial support is tax free as far as IHT is concerned. They can give up to £5,000 each (£10,000 in total) and this will not be included as part of the estate for IHT purposes. However, they must make the marriage gift before the big day.

## USING LOANS TO AVOID IHT

At the time of writing it was possible to use a will, a trust and a loan to reduce IHT. These schemes can take several forms. Some are offered by life insurance companies, others by solicitors.

For example, both partners leave everything to their spouses in return for an IOU of the nil-rate IHT band, whatever it may be at the time of death. When the first partner dies, the IOU (loan) is created and held in trust for the benefit of the children or other beneficiaries. However, the surviving spouse can use the assets to supplement income. On the death of the second spouse the value of the IOU is deducted from the estate before IHT is calculated. This means that both partners can make use of their nil-rate IHT band.

With loan-trust schemes offered by life insurance companies the individual makes an interest-free loan to the trust, which then invests this capital for growth. Once the loan is made, it then falls outside of the estate for IHT purposes. If the individual requires an income, then prearranged repayments of the loan – usually at 5 per cent per annum of the capital advance – can be made. As this money is required to finance expenditure, it will be spent and therefore not added to the estate for IHT purposes.

The minimum value of the trust is usually around £10,000. Loan trusts offered by insurance companies may have share-swap facilities so that the individual can turn an existing portfolio into a loan trust. Generally loan trusts invest in the insurance company's own bonds (usually with-profits bonds).

> ### ✎ Tax tip
>
> These schemes are only suitable for those who have assets other than the family home.

## Home Reversion Schemes

These schemes are suitable for those who have a valuable property but few free assets. Part of the family home is sold to a home reversion company (usually at a discount to the current valuation) and, in return, the home owner receives a lump sum but continues to live in the home. This lump sum is then passed on to the beneficiaries. Provided the donors survive for seven years after passing on the lump sum, it is free of IHT.

Some home reversion schemes require that interest is paid. In other cases no interest is paid and, instead, the home reversion company benefits when the property is sold upon death. If half a £500,000 property is sold to a home reversion company, and upon death it is worth £750,000, then the home reversion company receives £375,000 back for loaning £250,000. The beneficiaries receive £250,000 – which should fall into the IHT nil-rate band. Alternatively, depending on the type of scheme, the initial amount loaned, the outstanding debt, plus any accumulated interest is repayable upon death of the second spouse.

The discount to the current valuation at which the property is sold to the home reversion company depends on age. The older home owners are, the smaller the discount since life expectancy is shorter.

Contact Safe Home Income Schemes – 08702 416 060 – for details of home reversion schemes.

# OTHER WAYS TO ESCAPE IHT

## Second Homes

Those with spare cash but in need of an income could consider purchasing a second home as a buy-to-let property with some capital and a loan. This will provide an income for several years. However, when they are older, parents can gift the property to their children or grandchildren. As it is a gift without reservation, i.e. they do not live in it, receive an income from it or have any rights over it, it is potentially exempt from IHT provided the parents survive for seven years.

---

### ✏ Tax tip

Increasingly, parents are required to fund their children's education. One way to help with the costs is to buy a property in the town or city where their child is studying, and put it in his or her name. Alternatively, a loan for the purchase of the property can also be made in the child's name, with the parents acting as guarantors. The child can then live there and rent out rooms to pay for the loan and at the same time live in rent-free accommodation; they also benefit by getting a foot on the property ladder and from the capital appreciation of the property, which is usually tax free, and they receive an early inheritance (the capital down payment) which will also be free of IHT (provided the parents live for at least seven years after making the gift).

## Insuring the Bill

It is possible to buy life insurance to cover an IHT bill. Written as a joint life, second death policy – as it is only upon the death of the second partner that IHT is usually paid – the life insurance is written in trust for the beneficiaries and is therefore outside the estate for IHT purposes. It can, however, be expensive and costs around £11 a month for £10,000 of death benefit for a couple aged 60, rising to around £22 a month at seventy. If the potential liability is £100,000, the costs would be £220 a month – which may be too expensive for most retired couples.

---

### 🖊 Tax tip

Taking out a life policy so that heirs will have a lump sum to pay any IHT liability (which should mean no need to sell the family home) can be expensive. To cut the costs make potentially exempt transfers, which will fall outside of IHT after seven years, and then buy a seven-year life policy that will pay the IHT on those assets. As the policy is for a relatively short term, the premiums will be lower. Remember to take into account any increase in value of the assets. IHT liability is assessed on the value of the assets at the time of death, not at the time the gift was made.

---

Another option is a life assurance bond. These are not life insurance policies, but investments. They can be assigned to a trust and become a potentially exempt transfer (PET). However, investors can withdraw 5 per cent of the original capital invested each year over a 20-year period with no immediate tax liability. For more details on investment bonds see the section on WITH-PROFIT BONDS in CHAPTER 2: SAVINGS AND INVESTMENTS.

Note: Although life insurance payments upon death are free of income tax and CGT, they can still have an impact on IHT. This is because the lump sum – which will often be used to repay a mortgage – increases the size of the estate by reducing the debts and therefore the amount of IHT that needs to be paid. See the section LIFE INSURANCE AND TRUSTS later in this chapter.

## Moving on Down

If the family home is the main asset and exceeds the nil-rate band threshold, one of the simplest ways to cut a potential IHT liability is to sell the property, buy a smaller one and give the children or grandchildren the surplus. Provided the parents survive for seven years, there will be no – or less – IHT liability.

## Leaving Half the Property to Children

As has already been discussed, it is not possible for parents to give children the family home and then continue to live in it as this is known as a 'gift with reservation'. However, it is possible to leave part of the property to the children on the death of the first spouse.

As the family home is likely to make up the bulk of the estate, this can reduce its value significantly.

First the parents must change the way in which they own the house from a joint tenancy – in which assets automatically pass to the survivor on death – to 'tenancy in common'. The latter enables the property to be passed on to a third party rather than the other person who owns the property.

However, this will mean that the surviving spouse no longer has exclusive rights to all of the property, so before opting for this, parents should be sure that their children understand the implications. If the children run into financial difficulties they could be forced to sell the home and leave the surviving spouse homeless.

# TRUSTS

Discretionary trusts are a legitimate way to reduce an IHT liability. Provision to create a trust can be made when writing a will with the trust coming into existence on death (usually of the first spouse). They are known as discretionary trusts because income is distributed at the discretion of the trustees who hold assets in a trust.

A trust enables the first spouse to die to use up all of his or her nil-rate IHT band while still enabling the surviving spouse to benefit from the assets.

An amount up to the nil-rate band is subject to the provisions of the discretionary trust. Potential beneficiaries should be identified in the will. These beneficiaries will receive income from the trust and can take out loans against the assets of the trust and receive outright gifts of capital from the trust at the discretion of the trustees (which usually include the surviving spouse). However, while the beneficiaries benefit there is no IHT liability in respect of assets sheltered within the discretionary trust.

This does not mean, however, that no tax needs to be paid. The trust itself is taxed, with income taxed at 34 per cent. Capital gains are also taxable. Administering a trust can therefore be time-consuming and expensive so it is important to consult a solicitor and financial adviser before deciding which assets to shelter in the trust.

## Life Insurance and Trusts

Most life insurance or assurance policies can be put in trust if they are intended to provide money for dependants upon death. However, a policy intended to repay a mortgage cannot be written in trust as it is assigned to a mortgage lender.

Both new policies and existing ones can be placed under a trust with forms usually available from life insurance companies. These are standard trusts covering the majority of cases. They can take several forms:

- Flexible trust – this is a basic type used for family protection or IHT planning. Everything is left to chosen beneficiaries. The reason why it is called a flexible trust is that the person creating the trust, the settlor, can change the beneficiaries if circumstances change. In addition to life insurance policies, with-profits bonds can be written under this type of trust – although the settlor must survive seven years after setting up the trust for IHT not to apply to the original sum invested.

- Split trusts – these are protection policies that include both death and critical illness benefits. The latter pay out a lump sum if the policyholder is diagnosed with certain life-threatening illnesses. The trust enables the death benefits to go to the beneficiaries while still allowing the policyholder to have any critical illness benefits if they suffer from a serious disease before they die.

- Family trust – this is a lifetime interest trust for single premium bond investments such as with-profits bonds. The settlor has access to the policy while still alive but can avoid probate and leave the bond to named individuals when he or she dies. There are no IHT savings.

- Legacy loan trust – the settlor gets access to their money because they only make a loan to the trustees. They can ask for this loan to be repaid at any time. The trustees use the loan to invest in a with-profits bond or a capital bond. The estate is only liable for IHT on any of the loan that has not been repaid. Generally, these are suitable for older investors who need the income in the trust. Each year, as an element is repaid, the IHT liability reduces. No IHT is paid on any profits the bond makes.

## Reversionary Interest Schemes

These transfer assets outside the estate for IHT purposes while still giving the individual control over the assets – and the right to receive regular annual payments for them.

When assets are transferred into a reversionary interest scheme, which involves a series of insurance bonds – they are classed as potentially exempt transfers so there will be no IHT liability if the donor (known as the settlor) survives for seven years.

As these schemes are based on investments, the assets can continue to grow and provide an income. Different maturity dates of a series of bonds can ensure that one matures each year giving the settlor the option of withdrawing the maturity value as income. Alternatively, the money can be reinvested and remain outside the grasp of the Inland Revenue.

Held within a trust, the bonds will eventually be inherited by the beneficiaries – usually children or grandchildren. They get their name because the settlor has a 'reversionary right' to receive the maturity value of the underlying bonds.

## Bare Trusts

Returns on investments (such as interest or dividends) made by parents on behalf of their minor children are generally taxed as the income of the parents. This means that a parent cannot escape income tax on savings income by putting his or her savings in the name of a child. This rule is subject to a £100 limit for small amounts.

To get round this rule parents have, in the past, set up a trust. A trust for a minor child, in which the child has an indefeasibly (not able to be annulled) vested interest in the income and capital of the trust was known as a bare trust for tax purposes. This ensured that any income arising to the trust, which was not distributed, was treated as the child's even if the funds in the trust came from the parent. It therefore generally escaped tax. So parents could set up a trust to escape tax on their savings and investments and, at the same time, provide for their children's futures.

However, as from the 1999 Budget these bare trusts are no longer so tax efficient. Any income from trusts set up after that date is treated and taxed as that of the parent (subject to the £100 limit) as is any income arising to funds added to existing trusts after Budget day 1999.

---

✎ **Tax tip**

Just because the parent is now liable for tax on these trusts does not mean they are not useful for income tax and IHT planning. Grand-parents can make use of them – particularly if they want to help with school fees planning.

---

# PENSIONS

A pension is one of the most tax-efficient ways to escape IHT. Tax relief is given at the individual's highest rate on contributions to the pension. A tax-free lump sum can be taken on retirement and if the individual lives a long life he or she can benefit from an income in retirement. In addition, if the individual dies before retirement, the lump sum paid out by the pension fund (up to four times salary for those in occupational schemes) is not included in the estate for IHT purposes.

If the individual dies after retirement, the spouse (and possible other dependants) will receive a pension for life, which also escapes being included in the estate for IHT purposes (although the pension itself will be subject to income tax if, as a result, it pushes the individuals' annual income to a level above their personal tax allowances).

Death benefits from personal and stakeholder pensions also escape IHT. The policyholder needs to ensure that the insurance is written in trust for their beneficiaries.

# MAKING A WILL

Nearly 40 per cent of the population in the UK dies intestate, i.e. without a will, leaving confusion over who should receive any inheritance. Those who die intestate could find, as in the case of unmarried couples, that those closest to them receive nothing. Worse, if the state cannot trace anyone to inherit, the tax man gets the lot.

Writing a will is more than just a means of stating precisely the names of beneficiaries and what they will receive, it is also a means of minimizing tax bills.

---

✏ **Tax tip**

Although individuals can write their own will or use a will-writing pack, it is advisable to seek professional help unless the content of the will is very simple. This is because problems can arise after death if the individual's wishes are not made entirely clear.

---

**Warning:** A will needs to be kept up to date and changed in light of major life changes such as remarriage or divorce. If it is not, the wrong people may benefit. It also needs to be updated to reflect new assets.

---

✏ **Tax tips**

Married couples should think twice before writing a will leaving their estate to the surviving partner. By doing so they are failing to make the most of each spouse's IHT-nil-rate band (or exemption) on the first death. As the nil-rate band is £250,000 for the 2002/03 tax year, this gives a potential tax loss of £100,000 (40 per cent tax of the £250,000 nil-rate band). This is easily avoided.

Married couples with substantial assets and those of more moderate means but with property that is likely to exceed the IHT threshold, should write their wills making the most of the nil-rate band by giving away assets up to this threshold either outright or through trusts. Word the will referring to the 'nil-rate band available on the date of death' rather than specifying an amount. Leave the remainder to the surviving spouse.

Even if a will does not take full advantage of the IHT nil-rate band, all is not lost. It is possible to change a will after a person dies so that the inheritance is given in a more tax-efficient manner. As long as all the beneficiaries who would lose out as a result of a change agree, a deed of variation can change the way the assets are distributed. Where only a spouse is named in a will, it can be rearranged so that other members of the family inherit. A deed of variation, which is normally drawn up by a solicitor, must be done within two years of the death by written agreement. The beneficiaries must also sign an election for tax purposes. Providing a valid tax election is made within six months of the deed being signed, it will be backdated to the date of death. The rate of IHT at that date will be applied. There is only one potential problem: if the beneficiaries include minors, then the original will cannot be varied without the intervention of the Official Solicitor, as a child cannot give a valid consent. The Inland Revenue publishes a free leaflet IHT8: Alterations to an Inheritance Following Death.

## Doing it Yourself

Those who do decide to write their will themselves (without the help of a solicitor) should ensure they read any instructions carefully. Common mistakes include failing to state at the beginning of the will that it replaces all previous wills so that the executors (those looking after the individual's wishes after they die) know that they are following the instructions of the most recent will.

It is also important to make provision in case any beneficiary dies before the individual making the will. If they do, any gift that was intended for them will fall into the residue unless the will specifies that it should go to someone else. The residue is what is left over after all debts and expenses have been deducted and any gifts to beneficiaries have been given.

**Note:** It is usual for any inheritance tax due on a legacy received under a will to be paid by the executors of the estate before it is paid over. Those receiving legacies do not, therefore, have to pay any inheritance tax and neither do they pay income tax or capital gains tax. It should be specified in the will that a set sum be paid to a beneficiary net of tax. If the deceased stated that they wanted to leave £10,000 to an individual that person will receive the full amount, not a lower amount once inheritance tax has been paid.

Some people have been caught out by not having their will witnessed properly or by failing to sign or date it. The legal requirement is that the will must be signed by the individual in the presence of two independent signatories who do not benefit from the will. All three signatories must sign in each other's presence.

The will should be stored in a safe place but not so safe that it cannot be found.

## Who Gets What if No Will is Made

The rules depend on whether or not the deceased is married or not.
   If someone is married:

- Only the first £125,000 automatically goes to the spouse (this will include the deceased's share of the marital home).

- If the estate is worth more than this, and there are children, the spouse receives the first £125,000, and a life interest in half the remainder as well as any personal effects. Their children (or their children's children if they are no longer alive) get the rest.

- If there are no surviving children the deceased's parents will inherit half the balance in excess of £200,000 (with the spouse getting any personal effects).

- If there are no surviving children or parents, brothers and sisters of the deceased share in half the balance in excess of £200,000 (with the spouse getting the personal effects). If the brothers and sisters are no longer alive their children can inherit.

**Warning:** If no will is made a nephew or niece could inherit a share of the family home and a surviving spouse may be forced to sell the property to pass on that inheritance — even though the deceased had expressed a wish that the widow/widower continues to live in the home.

If the deceased was not married then:

- Any children inherit the entire estate with it shared equally between them or their issue.

- If there are no children the deceased's parents inherit with the estate shared equally between them.

- If the parents are no longer alive brothers and sisters, or their issue, then inherit.

- If there are none of the above still alive first grandparents, or if they are not alive, then aunts and uncles or their issue then inherit.

- If there are no relatives everything goes to the Crown.

# 6 Tax Saving for the Self-employed

This chapter is aimed at those who are considering becoming self-employed, are newly self-employed, or who have relatively small earnings from self-employment. As a business expands, its accounting requirements become more complex (particularly once staff are employed and the business needs to register for VAT). These larger businesses will generally need the services of an accountant.

Being self-employed has its advantages. Individuals do not have to account to a boss, can set their own hours, decide what work they want to do and can reward themselves with more pay the harder they work. In addition, they benefit from a far more favourable tax treatment than employees as they:

- Can deduct a far wider range of expenses from their income before calculating their taxable profits and therefore how much tax they pay.

- Pay lower National Insurance contributions (although this in turn reduces their right to some state benefits).

It is not surprising that casual workers and those on short-term contracts try to claim they are self-employed – that way they can pay less tax. However, the Inland Revenue is increasingly clamping down on those claiming to be self-employed and, as a result, even those who work for more than one company can find that they must be taxed as employees and cannot claim the tax breaks granted to the self-employed.

To convince the Inland Revenue, individuals who claim they are self-employed must generally meet the following criteria. They should:

- Determine what work they do, where they work and the hours – those paid for a job are generally self-employed while those paid by the hour or day are usually employees.

- Put their own money at risk – for example, if the project fails they lose financially – and bear any losses as well as keeping the profits made by the business.

- Have the trappings of a business – a business bank account etc. – and invoice for work done.

- Work for more than one employer.

- Provide the main tools and equipment to do the job and usually the premises.

- Be free to hire people to do work that they have taken on and pay them from their own pocket.

- Take responsibility for unsatisfactory work and correct it at their own expense.

In some cases, individuals may still be classed as self-employed even if they do not meet all of these criteria.

However, if someone is paid for their time (not for providing goods or services), works at the premises of one company and earns most (generally more than 75 per cent) of their earnings from that one source, they will usually be taxed as an employee.

---

✎ **Tax tip**

If an individual has the choice of being an employee or self-employed, in terms of tax they will generally be better off being self-employed. However, while they may pay less tax they will lose out in other ways – no holiday or sickness pay, no company pension scheme, no redundancy pay, no guaranteed salary or security of employment and no jobseeker's allowance if they stop working.

---

## Consultancy and Freelance Earnings

It is possible to be an employee and self-employed. For example, those who make money out of a hobby such as dressmaking or gardening may be classed as carrying out a trade. Or, a senior employee may earn a bit extra on the side being paid to write a freelance article or an executive may receive a commission for introducing business to another company.

These extra earnings must be declared. Even though the individual is an employee, these earnings must be included on the self-employment pages of the tax return. However, if the employee only earns isolated income or commission they do not need to bother. This extra income can simply be entered in the section following question 13 on the main tax return. These earnings can include profits from isolated literary or artistic activities. Bear in mind that it is the profits that must be declared, so any tax allowable costs can be deducted from the income earned.

---

### ✎ Tax tips

If an individual makes a loss on freelance earnings then this loss can reduce the tax paid on his earnings from employment. So, for example, if he needs to purchase a computer and, as a result, his earnings from self-employment turn into a loss, he can cut his overall tax bill. However, he cannot get away using part-time self-employment to cut the amount of tax he pays for ever. The Inland Revenue will probably want to see evidence that he is in business to make a profit not a loss.

If a business has an annual turnover below £15,000 (that is sales not profits), then the self-employed have to provide far less information for the Inland Revenue filling in just three lines of accounts (turnover, expenses and net profit) on their tax return. There is no need to prepare accounts.

---

## MAXIMIZING EXPENSES

Deducting as much as possible from earnings, to minimize taxable profits, is the easiest way to save tax. Generally the self-employed can only deduct expenses that are incurred 'wholly and exclusively' for business purposes. However, there are exceptions such as cars, which can also be used for private mileage. In these cases only the business proportion of any expenses can be claimed.

The self-employed should avoid items of expenditure that they are not allowed to claim or keep these costs to a minimum where possible:

- Any business entertainment such as business lunches with clients.

- Legal fees and fines for breaking the law – including parking fines.

- Travel between home and the workplace.

- Meals – except a reasonable amount for breakfast and evening meals on overnight trips.

- The initial cost of buildings and alterations and improvements to business premises (although these may qualify for capital allowances).

- Capital repayments on loans and hire purchase.

And the self-employed cannot deduct their own salary, National Insurance contribution, income tax payments, pension costs, life insurance or private medical insurance as expenses.

In addition, the self-employed cannot claim for any items of capital expenditure (the purchase of assets, equipment, tools, cars, furniture etc.). These are deducted as capital allowances not as business expenses.

---

### ✎ Tax tip

It may be more tax efficient to buy equipment with a loan or on hire purchase. In addition to freeing up capital to invest in other aspects of the business, it is possible to claim all the interest as a tax-allowable deduction. If equipment is purchased, only 25 per cent of its cost can be deducted in the first year (although there are exceptions – see CAPITAL ALLOWANCES below).

In addition to keeping those expenses that cannot be reclaimed to a minimum, the self-employed should ensure they claim every item of expenditure they can to reduce their taxable profits.

However, remember that this is money that must actually be spent. So although higher expenditure will result in a lower tax bill, it will also mean lower profits and less income.

The items of expenditure the self-employed should remember to claim include:

- The running costs of their own car if they use it (even only occasionally) for business – they can deduct a proportion relating to the amount of business usage. Costs that can be claimed include motor insurance, road tax, maintenance and fuel. If a car is hired, the costs can also be deducted.

- A proportion of the costs of running their home – if they use it mainly or even only part-time for business use. For details of what can be claimed see the WORKING FROM HOME section later in this chapter.

- Bank charges, loan interest and overdraft fees on business accounts but not any capital repayments of loans.

- Interest on loans from friends and relatives who have helped start the business (provided they do not have a say in how the company is run and the loan is covered by a written agreement).

- VAT – those who are not registered for VAT can still claim it back by including it in the cost of any items of allowable expenditure.

- Insurance – to cover business premises and equipment (including a proportion of household insurance bills if working from home).

- Wages – paid to others.

- Legal fees for debt collection and preparing trading contracts and employee service contracts and accountancy and audit fees.

---

### ✎ Tax tips

To cut down on paperwork, those who use their car for business can simply claim a mileage allowance rather than keeping motoring bills. They can claim the same amount as employees under the agreed mileage allowances (known as the fixed profit car scheme or FPCS). These allowances are:

**Rates for 2002/03**

Cars and vans:

| | |
|---|---|
| On the first 10,000 miles in the tax year | 40p per mile |
| On each additional mile over 10,000 miles | 25p per mile |

If the self-employed lease a car that is classed as 'expensive' – with an original cost of £12,000 plus, part of the lease rentals must be added back as a disallowable cost. So before leasing a Porsche, think of the consequences.

If a spouse or partner is on a low income and helps with the business (book-keeping, for example), pay them a decent wage. Salaries (so long as they are reasonable) are a tax allowable expense and can be deducted from profits. Provided the salary does not reach £89 a week (in the 2002/03 tax year) no National Insurance need be paid by the individual or the employer. Even if the pay is above that level, a salary could be worthwhile, particularly for higher earners as the spouse on the lower income will pay tax at the lower or basic rate rather than the higher rate.

### Example

*Carl Carpenter has been running his joinery business from home since he became self-employed two years ago. His wife, Caroline, looks after the paperwork, files any receipts, answers the phone and books appointments.*

*However, Carl does not pay her for this work believing that any wages would eat into his business profits and cost the couple money.*

*He is wrong. If he had paid Caroline a small wage of £87 a week the couple would have made significant tax savings.*

*Caroline's annual salary: £87 × 52 (weeks) = £4,524*

*This is below the personal allowance of £4,535 for the 2001/02 tax year. Caroline would therefore have paid no tax.*

*Carl's taxable profits were £40,000 in 2001/02. If he had paid Caroline a wage these would have been reduced to:*

*£40,000 – £4,524 = £35,476*

*This was still above the higher-rate tax threshold of £29,400*

*£35,476 – £4,535 (his personal allowance) = £30,941*

*This means he would have no longer paid higher-rate tax on £4,524 of profits:*

*£4,524 × 40% = £1,809.60*

So the Carpenters could have saved £1,809.60 in tax if Carl had paid Caroline a salary. In addition, Caroline would not have to pay any NICs and as an employer Carl would also escape having to pay employers NICs because her income was below the lower earnings limit.

---

### 🖉 Tax tips

Any expenses that have been incurred but not yet paid for can also be deducted. Where an expense covers more than one accounting period (for example, a 12-month service contract), the proportion that relates to each accounting period can only be deducted.

It is not possible to make a deduction for bad debts in case any customers fail to pay up or are slow payers – only specific debts can be deducted and only if it can be shown that the amount is unlikely to be recoverable.

When a one-man band becomes a two-man band it means lots of paperwork. Employing staff is the only way for most businesses to grow but it means becoming an employer. That entails working out income tax and NICs each pay day and paying these over (including employer's NICs) to the Collector of Taxes each month. However, if the amount of tax and NICs is less than £1,500 payments can be made every quarter. Employers are also required to give staff certificates (P60s) showing earnings, tax and NICs in the year, P11Ds showing taxable benefits and provide them with P45s when they leave employment.

If possible, use the services of someone else who is self-employed – that way there is little paperwork and no employer's NICs need to be paid. However, check that they are legitimately self-employed (see the criteria at the start of this chapter). If they should be taxed as employees, then the Inland Revenue could demand that the tax that should have been deducted from their pay is handed over.

## Capital Allowances

The cost of items of equipment that are for use, not for resale (in which case they are stock), cannot be claimed as an allowable expense with the full cost deducted from profits. Instead, tax relief is given through capital allowances.

The main drawback of capital allowances is that instead of being able to claim the whole cost when it is incurred (as is the case with expenses), the self-employed can only claim a proportion of the cost each year. This reflects the fact that the asset or equipment bought has a life of several years.

Generally 25 per cent of the cost can be deducted in the year of purchase and thereafter a writing-down allowance of 25 per cent of the remaining value can be claimed.

### Example
*Doris Dressmaker spends £3,000 on new sewing equipment for her seamstress business. She can claim the following capital allowances:*

*Year 1 (the year of purchase): 25% as a capital allowance*
   25% × £3,000 = £750
   *The equipment now has a written-down value of £3,000 − £750 =*
£2,250


*Year 2: In the second year she can claim 25% of this written-down value*
   25% × £2,250 = £562.50
   *The written-down value is now £2,250 − £562.50 = £1,687.50*


*She can continue to write down the asset in this way in subsequent years until it is completely written off, no longer used or sold.*


To simplify calculations, the self-employed can put all their plant and machinery into a pool of expenditure so they do not have to calculate each item separately. They can then take the written-down value of all the items in each pool and deduct 25 per cent.

Cars must be calculated separately or in their own pool if there is more than one.

Short-life assets, those with a useful life of five years or less, must be calculated separately.

When the asset is sold, given away or ceases to be of any use, a separate calculation must be made. A balancing charge must be made. This is a method of taxing any profit made from selling the asset, and the balance allowance compensates for any loss – if the asset is sold for less than the written-down value. If the item is scrapped the remaining written-down value can be deducted.

---

### ✏ Tax tips

It may be more tax efficient to lease equipment as it is possible to claim 100 per cent of leasing costs as a business expense but only 25 per cent as a capital allowance.

Small business can claim a first-year allowance of 40 per cent in the year of purchase for plant and machinery (but not cars, long-life assets or items for lease or hire) and up to 100 per cent of the cost of information technology purchases such as computers (in the current tax year). This will cut profits in the year of purchase. However, claiming these additional tax breaks may not always be wise.

## Example

*Craig Computer has set up a software business investing heavily in new computer equipment to get his venture off the ground. In his first year, his profits are likely to be very small but once he develops his software product he expects profits to rise sharply.*

*He has heard that he can deduct 100 per cent of the cost of his computers against his profits but is not sure whether this is wise.*

*Year 1: Pre-tax net profits £10,000 (these are after allowable expenses have been deducted but before capital allowances have been taken into account)*

*Option 1:*

*Capital allowance @ 100%*

*Cost of computer equipment £15,000*

*Capital allowance £15,000*

*Net profit/loss for tax purposes (£10,000 − £15,000) = −£5,000*

*Although this loss can be carried forward to offset future profits, Craig is worried about showing a loss on his accounts as he fears it may make it hard to get a loan from his bank if he needs finance to expand his business.*

*Option 2:*

*He decides to consider deducting the standard 25% capital allowance.*

*£10,000 (profits) − £3,750 (25% of £15,000) = £6,250.*

*This option means he would have to pay tax − which he wouldn't have to do if he made a loss using option 1.*

*He decides to consider the impact of his decision if his profits rose sharply to £35,000 in year two and he incurred no further capital expenditure.*

*Year 2:*

*Option 1:*

*If he had deducted 100 per cent capital allowances in year 1 he would have no capital allowances to deduct in year 2. However, he would be able to offset £5,000 of losses against his taxable profits bringing his profits down to £30,000.*

*Option 2:*

*Craig can deduct a capital allowance of £2,812.50 (£15,000 – £3,750 = £11,250 (written-down value) × 25% = £2,812.50). This reduces his taxable profits to £32,187.50. So he is worse off in both year 1 and year 2 and although he has capital allowances to carry forward to future years with Option 2, he decides Option1 leaves him better off.*

If assets are pooled then the calculation can work differently making it more advantageous if the first-year allowance is not claimed. Note that first-year allowances must be calculated separately.

## Example

*Barry Builder needs a new machine for his small home-renovation business and is considering deducting the 40 per cent first-year allowance concession given to small businesses. His accountant does two calculations to show him if this would be a good idea.*

*1. Assuming the first-year allowance was not available:*

| | |
|---|---:|
| Pool carried forward | |
| (the written-down value of past capital expenditure) | £4,000 |
| Additions (the new machine) | + £2,500 |
| Less sales proceeds | |
| (from selling various items of old equipment) | – (£6,000) |
| | £500 |

*Capital allowance @ 25% of £500 = £125 deducted from profits*

*2. Assuming 40% first year allowance*

| | |
|---|---:|
| Pool carried forward | £4,000 |
| Less sales proceeds | –(£6,000) |
| | –(£2,000) |
| Balancing charge | –(£2,000) |
| Less first year allowance | |
| £2,500 @ 40% | £1,000 |
| Balancing charge | –(£1,000) |

*Balancing charge of £1,000 is added to profits*

So by claiming a first-year allowance he would have lost out having £1,000 added to his profits instead of £125 deducted from his profits.

---

**✎ Tax tips**

It does not matter when a purchase is made during the year – even if an item of equipment is bought the day before the end of their accounting year, the self-employed can claim the full capital allowance for that year. So those realizing that they are set to make substantial profits and wishing to reduce these can bring forward the purchase of equipment to reduce profits.

Any equipment bought for private use (such as a computer) and then used in a business, can be claimed as a capital allowance. The amount claimed will be its market value at the time it is first used for business purposes.

When items are bought on hire purchase a capital allowance can be claimed on the original cost of the item (the cash down payment). However, the extra paid in interest or other charges should be claimed as a business expense.

---

# WORKING FROM HOME

Using the family home as an office has several advantages. There is no rent to pay for premises, no time is wasted commuting and home-workers can deduct some of the cost of running their home as an allowable business expense. Generally the self-employed can deduct a proportion of the following:

- heating

- lighting

- cleaning

- insurance

- mortgage interest or rent

- council tax (although this is open to interpretation – check with your tax office as current understanding is that only if a room is entirely used for business purposes can a proportion of council tax be deducted)

The proportion should be agreed in advance with the tax office. It should reflect actual usage.

## Example

*Harry Homeworker uses the dining room of his home as an office. His three-bedroom house has five rooms excluding kitchens and bathrooms and as he uses one exclusively for business he has agreed with his tax office that he can deduct a fifth of the household running costs as an allowable expense.*

| | |
|---|---|
| *Mortgage (interest only)* | *£  9,200 pa* |
| *Council tax* | *£    800pa* |
| *Gas* | *£    600 pa* |
| *Electric* | *£    300pa* |
| *Insurance* | *£    250pa* |
| | |
| *TOTAL* | *£11,150* |

*Business proportion 1/5 × £11,150 =        £ 2,230*

*Plus*
*Telephone (used only for business)  £ 1,000*

*TOTAL                £ 3,230*

*So he can deduct £3,230 pa as the cost of running his office from home.*

> ### ✏ Tax tip
>
> Watch out for CGT! Anyone using their home as an office could be liable for CGT on some of the profits they make when they sell their home. There are exemptions (the first £40,000 of gains are excluded). However, the easiest way to avoid CGT is to use a room 'mainly' for business not 'exclusively'. Although this means that the self-employed will be able to claim fewer expenses, it will avoid the risk of a hefty CGT liability. See CHAPTER 7: LAND AND PROPERTY for more advice.

# Starting Up

When starting in business, the self-employed need to decide on their accounting year. This is often the first 12 months of their business. They do not have to draw up accounts to 5 April in order to fit in with the tax year.

The self-employed are assessed on profits made in their accounting year ending in the tax year. If, for example, the business has an accounting year ending on 31 May then in the 2001/02 tax year they would pay tax on profits up to 31 May 2001.

> ### ✏ Tax tip
>
> The earlier an accounting year ends in the tax year, the longer an individual has between earning profits and paying tax on them. Although payments on account must be made – so tax in instalments must be paid in advance – if profits are increasing the self-employed have a long time in which to make any balancing payments.

For example, if their accounting year ends on 1 May 2001 then the tax year these profits fall into is the 2001/02 tax year ending April 2002 and, as such, the final tax due for that year does not have to be paid until 31 January 2003 – a delay of 21 months. If the accounting year ended on 1 April, then the tax on the profits made in the year to 1 April 2002 would have to be paid by 31 January 2003 a delay of only ten months.

When starting in business there is not normally an accounting year ending in the tax year so special rules apply.

- In the first year profits/losses actually made in that tax year are assessed.

- In the second year, the profits/losses of the first 12 months are assessed.

- In the third year, the profits made in the accounting year ending in that tax year are assessed.

As a result, profits can be taxed more than once in the early years. To compensate for this, overlap profits are paid when the business ceases.

---

### ✎ Tax tips

Individuals do not have to wait until they retire to tax back (overlap relief) on profits taxed twice when they first set up. They can change their accounting date and extend their accounting year to bring it nearer to 5 April and receive overlap relief. If, however, they change their accounting date and shorten their accounting year, more profits will be taxed twice.

If a loss is made in the first four years of a new business, these losses can be offset against total income in the three tax years preceding the tax year of loss. So those who were previously employees can use these losses to get a tax rebate on tax previously paid as an employee. Although this is a valuable concession, it may not always be the best alternative.

Any expenses incurred before trading starts can be claimed as pre-trading costs if they would have been allowable if the business had started. That means any rent paid before the business started trading can be deducted when arriving at taxable profits. Expenses as far back as seven years before the business starts can be claimed.

## Payments on Account

The self-employed pay tax directly to the Inland Revenue. Unlike employees who pay tax in regular instalments, usually monthly, with this tax deducted from their salary under PAYE, the self-employed pay tax in two instalments known as payments on account. These are on 31 January during the tax year and on 31 July shortly after the end of the tax year, with a final balancing payment on the following 31 January.

For the 2001/02 tax year these instalments would have been payable on 31 January 2001 and 31 July 2001, with a final payment, if necessary, on 31 January 2002. On this date, 31 January 2002, the first payment on account for the 2002/03 tax year is also due.

The amount payable for each instalment is usually half the tax liability of the preceding tax year.

---

✎ **Tax tip**

Payments on account are calculated as half the tax owing in the previous tax year. So those whose profits are rising rapidly do not have to pay all of their tax in advance. Provided they pay the required amount, no interest is charged on any extra tax due (however, the balance must still be paid by the final deadline).

---

See CHAPTER 8: DEALING WITH THE INLAND REVENUE for more tips on payments on account.

## Losses

Going into business to make a loss may seem like financial suicide. However, losses are not always bad. In the first years of a business, high investment in the future growth of the company can result in a loss, for example, but a much healthier business.

Losses can be used to reduce the individual's overall tax liability – this tax year or in the future.

A loss in an accounting year can be:

- Carried forward to set against profits from the same business in future years.

- Set against any other type of income in the current tax year – and if this does not use up the whole loss, it can be set against any capital gains for the year.

- Set against income in the previous tax year (provided the business was carried on in that year) – and if this does not use up the whole loss, it can be set against any capital gains for that year.

- Set against other income from the previous three tax years if the loss is incurred in the first four tax years of the business.

- Set against profits from the business over the previous three years if the loss is incurred in the last 12 months before the business ceases.

---

### ✎ Tax tip

Losses suffered by the self-employed can be set against any capital gains that arise in the same or the preceding year. Losses can also be used to reduce taxable income for the same or the previous year – for example, from employment if the individual is an employee who also has earnings (or rather losses) from self-employment. In these cases losses in the 2001/02 tax year must be claimed by 31 January 2004.

However, if losses are offset against general income they will reduce taxable income to zero with any remaining losses carried forward/ back. That means the individual cannot make use of his personal tax allowance.

# National Insurance

The self-employed pay National Insurance in two ways:

- Class 2

- Class 4

The rates and thresholds of these NICs are covered in detail in CHAPTER 10: NATIONAL INSURANCE.

---

**✏ Tax tip**

Those who are also employees may find that they have paid too much NICs. There is a maximum amount of NICs that an individual needs to make during the tax year. However, as Class 1 NICs are deducted from earnings from employment, once the self-employed contributions are made this can mean the contributions exceed this limit. An individual can get a refund of Class 2 contributions if they pay more than £2,579.20 in Class 1 contributions (the limit for the 2001/02 tax year was £2,589.65). They are entitled to a refund of Class 4 contributions if they pay more than £1,806.35 in Class 1, 2 and 4 contributions.

---

# Special Rules for Certain Professions

An author who starves for years while writing a book and is then taxed heavily in the one year he sells the book and earns a decent income, can escape some of this hefty tax burden. Creative writers and artists can average profits over two or more consecutive years provided the profits of the lower year are less than 75 per cent of the profits of the higher year. Instead of paying little or no tax in one year and a high tax bill in the next, the total tax bill for the two years should be lower. This tax concession applies to those who take more than 12 months to complete a work.

There are also special rules covering barristers, doctors, dentists, farmers, ministers of religion and Members of Parliament. Those falling into one of these categories should ask their tax office or accountant for advice.

# SELF-ASSESSMENT RULES

Self-assessment requires the self-employed to keep proper records of all business transactions. Failure to keep these for the required length of time – for five years after the date they send back their tax return – can result in a fine of up to £3,000.

Records that must be kept include details of:

- sales and other business receipts – generally invoices

- purchases and expenses – again invoices or bills

- amounts taken out of the business – details of payments for personal use (drawings)

It is advisable to maintain a separate bank account and keep the following accounts – either manually or on computer:

- cash book – summarising all entries and withdrawals from the bank account

- petty cash book – recording small transactions

---

✐ **Tax tip**

When drawing up accounts to show the profit or loss for the accounting year, it is important that any unpaid invoices are included in the total income for that year. Likewise any payments the self-employed owe (invoices they have yet paid) must be included in that accounting year – not in the accounting year when they are actually paid.

# 7 Land and Property

Property has, over the decades, proved to be a wise investment. Not only have property prices risen, but the profits (gains) made on the sale of a family home are usually tax free. In addition, property can be a worthwhile investment for those looking for a steady income stream combined with capital growth or an alternative to stocks and shares.

## TAX AND THE FAMILY HOME

### Profits on Sale of the Family Home

Those who have lived in their only or main home since they purchased it and who have not rented out all or part of it or used part of it for business or purchased it to resell at an instant profit, should not read this section. They should not be liable for CGT on the sale of their property.

However, those who have:

- rented out all or part of the property

- used the property to run a business

- owned more than one home

- were away from the home for more than three years in total

- sold off part of the property (for example, converted into self-contained flats which were sold off or built a home in the garden which was then sold)

may find that they are liable for CGT when they sell their property.

**Note:** A married couple living together have an exemption for only one property – the husband and wife cannot each claim that they own separate properties unless they no longer live together.

---

### ✎ Tax tips

On marriage, the Inland Revenue allows a couple to own two properties with both qualifying for private residence relief for up to 12 months. This is to allow couples the chance to sell one or both homes before buying a new family home. In the meantime the newly-weds can benefit from the capital appreciation of both properties (free of tax) and can earn an income from one property by renting it out (with this rental income subject to income tax).

New homeowners are allowed up to 12 months to move into their home after buying it (for example, to allow for renovations or because it was not possible to sell the previous property). In some cases this may be extended by a further 12 months.

The last three years of ownership of a home are treated as qualifying for the private residence relief regardless of whether or not the owner lives in the property but provided the property has previously been his main residence. This means a homeowner can rent out the property or use it for businesses without jeopardizing the fact that profits on the sale of the home are free of CGT.

Make the most of the fact that the family home (principal private residence) escapes CGT. It is one of the few investments that is exempt. It is not unknown for small-scale property developers to move into homes they are renovating. They can then add value to the home and sell it for a profit but escape paying tax on this gain. However, watch out – the Inland Revenue will clamp down on those it believes buy a home as one of a series that are bought in order to make money. The same will apply if someone buys a property at a large discount (for example, from their employer or a relative) and then sells it shortly afterwards at a large profit.

The exemption of the main family home from CGT only covers the property and grounds of up to 0.5 hectare – larger if the grounds are 'required for the reasonable enjoyment' of the property. However, if the owners purchase an adjacent field – for example, to use for an additional garden, stabling horses or growing produce – the Inland Revenue could decide that this is not 'required' for the enjoyment of the property. This is a bit of a grey area with several judgements interpreting the rules. Before making any purchase of this sort take professional advice.

Separate buildings, for example, a gardener's cottage, could also fall outside the definition of 'residence' as could any other separate building. Once again, it is important to seek advice.

The gains made on selling off part of the garden to a developer (to build another home) will also be liable to CGT even if the garden is less than 0.5 hectare.

## Working from Home

Someone who occasionally takes work home is not affected by the ruling that the property cannot be used for business and escape CGT. Only those who claim the use of part of their property as a tax-allowable expense need worry.

It is the self-employed and those who have extra earnings (for example, for writing, consultancy or even dressmaking) who could get caught out by this rule.

If they claim part of the running costs of the property (including the mortgage) as a deduction when calculating their profits then they will lose the private residence relief on the proportion of the property used as an office.

### Example
*Susan Seamstress gave up work when she started a family but was under pressure to return to employment for financial reasons. After being talked into making curtains for several relatives she realized that she could combine her hobby with looking after a family and earn an income. Her business quickly flourished and when the family bought a new home she turned the fourth bedroom into her workshop claiming a proportion of the*

*running costs of the property as a tax-allowable deduction when calculating her profits.*

*The property had six rooms excluding kitchen and bathrooms (two living rooms and four bedrooms).*

*She therefore agreed with her tax office that she deduct one sixth of the running costs of the property.*

*As a result, when she comes to sell the property she could have to pay CGT on one-sixth of the profits if she continued to use the room exclusively for business for the entire period of ownership of the property.*

---

### ✎ Tax tip

The key word in this rule is 'exclusively'. If Susan had used the room partly as a workshop and partly as the family laundry room, she would escape any potential CGT liability. So, for example, someone who uses the dining room as an office but also occasionally uses it to entertain is not using that room 'exclusively' for business and therefore escapes CGT. If they had four rooms excluding kitchens and bathrooms, they could therefore claim a proportion of a quarter of the running costs of the property rather than the entire quarter. This proportion should be agreed with the person's tax office and should reflect the usage of the room for business and private use.

## Renting Out Part of the Property

If only part of a property is let (for example, the basement), then the owners will only lose the exemption on that part of the home. If there were three floors, two floors (or two-thirds of the gain) would be exempt and one-third potentially liable for CGT.

Even then, the gain will often be exempt as gains of up to £40,000 are not subject to CGT. As both a husband and a wife (if they own the property jointly) can each claim the exemption against their share of the gain, many homeowners may escape CGT.

# Second Homes

Only the main family home is exempt from CGT. A second home is not if a married couple lives together – even if the couple own the two properties in separate names.

Generally the property that is their main residence will be the one that qualifies for private residence relief. However, owners can elect to treat a different property as the main residence and may even vary this. This election must be made within two years of the date the second residence was bought.

> ### ✎ Tax tip
>
> If possible, elect the property which is likely to have the largest capital gain as the main residence. That way CGT will be paid only on the sale of the less valuable property and the potential tax liability will be lower. However, bear in mind that CGT reduces the longer an asset is held. So this could affect the tax liability. See CHAPTER 10: CAPITAL GAINS TAX for more tips.

# Living Away from Home

To qualify as a main residence, the individual must live in it and not be away from it for more than three years in total. There are exemptions:

- The last 36 months of ownership are exempt from CGT (even if the property is let during this time).

- If an individual is required to live in job-related accommodation he or she can still nominate the family home as his or her main residence.

- If an individual's job requires he works abroad and his duties are performed overseas which means he cannot live in his home, it can still be counted as his main residence.

- If an individual has to work elsewhere in the UK he is allowed a period of up to four years during which the home is still classed as his main residence.

- In addition, a further period of absence of up to three years can be treated as qualifying for private residence relief provided the homeowner lives in the home before or after this time spent away.

In other cases the gain is calculated on the proportion of the period of ownership of the property that it was not occupied by the owner.

### Example

*Simon Stockbroker bought a home in 1995 which he rented out for the first two years and then moved into it in 1997. It was his main home until 2000 when he moved in with his girlfriend. He let the property for another year before selling it. The profit he made on the property when it was sold was £100,000.*

   *His gain is calculated as follows:*

   *2/5 (two years out of five)* × *£100,000 = £40,000*

   *Only the first two years the property was let count towards the taxable gain as the last 36 months of ownership qualify for an exemption even if the property was let during this time.*

   *If he had occupied the property before letting it out, the first two years may have been exempt as owners are allowed to be away from the home for up to 36 months provided they live in the property immediately preceding and succeeding the absence.*

   *If Simon had to work abroad during the first two years because his employer required this (his duties were performed overseas), all of the gains would be free of tax.*

   *As it is, the gain is £40,000 which falls within the exemption where a property has been let of £40,000 so he will not face a CGT liability.*

To work out a gain take:

- The number of complete months since 31 March 1982 that the property was owned.

- Then deduct any months since 31 March 1982 it was NOT occupied as the owner's main residence (but discount the last 36 months).

- Deduct any period the owner had to work overseas or elsewhere in the UK (if part of this time falls within the last 36 months do not count it again).

- Deduct any further period of absence which was both preceded and succeeded by the individual occupying the home as his main residence (subject to a maximum of 36 months and again ignoring the last 36 months).

That gives the number of months that are potentially taxable.

Then divide this by the months of ownership since 31 March 1982. That will give the proportion of the gains that are subject to CGT.

So if a home was owned for 100 months but ten months are taxable then 1/10 of the total gain is taxable. This amount will then be reduced by the individual's CGT allowance and taper relief.

However, if the property is let the first £40,000 is exempt.

There is one other exemption. If an individual owns a property occupied by a dependent relative (widowed mother-in-law, infirm parent etc.) who lives there rent free, and the property was occupied by them before 6 April 1998, then it is exempt from CGT.

## INCOME FROM THE FAMILY HOME

The home we live in is usually the biggest asset we own. However, it is a drain on our finances. Properties cost money to run and produce no income. There is a way to remedy this – and escape tax on the income.

## Rent a Room

Homeowners (or tenants) who let part of their only or main home as furnished accommodation may not have to pay tax on their rental income if they qualify for rent-a-room relief.

This enables them to receive up to £4,250 in gross rent (before expenses) in a tax year free of tax.

It is only available if the owner rents out:

• One room only (if two people own the property they can let out a room each but the allowance is halved to £2,125).

• The room is in the main home and is furnished.

The tax break can sometimes be claimed by those who let rooms for a business (such as a guest house). See the section later in this chapter.

In much of the country this limit (just below £82 a week) may be sufficient but in the south-east, some homeowners may find that their rents exceed this threshold. They cannot get round the rule by charging extra for meals, cleaning, laundry or bills – any charges must be added to the rent received when calculating the gross rent. It is not possible to deduct expenses – their share of the gas or electricity – either.

If two people own a property they cannot each claim the allowance – it will simply be divided so they receive £2,125 each.

Claiming the rent-a-room allowance is easy. Those who do not need to fill in a tax return do not have to tell their tax office provided the rent falls within the £4,250 p.a. limit. Those who do receive a tax return will find a box on the land and property pages relating to the rent-a-room allowance.

If the rent from the lodger exceeds £4,250 then the homeowner can either decide to stay within the rent-a-room scheme and pay tax on the excess. Or they can pay tax on the rent above the threshold.

---

✎ **Tax tips**

Homeowners are generally better off claiming the rent-a-room relief and then paying tax on the rent in excess of £4,250. Although they cannot claim any expenses (the cost of providing meals, heating, light, laundry services etc.) as a tax-allowable deduction, if these expenses do not exceed £4,250 they will be better off. If the expenses are higher (which will be unlikely) they can opt out of the rent-a-room scheme and opt to be taxed in the same way as rental income and thus deduct any expenses before paying tax on their profits.

Lodgers do not jeopardize the private residence relief (the relief which means the main home is exempt from CGT) if the lodgers mix and eat with the family.

## Letting a Home

Those planning to work or travel overseas or who move in with a partner or spouse and then want to rent out their existing home can be taxed in two ways:

- income tax on rental income

- CGT on any profits made when they sell the home

The latter is covered earlier in this chapter.

Rental income is taxed in the same way as earnings with the rents (minus expenses) added to earnings from employment or self-employment and taxed at the individual's top rate of tax. Unlike savings income, which is taxed at 20 per cent, rental income falling within the basic-rate band is taxed at 22 per cent.

Those who rent out their property as a guest house or B&B are covered by different rules (they are classed as running a business and therefore are classed as self-employed).

The property owner pays tax on the rents due (even if not received) during the tax year less any expenses 'wholly and exclusively' incurred in renting out the property.

If the property is let in part (the basement, for example) or only for part of the year, only a proportion of these expenses can be deducted. If the property is let for only six months, then the expenses can only be claimed for those six months and annual costs will be halved.

Allowable expenses include:

- water rates

- ground rent

- council tax

- repairs and redecoration (but not improvements or additions to the property)

- wear and tear – 10 per cent of the rent minus certain items (see below)

- gas and electricity bills

- management expenses, which include phone bills, accountants' fees and the cost of rent collection

- legal fees in drawing up a new tenancy agreement or renewing an agreement

- insurance premiums (and valuations)

- estate or letting agent's fees

- advertising costs

- cost of services provided – the gardener's wages, for example

- cost of preparing an inventory

- interest on any mortgage on the property (but not repayment of the capital)

Wear and tear can be claimed in one of two ways on fully furnished properties:

1. Renewal basis – when items need replacing then the cost of replacing them can be claimed (but it is not possible to improve on what was there before, so an old TV cannot be replaced by a state-of-the-art flat-screen home-movie centre).
2. Ten per cent of the rent (less council tax, water rates and other services which are normally paid by the tenant but are, in fact, paid by the landlord).

**Note:** Once decided, it is not possible to change the way wear and tear is calculated.

With so many allowable deductions, most homeowners can keep their income tax bill from rental income to the minimum.

### Example

*Harry Homeowner and his family want to move out of the city and try life at a slower pace in the country. However, they are reluctant to burn their bridges just in case they want to return. So they rent a farmhouse and rent out their London property. The aim is to provide enough income to pay the mortgage and cover costs as well as providing a modest income.*

*Harry calculates his taxable income from renting out the home as follows:*

| | | |
|---|---|---|
| *Rent @ £2,000 a month × 12 months* | | *£24,000* |
| *Less allowable expenses* | | |
| *Mortgage interest* | *£12,000* | |
| *Management expenses:* | | |
| *Letting agent 15% of gross rent* | *£ 3,600* | |
| *Advertising* | *£ 500* | |
| *Water rates* | *£ 300* | |
| *Wear and tear 10% of rent* | *£ 2,400* | |
| *Legal costs* | *£ 300* | |
| *Insurance* | *£ 1,000* | |
| *Inventory* | *£ 200* | |
| *Bills and council tax will be paid by the tenant.* | | |
| | | |
| *TOTAL* | *-£20,300* | |
| | | |
| *PROFITS FROM RENTAL INCOME* | | *£ 3,700* |

*As the property is owned in both Harry and his wife Harriet's names, the profits will be split.*

Anyone planning to rent out their home should inform their mortgage lender first. Lenders will want to ensure that they can have vacant possession of the property should the borrower fall into arrears so they need to know that any tenant will not become a sitting tenant. Short-term tenancy agreements (now standard) are usually all that is required to satisfy the lender.

## INCOME FROM PROPERTY

Income from property – other than the owner's main home – can be treated in a number of ways.

- Income from a guest house, hotel or B&B is classed as business income and declared on the self-employment pages of the tax return.

- Income from renting a second home or a home bought with a buy-to-let mortgage is declared on the land and property pages of the tax return.

- Letting a home overseas is declared using the foreign income pages of the tax return. Homes overseas are subject to the same rules as UK property. However, non-resident landlords must deduct tax from the rent and pay the tax each quarter to the Inland Revenue (unless they apply to the Inland Revenue Financial Intermediaries and Claims Office FICO – call 0151 472 6000).

### Buy to Let

Every week nearly 800 homes are bought as investments by private landlords with the popularity of buying to let continuing to grow according to latest figures from mortgage lenders. Why? Because buying to let can represent an attractive investment, offering a good income and the prospect of long-term capital growth. The ability to benefit from a far larger investment than the individual can actually raise, through gearing (borrowing to invest), boost these gains. With a £20,000 deposit an individual can buy a £100,000 property and benefit from the income and growth on that full £100,000 whereas they could buy only £20,000 of shares with the same amount of capital.

A typical rental yield is around 7 per cent a year, so on a £150,000 property the yield would be roughly £875 per month or £200 a week which should cover the mortgage. However, investors in buy-to-let properties are generally advised to charge around 30 per cent more than their borrowing costs to cover periods when there are no tenants and the costs of letting out the property (management fees, advertising costs etc.).

As with other rental income, the amount that is taxable is the rent received minus allowable expenses including any interest paid on a buy-to-let mortgage. These expenses are detailed in the section LETTING A HOME.

Many buy to lets are leasehold properties. In these cases landlords can also offset services charges and ground rents.

---

### ✏ Tax tips

The cost of furnishing a flat or house cannot be deducted as an allowable expense. Although this is not an issue for those letting an existing home which is already furnished, for new buy-to-let landlords it can represent a significant cost particularly as the better quality the furnishings (and therefore more expensive) the higher the rent. Only wear and tear can be claimed (generally 10 per cent of the rent). To get round this restriction, landlords can rent the furniture and claim the full costs of renting it as an allowable expense.

If a buy-to-let landlord makes a loss – if, for example, the initial costs of furnishing a property and advertising it do not cover the costs of the mortgage – then they can use this to offset future rental profits by carrying the loss forward to the next tax year.

Buy-to-let investors cannot claim the deposit paid on the property (generally at least 20 per cent of the purchase price) as an allowable expense. However, they can claim the interest they pay on the loan taken out to buy or improve the property. As a result, it pays to borrow as much as the individual can afford or is allowed.

## Furnished Holiday Lettings

Those who let property on a commercial basis for at least 140 days during each 12-month period (with the property actually let for seventy or more of these days) and who only have short-term tenants (for less than 31 days in one go for at least seven of the 12 months) are taxed differently. They are treated as letting furnished holiday accommodation and therefore get some of the concessions due to those taxed as receiving business income (guest houses and B&Bs) that are not available to other private landlords. See below.

## Letting as a Business

Many homeowners strapped for cash or wanting to boost their income look to their property as a means of generating earnings. They may not realize that letting out the odd room to paying guests or even turning their rambling home into a guest house means that they are running a business, but they are and they are taxed as being self-employed (unless they register as a company). The rules for self-employment are covered in CHAPTER 6: TAX SAVING FOR THE SELF-EMPLOYED.

Generally property owners will be running a business rather than receiving rental income if they provide services such as meals and laundry that are beyond those normally offered by a landlord for a tenant. Business income from a property (even if the owners also live there) is covered on the self-employment pages, not the land and property pages of the tax return.

The main tax advantages to running a business (being taxed under Schedule D) rather than receiving rental income are:

- Capital allowances may be claimed – in layman's terms this means that some of the cost of buying furniture and furnishings, electric and heating systems and even burglar alarms can be claimed. With other types of rental income (non-business income) a deduction for wear and tear can only be claimed.

- Pre-trading expenses can also be claimed – this is the cost of setting up the business before lettings actually began.

- Any losses can be used to reduce the individual's tax bill – with other types of property income the losses can only be offset against profits from other properties. With business income any losses can reduce the individual's taxable income from employment, for example.

## Guest Houses and B&Bs

There is a difference between taking in a lodger (or a series of lodgers) and taking in guests. In the latter case, the guests tend to stay for only short periods and they are usually provided with services – for example, meals and cleaning. In this case the lettings amount to a trade and should be taxable as earnings from self-employment rather than income from property.

---

### ✎ Tax tip

Even if lettings amount to a trade, rent-a-room relief may still be claimed provided the room is let in the owner's main home. This means that the first £4,250 of lettings income is tax free. If the business is small – with only occasional guests – and rents are below this level then they will be entirely tax-free. Even if they are above this level, it may still be worthwhile claiming the relief. Ask for Help Sheet IR223.

# 8 Dealing with the Inland Revenue

In addition to dealing with enquires regarding taxation, the Inland Revenue, since it merged with the Contributions Agency in April 1999, also handles:

- National Insurance contributions

- statutory maternity pay

- statutory sick pay

The Revenue also deals with the working families' tax credit and the disabled person's tax credit, which replaced family credit and the disability working allowance in October 1999, and the new tax credits, the children's tax credit and the pensioners' tax credit.

## HOW TO CONTACT THE INLAND REVENUE

Individuals can contact the Inland Revenue by telephone, letter or in person and can also find out information and download and print out leaflets about tax on the internet at www.inlandrevenue.gov.uk.

Those who are already dealing with a tax office regarding a particular matter should carry on dealing with that particular office.

If the enquiry is about a tax return, contact the Inland Revenue office listed on the front of the tax return.

Those who do not know which tax office handles their affairs should ask their employer (the payroll department) who should be able to provide this information. The same applies to those in receipt of company (occupational) pensions which are paid with tax already deducted (through PAYE).

The self-employed and other taxpayers (who are not employees) usually have their tax affairs handled by their local tax office.

The address and telephone numbers of tax offices – as well as Inland Revenue enquiry centres – are listed in the local phone book under Inland Revenue.

## Asking for Help by Phone

Simple problems, requests for forms and enquiries about tax payments can often be handled over the phone – so there is no need to go to the bother of writing a letter.

The numbers taxpayers should find most useful are listed at the end of this chapter.

---

> ### ✎ Tax tip
>
> Always keep a written record of any telephone conversation with the Inland Revenue particularly if any advice is given (for example, 'you don't need to fill in that form' or 'we will send you a tax demand'). If there is any dispute you will need evidence of all conversations.

---

## Asking for Help in Writing

First, taxpayers need to check that they know which tax office to write to. The details should be listed in any recent correspondence, or on the front of the tax return, or can be obtained from employers. It is important that any reference number is included in correspondence.

For National Insurance enquiries taxpayers should contact their local Inland Revenue (NIC) office.

## Asking for Help in Person

Most Inland Revenue offices are open to the public from 8.30 a.m. to 4.30 p.m., Monday to Friday, and some are also open outside these hours.

Any Inland Revenue Enquiry Centre or Tax Office should be able to deal with tax and NIC queries. Booklets and leaflets are also available.

Addresses are listed under Inland Revenue in the phone book.

# INLAND REVENUE TAX ASSESSMENTS

Taxpayers may be shocked to find that the Inland Revenue can make mistakes – even when it comes to issuing demands for large amounts of tax.

Check – or ask an accountant to check – any demand for tax owing or any statement detailing the amount of tax to be refunded. Assessments can be wrong. In some cases this is because the correct or most up-to-date information has not been supplied so the tax office has to make an assumption.

---

### ✎ Tax tip

The Inland Revenue will make an estimate of income or rely on last year's figures, if a taxpayer fails to supply the most recent information. To avoid a larger than necessary bill it is up to the individual taxpayer to supply these details – it is not the Inland Revenue's job to track information down.

Pay particular attention to tax relief. If, for example, a claim has been made to carry back a pension contribution, check that this has been taken into account in any tax calculation.

If it is not possible to agree a final amount with the tax office, then an appeal can be lodged. (Inland Revenue leaflet IR37 sets out the details.)

If the taxpayer does not agree with that appeal, then an appeal can be made to independent commissioners.

# INLAND REVENUE MISTAKES

As we have already discussed, mistakes by the Revenue are not unknown and not uncommon. For example, some 400,000 letters were sent out in April 2001 demanding unpaid self-assessment and warning recipients to pay up or else. However, many of the demands were sent in error to those who owed nothing. In one case the taxpayer was told to pay a bill for £17,000 that had already been paid.

> ### ✎ Tax tips
>
> Taxpayers who have paid too much tax because of an error by the Inland Revenue can reclaim a repayment (as one would expect) going back up to 20 years.
>
> Anyone who finds that their tax office says that this is too far back should ask for a copy of the Inland Revenue's own Code of Practice and look for the section 'Mistakes by the Inland Revenue'. Look under the heading 'Late Claims' where how to claim back tax for years past is explained.
>
> If the Inland Revenue has made a mistake, the taxpayer can ask for some costs to be paid (postage, professional fees, lost earnings etc.). These will generally only be paid if the mistake was serious. See the Inland Revenue Code of Practice 1 for details.

If the Inland Revenue has demanded too much tax and needs to give a repayment then it should pay interest. The interest rate on repayments of income tax and NICs is currently 2.5 per cent (the rate set in November 2001) which is higher than the rate paid on most interest-bearing current accounts. However, it is far lower than the rate the Inland Revenue charges to those who are late paying tax – currently 6.5 per cent for income tax.

# Problems with the Revenue

Taxpayers should expect a fair, effective and confidential service. If they do not receive this, they can complain. The Inland Revenue's service standards are set down in the Charter for Inland Revenue Taxpayers and the Charter for National Insurance Contributors.

---

### ✎ Tax tip

If the Inland Revenue fails to reply to a query within six months (after its 28-day target) it should waive interest on unpaid tax that arose during the period of delay. If any tax was owed by the Inland Revenue, it should pay interest to cover the delay and also pay any reasonable costs.

Often a problem occurs because paperwork has been lost or information has not been provided. In these cases it is up to the individual taxpayer to solve the problem – even though it can take time.

---

### Example

*Sam Salary has been employed by just two companies during his working life, has never had to pay higher-rate tax and has no untaxed savings. So he has had no need to contact the Inland Revenue. However, this year his earnings exceeded the higher-rate threshold and he wanted to claim back higher-rate tax relief on his pension contributions. He contacted his tax office to be told he had failed to send back the tax returns sent to him over the last three years and owed a substantial amount in fines. The tax returns had been sent to an address he lived at briefly when switching jobs. Worse – bailiffs had been sent round to this home to collect the unpaid debt and he was worried that would leave him on a credit black list. The fines had been imposed despite the fact that he:*

- *did not need to fill in a tax return*

- *did not owe any outstanding tax*

- *did not live at the address the tax returns were sent to (even though the Inland Revenue knew his correct address as it was supplied by his employer).*

*After 23 telephone calls during which the Inland Revenue gave him conflicting advice he was finally informed that the tax office had dropped its court action (the distress warrant was withdrawn). He received no compensation.*

## Making a Complaint

The first step is to ask for leaflet IR120 You and the Inland Revenue, which sets out the standards of service taxpayers can expect. If taxpayers feel that these have not been met, the leaflet then gives guidance on how to complain.

The next step is to complain to the officer in charge of the tax office. If this does not resolve the problem, the next stage is to contact the regional controller.

If this response is not satisfactory, there is an independent adjudicator who can rule on the handling complaints – excessive delays, mistakes etc. The adjudicator can be contacted on 020 7930 2292. More details are available at www.open.gov.uk/adjoff.

# IF THE TAXPAYER MAKES A MISTAKE

Even if it is the individual taxpayer who is to blame for an overpayment of tax, all is not lost. Those who pay too much tax as a result of their own mistake can claim repayment up to six years later.

Taxpayers who have failed to ask for certain tax allowances (for example, because they did not know they were entitled to the allowance), can also claim these allowances retrospectively.

Self-assessment put the onus on calculating tax owed on to the individual taxpayer (although it is still possible to ask the Inland Revenue to do the calculation). However, there were fears that this would lead to abuse of the system. As a result, the Inland Revenue spot checks a number of tax returns each year and also looks more closely at those it believes are incorrect or incomplete. There are two types of enquiry:

- Full enquiry – this looks at the tax return as a whole.

- Aspect enquiry – this looks at one aspect of the tax return. For example, a claim to carry back a pension contribution.

If the Inland Revenue starts an enquiry it must:

- inform the taxpayer that an enquiry is being started

- tell the individual about his rights and responsibilities

- ask what information is required

- allow the individual to have professional representation

Taxpayers worried that they may be investigated at any time can rest easy after a year. The Inland Revenue must tell the individual within 12 months of the filing date (31 January) or the actual date the return was submitted, if this was later, if it intends to start an enquiry.

---

### ✎ Tax tip

Even if an individual makes a mistake on their tax return, all is not lost. It is possible to amend a tax return and assessment provided it is done within 12 months of the date it was sent back. In most cases no penalty will be charged, however there will probably be interest to pay on any tax that should have been paid earlier.

---

# TAX RETURNS

Some nine million taxpayers are sent a tax return each year. Anyone sent a return must fill it in and return it by the deadline (31 January following the end of the tax year to which the return relates).

It is the taxpayer's responsibility to ask for a tax return – not the Inland Revenue's responsibility to send a form out to every taxpayer who needs to fill one in.

Anyone who receives any new and untaxed sources of income during a tax year has six months – until the 5 October following the end of the tax year – within which to declare this to the Inland Revenue. They should then be sent a tax return.

When filling in details of income and allowances, it is possible to make a few pounds by using rounding. Round down income to the nearest pound – that means that if savings interest, for example, is £20.95, write £20. Do the opposite for outgoings. Round up to the nearest pound. That means rounding up £19.01 to £20. It is also possible to round up tax credits and tax deductions.

# DEADLINES AND FINES

One of the easiest ways to cut the amount given to the Inland Revenue is to meet all the deadlines and avoid the fines and penalties imposed on those who fail to return their completed tax returns or pay tax owed on time.

## Tax Returns

Anyone sent a tax return must complete it and send it back to reach their tax office by 31 January following the end of the tax year to which the tax return applies.

✎ Tax tip

Don't wait until the last minute. There are benefits to filing your tax return early. Taxpayers who send back their returns by 30 September (so for the tax year ending 5 April 2002 by 30 September 2002) will have their tax bill calculated for them by their tax office. This saves them having to do the complex calculation themselves or having to pay an accountant to do this for them.

## *Fines and Penalties*

- There is an automatic penalty of £100 for returns received after 31 January.

- If the tax return is still outstanding after 31 July there will be a further £100 automatic penalty. If the return is still outstanding after these fines, the Inland Revenue can charge a further penalty of up to £60 a day.

These fines apply to those responsible for the tax return of a trust or estate. However, the penalty payable can never exceed the balance of tax due.

---

### ✎ Tax tip

In theory, this fine is automatic. However, the Inland Revenue can be a little flexible. If taxpayers miss the deadline by a day or two they may escape the penalty.

Those sent a tax return in the three months before the 31 January deadline may be given a little more time to complete the form. Check the date with the Inland Revenue office listed on the front of the tax return.

The most common error is not to sign and date the tax return on page 8. Forgetting to sign could cost taxpayers a fine.

---

## Payment of Tax

Payments of any tax owed for a tax year must reach the Inland Revenue by 31 January following the end of the tax year for which the tax is owed.

For example, tax returns for the year 6 April 2001–5 April 2002 must be returned by 31 January 2003 and any tax outstanding paid by this deadline.

> ### ✎ Tax tip
>
> Employees and those in receipt of company pensions who owe less than £1,000 in tax do not have to pay this bill by 31 January if they file their tax return by 30 September. This is because the Inland Revenue can collect the tax owed through the taxpayer's next year's PAYE tax code. That way they have even longer to pay. So they are effectively being given an interest-free loan.

## Fines and Penalties

- Interest is charged on payments received after 31 January. The current rate is 6.5 per cent.

- If the payment is still outstanding after 28 February there may be an automatic 5 per cent surcharge.

- If the tax owed is still not paid by 31 July there may be a further 5 per cent surcharge.

> ### ✎ Tax tip
>
> Those who have difficulty in paying their tax bill should not bury their heads in the sand. Tax offices can often come to arrangements to those in difficulty allowing them to pay the tax owed in instalments.

## Avoiding the Fines

It is not possible to blame a third party for a late payment or the late filing of a tax return. Even if an accountant misses the deadline, it is the client who pays the fine. However, taxpayers should try to claim back any fines if it is the accountant or tax adviser's fault.

It is possible to appeal against penalties and surcharges. However, individuals need a very good excuse. 'I had flu' will not count because the taxpayer has had months to complete a tax return and being ill at the last minute is a poor excuse. Being hospitalized and seriously ill, on the other hand, may be an acceptable reason.

Ask for Inland Revenue booklets SA/BK6 and SA/BK7 for more help with what constitutes a 'reasonable case'.

Filling in the tax return on time is easier said than done. Apart from the complexity of the tax return, individuals often find it hard to complete their return because they do not have the relevant paperwork to hand. To help avoid this problem, here is a check list of the most vital pieces of paper.

## Employees

- P60 Certificate of Pay: this states how much income tax and National Insurance was paid in the tax year. Employers should have given this to staff by 31 May following the end of the tax year.

- P45 (Part 1A): if the individual left a job during the tax year.

- P11D or P9D: if the taxpayer received any employee benefits such as a company car or are paid expenses. This form should be given to staff by employers by 6 July.

- Notice of Tax Coding: employees may have received one or more of these during the tax year. It tells individuals what tax allowances they have been getting and which employee benefits have been taxed at source.

- Details of any business expenses including expenses sheets or receipts.

- Pay slips for those missing any of the above forms.

> ### ✎ Tax tip
>
> Do not risk paying a fine because of a mislaid piece of paper. Employees should write to their employer's payroll or accounts department to request duplicate documents. However, if these do not arrive on time they should estimate the amount or calculate the figure for themselves from pay slips and then make a note in the 'additional information' box on the tax return stating that the figures are provisional. Once the duplicate paperwork arrives they can then write to their tax office with the correct figures.

## Pensioners

Paperwork they will need includes:

- Details of how much state pension was received during the tax year along with any other state benefits. Those who have not received this information should contact their local Benefits Agency office (part of the Department of Social Security) for a statement.

- Details of any company pension received. These should have been paid with tax already deducted. This will be detailed on form P60, which should be sent out by the employer by 31 May following the end of the tax year.

- Records of how much was received from any annuities bought with the proceeds of a pension fund.

## Savers/Investors

Tax-free savings such as ISAs (and their predecessors PEPs and TESSAs) do not have to be included on the tax return. Documents needed include:

- Bank and building society passbooks and any annual statements.
- Share dividend tax vouchers which are attached to dividend cheques.

- Unit trust or investment trust annual statements.

- National Savings documents but not those relating to tax-free schemes such as fixed-interest savings certificates, index-linked savings certificates or any winnings from premium bonds.

- Personal pension contribution statements.

> ✎ **Tax tip**
>
> If any of the required information is not available, enter a best estimate on the tax return but clearly identify it as such in the additional inform- ation box. Once an accurate figure has been obtained the tax office must be informed.

## PAYMENTS ON ACCOUNT

Although taxpayers have up to 21 months to settle their tax liability (that is from the start of one tax year to the 31 January following the end of the tax year), the Inland Revenue is not that generous in practice. Anyone who receives income that has not already been taxed is usually asked to make some interim tax payments. These are known as payments on account.

These payments are due in two instalments:

- 31 January – this is towards the end of the tax year for which the tax is due

- 31 July – this is just after the end of the tax year for which the tax is due

Generally the payments on account are half the amount of tax owed in the previous tax year less any tax deducted at source (for example, savings interest paid net, earnings from employment paid under PAYE etc.) and less any CGT.

Any balance is settled by the 31 January following the end of the tax year.

The types of income that may be subject to payments on account are:

- income from self-employment

- savings interest earned gross

- income from property

Employees – even if they earn some interest gross – will not usually have to make payments on account because this tax can be collected through their PAYE tax code (unless the tax owed exceeds £1,000). Those who want tax collected via their PAYE code need to file their tax return by 30 September (after the end of the tax year).

---

### ✎ Tax tips

Paying tax owed through PAYE makes life easy. However, it is not always financially astute. For example, taxpayers who expect their untaxed income to fall in the following tax year will still be taxed as if they had a higher level of untaxed income. This overpayment will have to be claimed after the end of the tax year. In addition, paying tax on account gives the individual more time to pay their tax as it is not collected monthly through their salary.

Those who have a total income tax liability (less deductions) in one tax year of £500 or less will not usually have to make payments on account. The same applies to those who receive at least 80 per cent of their income with tax deducted at source – for example, through PAYE. These taxpayers have until the 31 January following the end of the tax year for which the tax is due, to settle their tax liability.

Payments on account are usually half the tax owed for the year before. This means that those who are likely to earn less in the next tax year, will pay too much tax. To avoid this overpayment, they can ask to have their payments on account reduced. However, they will have to give a good reason (maternity leave, sickness, loss of a contract etc.).

To calculate payments on account:

- Add up the total tax liability for the tax year (for example, 2001/02) including all gross income but excluding income paid with tax deducted at source and any CGT liability.

- Divide this amount by two – paying one instalment on 31 January (for example, 31 January 2002) and the second on 31 July (for example, 31 July 2002).

To calculate reduced payments on account:

- Estimate the profits and gross income for the coming tax year. Be realistic. Take into account increases in expenditure or costs and any reductions in expected income.

- Divide this amount by two – paying one instalment on 31 January (for example, 31 January 2002) and the second on 31 July (for example, 31 July 2002).

- Inform the Inland Revenue that payments on account have been reduced. Those who calculate their own tax bills can tick box 18.7 on the tax return, calculate their reduced payment and then explain why in the 'Additional Information' section. If the Inland Revenue does the tax calculation, it will send claim form SA303 with the tax statement. This form should be filled in by those wishing to reduce payments on account.

Taxpayers should not be tempted to reduce their payments on account just to save paying tax today. Interest will be charged if an individual asks to reduce their payments and gets their sums wrong. However, the rate of interest – it is variable and currently stands at 6.5 per cent – may be cheaper than a bank loan or overdraft.

Those who are likely to see their income – and therefore tax liability – rise substantially do not have to increase their payments on account. Provided they pay the requested amount, no interest is charged (however, the balance must still be paid by the final deadline).

Those who suffer a sudden drop in income – and therefore tax liability – and, as a result, overpay when making their payments on account, should receive interest on the amount overpaid. The interest they receive is at a variable rate set once a year by the Inland Revenue. It is currently set at 2.5 per cent.

# USEFUL NUMBERS

In most cases taxpayers do not need to write to their tax office as most enquiries can be handled by telephone. Taxpayers should contact their tax office direct for any specific enquiries. However, for general enquiries there are special help lines. In addition, the Inland Revenue has order lines so that taxpayers can request free leaflets and booklets and any forms required to make elections or reclaim tax.

### Help with tax returns
During normal working hours contact your own tax office. During the evening and at weekends call 0845 9000 444.

### Requests for leaflets
Taxpayers who need supplementary pages (for example, the CGT pages) in order to complete their tax return, because these were not included in the form sent, or who require leaflets to help them to complete their tax return should call 0845 9000 404. The lines are open seven days a week from 8 a.m. to 10 p.m. Other leaflets are also available by calling this number. The tax return and help sheets can also be downloaded from the Inland Revenue's self-assessment pages at www.inlandrevenue.gov.uk.

### Taxback Helpline
For those paying too much tax on their bank or building society interest – mainly non-taxpayers such as pensioners. Call 0845 077 6543.

## Enquiries about Class 2 National Insurance Contributions (NICs) paid by the self-employed

Call 0845 9 15 46 55. Lines are open from Monday to Friday from 8.30 a.m. to 5 p.m.

## Working families' tax credit (WFTC)

Call 0845 609 5000. Lines are open Monday to Friday from 7.30 a.m. to 6.30 p.m. In Northern Ireland call 0845 609 7000.

## Disabled persons' tax credit (DPTC)

Call 0845 605 5858. Lines are open from Monday to Friday from 8.30 a.m. to 4.45 p.m. In Northern Ireland call 0845 609 7000.

## Children's tax credit

Call 0845 300 1036. Lines are open from 8 a.m. to 10 p.m. seven days a week. Parents need to fill in form CTC1 to claim the credit.

## Individual Savings Account

Call 0845 604 1701 for enquiries about the tax rules for ISAs which are not covered in the Inland Revenue leaflets. Lines are open from 8.30 a.m. to 4.30 p.m. Monday to Friday.

## Help with the Construction Industry Scheme (CIS)

Contractors who need help can call 0845 7 33 55 88. Lines are open from Monday to Friday from 8.30 a.m. to 5 p.m.

## National Insurance: Self-employed Helpline

Call 0845 91 54655. Lines are open 8 a.m. to 5 p.m. Monday to Friday for help with Class 2 NICs.

## Coming clean

The tax and benefit advice line offers people operating in the hidden economy confidential help and information to help them put their affairs in order. Open 8 a.m. to 8 p.m. Monday to Friday and until 5 p.m. on Saturday and Sunday. Call 0845 608 6000. All calls are charged at local rates.

# 9 National Insurance

Although this is technically not a tax, moves to bring the tax and National Insurance systems into line for employees and the merging of the two so they are both now handled by the Inland Revenue (National Insurance was previously handled by the Department of Social Security) means that no book about saving tax would be complete without some guidance about National Insurance.

As from April 2001, the amount that employees can earn before paying National Insurance has been brought into line with the amount that can be earned before paying income tax.

There are four types of National Insurance Contributions (NICs) which are payable:

- Class 1, payable by employees

- Class 2, paid by the self-employed as a flat-rate contribution

- Class 3 which is a voluntary contribution

- Class 4, paid by the self-employed and based on profits

Contributions are payable from the age of 16 until state retirement age but not after then (even if the individual carries on working).

Paying NICs gives an individual the entitlement to certain state benefits. However, so that those who are not in work do not lose out, they may be able to get credits instead of having to pay contributions.

Credits are given to those who are:

- Unemployed or sick for full weeks (Sunday to Saturday). They will normally have to make fortnightly labour market declarations at an Employment Service Jobcentre (Social Security office in Northern Ireland) or send in medical certificates to their nearest Social Security office to get the credits.

- Entitled to Maternity Allowance or Invalid Care Allowance.

- Entitled to Statutory Sick Pay or Statutory Maternity Pay.

- Taking a course of approved training.

- Receiving Disability Working Allowance (DPTC).

- Required to attend jury service and do not have earnings exceeding the lower earnings limit from employed earner's employment and are not self-employed, a man aged 60 or over.

# EMPLOYEES

Class 1 contributions are deducted as a percentage of earnings. These include:

- salary (before deduction of pension contributions)

- overtime

- commission and bonuses

- holiday pay, statutory sick pay and maternity pay

---

### ✎ Tax tip

While employees pay income tax on the value of benefits in kind (the perks of the job such as a company car), they do not have to pay NICs on these benefits. It is usually more tax-efficient to opt for the benefit rather than taking the equivalent salary increase instead.

Only earnings between the lower earnings limit and upper earnings limit are subject to NICs (although 1 per cent will be paid on earnings above the upper limit from 2003 when the rate of Class 1 contributions rises to 11 per cent) and no NICs are deducted from earnings below a certain limit. As with income tax the starting threshold is £4,615 (the same as the basic personal allowance for 2002/03) and the upper limit is £30,420 (almost the same as the higher-rate tax threshold which is £29,900 of taxable earnings).

## CLASS 1 NATIONAL INSURANCE CONTRIBUTIONS

| 2001/02 | 2002/03 |
|---|---|
| Lower earnings limit £72 | Lower earnings limit £75 |
| Up to £87 per week – nil | Up to £89 per week – nil |
| £87–£575 per week – 10% | £89–£585 per week – 10% |
| Above £575 per week – nil | Above £585 per week – nil |

Contracted-out employees (those in company pension schemes that are opted out of SERPS) pay a lower rate of NICs. The 10% rate drops to 8.4% for the 2001/02 tax year and a rebate of 1.6% is given on earnings between £72 and £87 a week.

### Example

*Max Earner was paid £39,000 a year gross (before deduction of tax and NICs) in 2001/02. This gave him weekly earnings of £750. He therefore paid National Insurance of:*

| | |
|---|---|
| *Up to £87* | *= nil* |
| *£87–£575 = £488 × 10%* | *= £48.80* |
| *earnings above £575* | *= nil* |
| | |
| *TOTAL NICs* | *= £48.80* |

*Even if Max received a pay rise he would not pay any more NICs as he had paid the maximum amount already.*

NICs work differently to income tax when someone loses their job or suffers a dramatic fall in income. NICs are paid at a flat rate on earnings so no rebate is due if the employee only works for part of the year. However, with income tax, the tax allowance is used to offset income earned in the entire tax year so, in some cases, a rebate of income tax may be due.

> ### ✎ Tax tip
>
> Those with more than one job or who are employees earning a bit extra with some self-employed or freelance earnings are liable to pay NICs on all their earnings. However, there is an annual maximum limit on the amount of contributions employees need to pay. In this case, the individual can either ask for a refund or can, if they know they will exceed the limit, apply for a deferment by completing form CF379 before the start of the tax year.
>
> The maximum amount of Class 1 contributions payable by employees is £2,579.20 for the 2002/03 tax year.

## Reduced Rates for Married Women

Married women and some widows used to be able to choose to pay Class 1 contributions at a reduced rate when employed and to pay no Class 2 contributions when self-employed (though Class 4 contributions were still payable in full). This was called 'reduced liability'. The rate of Class 1 contributions drops to 3.85 per cent (from 10 per cent) for those who have a valid election certificate.

This choice is no longer available, but those who already had reduced liability on 12 May 1977 may keep it unless:

- Their marriage ends in divorce or is annulled.

- Their marriage ends because they are widowed and they do not qualify for Widow's Benefits.

- Widow's benefits end (other than on remarriage).

- They have not been liable to pay NICs for two consecutive tax years after 5 April 1978 and have not been self-employed in those tax years.

| ✎ Tax tip |
| --- |

Paying reduced NICs may save money in the short term, but it could be a false economy because they do not count as contributions towards the basic state pension or other contributory benefits. So the married woman (or widow) could be left with a much lower pension or no pension of her own on retirement. To qualify for the full state pension, individuals must make contributions for 90 per cent of their working lives.

# THE SELF-EMPLOYED

The self-employed can pay both Class 2 contributions (which are paid at a weekly flat rate of just £2 a week payable either monthly by direct debit or by quarterly bill) and Class 4 contributions based on their annual profits. However, if earnings are below a certain amount – net earnings of £4,025 a year for the 2002/03 tax year – the self-employed do not have to make Class 2 contributions.

Class 2 contributions ensure that the self-employed are entitled to certain state benefits including the basic state pension, maternity allowance and incapacity benefits. However, there are two benefits they do not receive. Unlike employees, self-employed NICs do not give the self-employed an entitlement to the additional retirement pension or to jobseeker's allowance.

Class 4 contributions are only payable on profits falling between the lower limit of £4,615 (£4,535 for the 2001/02 tax year covered by the tax return issued in April 2002) and an upper limit of £30,420 (£29,990 for the 2001/02 tax year). They are paid at 7 per cent on these earnings (rising to 8 per cent in 2003) giving a maximum Class 4 NI liability of £1,806.35 (£30,420 − £4,615 = £25,805 × 7% = £1,806.35). As from April 2003, profits above the upper profits will also be subject to NICs at 1 per cent.

Class 4 contributions are paid on taxable business profits.

> ### ✐ Tax tips
>
> Those who are employed and self-employed should ensure they do not overpay NICs. They can ask to defer payment of both Class 2 and Class 4 contributions if they pay the maximum Class 1 contributions. Only the Inland Revenue National Insurance Contributions Office may agree a deferment. Ask for leaflet CA72.
>
> If the self-employed have failed to register, or are not yet registered, as self-employed they should ring the NICO Contact Centre on 0845 9154655. Failure to pay Class 2 contributions could mean they lose their entitlement to some state benefits.
>
> Losses suffered by the self-employed in past years can be offset against profits in future years for tax purposes and for the purposes of calculating Class 4 NICs profits.

# VOLUNTARY CONTRIBUTIONS

A voluntary tax? Sounds like a silly idea. After all, why would anyone want to pay money to the Inland Revenue if they did not have to? The answer is simple. So that they can preserve their entitlement to the basic state pension when they retire.

Those who are:

- Not employed or self-employed (but not registered as unemployed).

- Self-employed but earning less than the lower limit for Class 2 contributions (£4,025 per annum for the 2002/03 tax year).

can pay Class 3 contributions. The rate for the 2002/03 tax year is £6.85 a week.

# 10 Indirect Taxes

These are the taxes we do not always realize we are paying. Some of them are so-called stealth taxes – hidden ways in which the government raises extra revenue without having to put up the rate of more high-profile taxes such as income tax.

Some 25 per cent of tax revenue is in the form of income tax followed by NICs and then corporate tax. These three taxes alone account for about half of total government revenue. A further third of government revenue is in the form of taxes on expenditure including VAT. The remainder is raised by other indirect taxes including excise duties on petrol, alcohol and tobacco.

As a result, the average taxpayer works for the government from New Year's Day until early to mid-June (known as tax freedom day) with the equivalent of all of these earnings going in tax. It is only after that point in the year that all earnings would be tax free (if we were taxed in this way).

## STAMP DUTY

The Chancellor raises more tax from stamp duty than from CGT and IHT combined. Recent hikes in the rate of duty paid on the purchase of property are likely to yield even more for his coffers.

It is charged as follows:

### SHARES

Stamp duty is charged at 0.5 per cent on the sale of shares and other securities (it is paid when they are purchased) with the duty rounded up to the next £5. So a £1,000 share purchase leads to a £5 stamp-duty charge.

## PROPERTY

Stamp duty increases depending on the value of the property. It is paid by the purchaser of the property and not by the vendor.

| PROPERTY VALUE | RATE |
| --- | --- |
| Up to £60,000 | Nil |
| £60,001–£250,000 | 1% |
| £250,001–£500,000 | 3% |
| £500,000+ | 4% |

Once again the duty is rounded up to the next £5.

Stamp duty does not work like other taxes with the nil rate acting as a tax allowance. (For example, with IHT no tax is paid on amounts falling within the nil-rate band.) Instead, the duty is paid on the entire amount.

Note: the nil-rate band for properties in disadvantaged areas was increased to £150,000 from 30 November 2001. For a list of these areas see the Inland Revenue website www.inlandrevenue.gov.uk or contact the stamp taxes helpline on 0845 603 0135.

## Example

*Penny Property is moving up the property ladder and buying a house worth £300,000.*
*This falls into the 3% band and therefore the stamp duty she must pay is:*

*3% × £300,000 = £9,000*

---

### ✎ Tax tip

Homebuyers purchasing a property that falls just above a new stamp-duty threshold should consider negotiating a reduced purchase price and then agreeing to make a separate payment for additional items such as curtains, the dishwasher or washing machine. This can save them a considerable amount.

## Example

*Nicky Nurse could only just afford the £61,000 property she set her heart on until she calculated the stamp duty. This would put the property outside of her reach.*

*£61,000 × 1% stamp duty = £610*

*She managed to negotiate the price down to £59,900 and agreed to pay the vendors an additional £1,100 for certain items of fixtures and fittings.*

*As a result, the vendors received the price they wanted, but Nicky saved herself £610 in stamp duty.*

# VEHICLE EXCISE DUTY (VED)

VED, or road tax as it is more commonly known, has to be paid on all vehicles. However, it can be paid at a lower rate if your car is environmentally friendly. As from 1 March 2001 all new cars registered in the UK pay VED according to the amount of carbon emissions that their car produces. Cars registered before then pay a different rate of VED. The rate ranges from £90 to £160 and depends on whether or not the car is classed as a small car.

Following the 2002 Budget, low carbon emitting cars will now pay £100 less than high-polluting vehicles – qualifying for a further £30 discount. These include the most efficient Ford Fiestas, Vauxhall Astras, Peugot 206s and Honda Insights.

---

### ✎ Tax tip

Owners of cars between 1200cc and 1549cc who purchased a VED between 1 November 2000 and 30 June 2001 were eligible for a rebate of up to £55 for each annual licence or £27.50 for each six-months licence. The DVLA should have contacted eligible motorists in July 2001. If, for some reason, the driver had moved or did not receive a rebate, he should claim it now.

# OTHER INDIRECT TAXES

## Fuel Duty

Once again, motorists can save tax by being more environmentally friendly. Duty on unleaded petrol is 48.82 pence per litre, much higher than the 45.82 pence per litre charged on ultra-low sulphur petrol. Further duty incentives favouring sulphur-free fuels are planned for 2003.

## Tobacco and Alcohol Duty

Smuggling accounted for 22 per cent of the cigarette market in 2000 and although the government is trying to clamp down on this illegal trade, it is likely to remain at this level following a 6p per packet duty rise in the 2002 Budget.

Duty following the 2002 Budget tax year has been set at:

| | |
|---|---|
| Beer (pint)* | 28p |
| Wine (75cl bottle) | 116p |
| Spirits (70cl bottle) | 548p |
| 20 cigarettes | |
|    specific duty | 118p |
|    plus ad valorem | 22% of retail price |

* The rate is halved for small brewers from summer 2002.

VAT is charged on top.

**Warning:** Any tobacco purchased over the internet should be liable to UK taxes unless the site arranges for payment of these taxes. These products are liable to seizure.

## Air Passenger Duty

A relatively new way to tax the population, this duty is charged at £15 for destinations within the EU (which will be extended to 30 European countries from November 2002) and £20 for destinations outside the EU.

## Insurance Premium Tax

This is charged at a standard rate of 5 per cent on all policies sold (with a higher 17.5 per cent rate for travel insurance and some insurance for domestic electrical appliances).

## Value Added Tax (VAT)

The rate of VAT is 17.5 per cent on most goods and services apart from certain specific items which are zero rated:

- food for human consumption

- sewerage services and water (but not bottled water)

- books and newspapers

- construction and sales of new dwellings

- transport

- caravans and houseboats

- gold

- drugs, medicines, aids for the handicapped

- clothing and footwear

    In addition some items are exempt from VAT including:

- land

- insurance

- postal service

- betting, gaming and lotteries

- finance

- education

- health and welfare

- burial and cremation

- trade unions and professional bodies

- cultural services

VAT on domestic fuel is charged at a lower rate of 5 per cent.

Any business with a turnover of £55,000 or above the 2001/02 threshold) – or expected to be above this threshold in the next 12 months – must register for VAT and charge it on goods and services sold paying the VAT over to Customs & Excise.

# Useful Tables and Charts

## INCOME TAX

## Tax Allowances

| (age at 5 April–end of tax year) | 2002/03 | 2001/02 |
|---|---|---|
| *Basic personal allowance* | | |
| Under 65 | £4,615 | £4,535 |
| 65–74* | £6,100 | £5,990 |
| 75 years and over* | £6,370 | £6,260 |
| *Married couples allowance* | | |
| Under 65 | nil | nil |
| 65–74* | £5,465 | £5,365 |
| 75 years and over* | £5,535 | £5,435 |

* Excess above basic personal allowance reduced by £1 for every £2 of income over:

|  | £17,900 | £17,600 |
|---|---|---|

with personal allowance reduced to basic personal allowance and then married couples allowance reduced but not to below the minimum married couples allowance of:

|  | £2,110 | £2,070 |
|---|---|---|

## Tax Rates and Bands

|  |  | 2002/03 | 2001/02 |
|---|---|---|---|
| Starting rate | 10% | £0–£1,920 | £0–£1,880 |
| Basic rate | 22% | £1,921–29,900 | £1,881–£29,400 |
| Higher rate | 40% | over £29,900 | over £29,400 |

| | |
|---|---|
| Basic rate on savings | 20% |
| Basic rate on dividends | 10% |
| Higher rate on savings | 40% |
| Higher rate on dividends | 32.5% |

# TAX CREDITS

| | 2002/03 | 2001/02 |
|---|---|---|
| Children's tax credit | £5,290 pa @ 10% | £5,200 pa @ 10% |
| Working families' tax credit | £60 pw basic* | £59 pw basic |

* A £2.50 a week increase will apply from June 2002.

# SAVINGS AND INVESTMENTS

## ISAs

| ISA | MAXI | MINI |
|---|---|---|
| Overall limit | £7,000 | £7,000 |
| Cash | £3,000 | £3,000 |
| Stocks & shares | £7,000 | £3,000 |
| Life assurance | £1,000 | £1,000 |

## Occupational Pensions

| | 2002/03 | 2001/02 |
|---|---|---|
| Maximum pensionable earnings | £97,200 | £95,400 |
| Maximum employee contribution 15% | £14,580 | £14,310 |

# Personal and Stakeholder Pensions

Maximum contribution to stakeholder pension      £3,600 pa
   With no earnings required

Maximum contributions % of net relevant earnings
   To both stakeholder and personal pensions

Age on 6 April (start of tax year)

| | |
|---|---|
| 35 or less | 17.5% |
| 36–45 | 20% |
| 46–50 | 25% |
| 51–55 | 30% |
| 56–60 | 35% |
| 61–74 | 40% |

Maximum pensionable earnings for 2002/03 £97,200

# CAPITAL GAINS TAX

Annual exemption allowance

| 2002/03 | 2001/02 |
|---|---|
| £7,700 | £7,500 |

# INHERITANCE TAX

Nil-rate threshold

| 2002/03 | 2001/02 |
|---|---|
| £250,000 | £242,000 |

Rate of tax on estate in excess of threshold

| | |
|---|---|
| 40% | 40% |

# NATIONAL INSURANCE

| Class I: for employees | 2002/03 | 2001/02 |
|---|---|---|
| Lower earnings limit | £75 pw | £72 pw |
| Primary threshold | £89 pw | £87 pw |
| (at which NICs are payable) | | |
| Upper earnings limits | £585 pw | £575 pw |

## Employee contributions

| Contracted-in | 2002/03 |
|---|---|
| £0–£89 pw | 0% |
| £89–£585 pw | 10%* |
| Over £585 pw | no further contributions |

\* Increases to 11% from April 2003 with 1% payable on earnings over £595.

| Contracted-out* | |
|---|---|
| £0–£89 pw | 0% |
| £89–£585 pw | 8.4% |
| Over £585 pw | no further contributions |

\* Employee is a member of an occupational pension scheme that is contracted-out of SERPS, the state top-up pension scheme

## Self-employed contributions

| Class 2 | 2002/03 | 2001/02 |
|---|---|---|
| Contribution where earnings over | £4,025 pa | £3,955 pa |
| Flat weekly rate | £2 pw | £2 pw |

| Class 4 | 2002/03 | 2001/02 |
|---|---|---|
| Contributions on earnings between | £4,615–£30,420 | £4,535–£29,900 |
| Rate | 7% | 7% |

# STAMP DUTY

## Land and property

| | |
|---|---|
| If total value under £60,000 | nil* |
| £60,00–£250,000 | 1% |
| £250,000–£500,000 | 3% |
| Over £500,000 | 4% |

* In disadvantaged areas this is £150,000

**Securities**

0.5%

# INLAND REVENUE INTEREST RATES

## Interest charged on late payments

| | | |
|---|---|---|
| Income tax, NICs and CGT | from 6/11/01 | 6.5% |
| Inheritance tax | from 6/11/01 | 3% |

## Interest paid to taxpayers on repayments

| | | |
|---|---|---|
| Income tax, NICs, and CGT | from 6/11/01 | 2.5% |
| Inheritance tax | from 6/11/01 | 3% |

## Official rate of interest

Rate assumed for beneficial loans: 5%

# Useful Leaflets and Forms

Inland Revenue leaflets and fact sheets are free, written in plain English (as well as some other languages) and are available from Inland Revenue enquiry centres and tax offices as well as on the internet at www.inlandrevenue.gov.uk or by calling 0845 9000 404.

These are some of the more useful leaflets:

## GENERAL INCOME TAX

IR90: Tax Allowances and Reliefs
IR121: Income Tax and Pensioners
IR33: Income Tax and School Leavers
IR171: Income Tax. A Guide for People with Children
IR41: Income Tax and Job Seekers
IR60: Income Tax and Students
CTC/FS1: Factsheet: Working Families' Tax Credit (WFTC), Disabled Person's Tax Credit (DPTC), and Childcare
CTCR/1: Children's Tax Credit
IR65: Giving to Charity by Individuals
IR115: Tax and Childcare
IR45: What To Do About Tax When Someone Dies

## EMPLOYEES

IR34: Pay As You Earn
4P3(T): PAYE: Understanding Your Tax Code
IR207: Non-taxable Payments or Benefits for Employees
IR208: Payslips and Coding Notices
IR125: Using Your Car for Work

IR172: Income Tax and Company Cars

IR143: Income Tax and Redundancy

IR2002: The All-Employee Share Ownership Plan. A Guide for Employees

# SELF-EMPLOYED

IR222: How to Calculate Your Taxable Profits

IR227: Losses

IR229: Information From Your Accounts

# SAVINGS AND INVESTMENTS

IR110: A Guide for People with Savings

ISA1: The Answers on ISAs. Your Guide

IR297: Enterprise Investment Scheme and Capital Gains Tax

IR298: Venture Capital Trusts and Capital Gains Tax

# SAVING FOR RETIREMENT

IR78: Looking to the Future. Tax Reliefs to Help you Save for Retirement

# LAND AND PROPERTY

IR87: Letting Your Home

IR250: Capital Allowances and Balancing Charges in a Rental Business

IR283: Private Residence Relief

# CAPITAL GAINS TAX

CGT1: Capital Gains Tax – An Introduction
IR279: Taper Relief
IR280: Rebasing – Assets Held at 31 March 1982
IR281: Husband and Wife, Divorce and Separation
IR284: Shares and Capital Gains Tax
IR287: Employee Share Schemes and Capital Gains Tax
IR293: Chattels and Capital Gains Tax

# INHERITANCE TAX AND TRUSTS

IHT3: Inheritance Tax. An Introduction
IR152: Trusts. An Introduction
IHT2: Inheritance Tax on Gifts
IHT8: Alterations to an Inheritance Following a Death
IHT15: Inheritance Tax. How to Calculate the Liability

# NATIONAL INSURANCE

CA01: National Insurance for Employees
CA02: National Insurance Contributions for Self-employed People
   with Small Earnings
CA04: National Insurance Contributions, Class 2 and Class 4:
   Direct Debit – the Easier Way to Pay

# DEALING WITH THE INLAND REVENUE

SA/BK8: Self Assessment. Your Guide
SA/BK7: Self Assessment. Surcharges for Late Payment of Tax
SA/BK6: Self Assessment. Penalties for Late Tax Returns
IR120: Tax, Collection, NICs and Accounts Office. You and the
   Inland Revenue

A01: How to Complain About the Inland Revenue
IR37: Appeals Against Tax
IR167: Charter for Inland Revenue Taxpayers

# USEFUL FORMS

CTC1: Claim Form for the Children's Tax Credit
R85 Savings: Application to Receive Interest Without Tax Taken Off
CA5601: Application to Pay Class 2 National Insurance Contributions by Direct Debit

# Index